The Army Corps
of the
First World War

Michael Scott

The Naval & Military Press

Published by

The Naval & Military Press Ltd
Unit 5 Riverside, Brambleside
Bellbrook Industrial Estate
Uckfield, East Sussex
TN22 1QQ England

Tel: +44 (0)1825 749494

www.naval-military-press.com
www.nmarchive.com

For those who wish to find out more about the British Army's hierarchy during the Great War we recommend these scholarly reference works published by the Naval & Military Press.

A Record of the Battles and Engagements of the British Armies in France and Flanders by Capt. E. A. James

A survey, in chronological order, of all battles, actions, engagements etc. published by the Battles Nomenclature Committee in 1921, showing which formations took part, down to brigade level.

British Regiments also by the then Brig. E. A. James

One of the most used and most useful works of reference on the Great War ever published. In this marvellous volume is listed every cavalry and Yeomanry regiment, every battalion of every infantry regiment – Regular, Territorial or other – that existed during the Great War.

Order of Battle of Divisions compiled by Major A. F. Becke

These five volumes give details of every division with its component brigades, battalions, artillery, engineers, medical support etc., units and record of any changes. There are also organisational tables for divisions in the various theatres of war. Included are the names of GOCs and brigade commanders and senior staff officers. Each division has a brief history listing the operations and battles in which it was engaged and the corps to which it was subordinated at the time.

Find out more at
www.naval-military-press.com

Contents

Introduction	2	XIX Corps	163
Cavalry Corps	3	XX Corps	168
I Corps	15	XXI Corps	174
II Corps	29	XXII Corps	178
III Corps	41	XXIII Corps	182
IV Corps	52	XXIV Corps	192
V Corps	64	Reserve Corps	192
VI Corps	76	ANZAC Corps (1915)	193
VII Corps	83	I ANZAC Corps	197
VIII Corps	92	II ANZAC Corps	200
IX Corps	102	Australian Corps (1918)	203
X Corps	112	Canadian Corps	207
XI Corps	120	Indian Corps	215
XII Corps	126	Indian Cavalry Corps	218
XIII Corps	129	Desert Mounted Corps	221
XIV Corps	135	Tigris Corps	225
XV Corps	141	Mesopotamian I Indian Corps	232
XVI Corps	148	Mesopotamian III Indian Corps	236
XVII Corps	152	Appendix A – Corps Commanders	239
XVIII Corps	158		

Introduction

As I sit here in the coronavirus epidemic and British 'soft lockdown', I like to feel that in this work, I have achieved something from 2020 more than a little gardening. I was in the process of writing a divisional history. I came to the point at which the division about which I was writing left its first Corps and I could not easily find to which Corps it had moved. I looked for a reference work which could give me the answer relatively easily and discovered nothing existed. There are partial works such as the excellent website, the Long Long Trail, by Chris Baker which I highly recommend. But he focuses on the Western Front and I needed something more.

Hence, I started to research and decided to put something together that covered the Army Corps of all campaigns and theatres of the First World War. My divisional history has been put aside but may now be taken up once more. So, I began research which became this book.

I have to put in some caveats. First, what do I mean by 'Corps'. In the terms of this work, I mean the infantry and cavalry Army Corps, rather than a 'regimental' type unit that has Corps in its name. Hence, no Tank Corps, Royal Flying Corps, Kings Royal Rifle Corps or Royal Army Service Corps or similarly titled formation.

Second, dates. Movement of divisions between Corps did not happen instantly. I have tried to use the date of movement as the date at which the Divisional Headquarters moved from one Corps to another. But, sadly, the dates I have used must be accepted as being a little fluid. This is further compounded by the fact that war diaries and divisional or Corps records do not always accurately reflect, or even record, movement between Army Corps. I have done the best to track dates of movement as possible from the records. In addition, a division was sometimes moved from one Corps to another for administrative or tactical purposes which was not a full move. I have also used an arbitrary cut-off date for coverage of each Corps as being the date of the armistice for the theatre or campaign in which the Corps was located at the end of their war.

Third, what is this book meant to be? I have created a simple reference work. There are no detailed histories of each Army Corps, nor are there intended to be. I leave it to others to create more detailed histories for the various Corps.

I must thank the National Archives for access to the war diaries. I also want to mention the Divisional War Diaries made available by Naval and Military Press and thank Gary and Chris.

Cavalry Corps

History

The Cavalry Corps began to form at Doullens on 10 October 1914, under Lieutenant General Sir Edmund Allenby, with the 1st and 2nd Cavalry Divisions. Its task at that time was to support II Corps and secure the Mont des Cats and Mont Noir south of Ypres and north of Bailleul. It was then tasked to secure the Messines Ridge south of Ypres holding the line between III and IV Corps. It was planned to push forward from Messines but they became engaged in heavy fighting on the ridge in October 1914. During this battle, the 3rd Cavalry Division joined the Corps for a brief period British Expeditionary Force returning later in the year, thus for most of the war the Corps was made up of these three divisions.

In 1914, prior to the start of the First World War, there were just over 15000 men serving in 31 cavalry regiments. The British Army had three 'Household' and 28 line cavalry regiments all within the 'Regular' army. The Territorial Force also had cavalry, in the form of Yeomanry, tied to county affiliations, of which there were 55 units. Of the regular cavalry, 6000 men were overseas. The four cavalry brigades in the United Kingdom had three cavalry regiments in each brigade. These four brigades formed the Cavalry Division, which became the 1st Cavalry Division, on formation of the 2nd Cavalry Division in October 1914 and thus the Cavalry Corps. There was a fifth, independent, brigade, which became part of the 2nd Cavalry Division upon its formation.

The Corps was involved in First Ypres in 1914, Second Ypres and Loos in 1915 serving on the Western Front throughout its existence, although often it served as dismounted troops. However, when dismounted, the cavalry division was the equivalent of two weakened infantry brigades with less artillery than the infantry division. Often, the brigades and regiments of the Cavalry Corps would be under direct command of the Armies or 'loaned' out to other Corps. While under command of other Corps they remained also under command of the Cavalry Corps. This was particularly true in the period of major battles and campaigns. Their role as cavalry set them aside from other elements of the army.

The Corps was broken up on 12 March 1916 but re-established in the following September for action during the Battles of the Somme. At this time, it contained five divisions. These were the 1st, 2nd and 3rd Cavalry Divisions. With them were the 4th and 5th Cavalry Divisions, formerly the 1st and 2nd Indian Cavalry Divisions.

It continued in this configuration, being involved in the Battle of Cambrai, until the 4th and 5th Cavalry Divisions moved to the Middle East in March 1918. The remainder of the Corps was involved in the battles of 1918 on the Somme, the Lys and the Advance to Victory.

The Corps ended the war in Belgium east of Mons. It subsequently was involved in the advance to the German border after the Armistice.

Commanding Officers

10 October 1914	Lieutenant General Edmund Henry Hynman Allenby (sick 19 April 1915)
19 April 1915	Major General Sir Julian Hedworth George Byng (acting)
4 May 1915	Lieutenant General Edmund Henry Hynman Allenby
7 May 1915	Lieutenant General Sir Julian Hedworth George Byng
16 August 1915	Lieutenant General Sir Hew Dalrymple Fanshawe
23 October 1915 – 12 March 1916	Lieutenant General The Honourable Sir Cecil Edward Bingham
4 September 1916	Lieutenant General Sir Charles Toler MacMorrough Kavanagh

Field Marshal Edmund Henry Hynman Allenby, 1st Viscount Allenby, GCB, GCMG, GCVO, (23 April 1861– 14 May 1936) was commissioned as a Lieutenant in the 6th (Inniskilling) Dragoons in May 1882 and was promoted to Captain in 1888, Major in 1897, Lieutenant Colonel in January 1901 and Colonel in April 1901. He took part in the Bechuanaland Expedition of 1884–85. He entered the Staff College in the same cohort as Haig after which he became Brigade Major to the 3rd Cavalry Brigade in Ireland. He served in the South African Wars with the Inniskillings where he was Mentioned in Despatches, moved to the New South Wales Lancers, being again Mentioned in Despatches and was awarded the Order of the Bath (CB) in 1902. He took command of the 5th Royal Irish Lancers in 1902 and was promoted to Brigadier General in 1905 taking command of the 4th Cavalry Brigade in 1906. He was promoted to Major General in 1909 and was appointed Inspector-General of Cavalry in 1910. At the start of the war he was given command of the Cavalry Division leading them in the Retreat from Mons and First Ypres where the division is considered to have done well. Allenby was promoted to temporary Lieutenant General on 10 October 1914 and made commander of the Cavalry Corps. He was given V Corps in May 1915 during Second Ypres. In October 1915, Allenby was promoted to lead the Third Army and made a full Lieutenant General leading them into the Battle of the Somme. In 1917 Third Army was involved in the Battle of Arras despite Allenby requesting a change to the plans due to the German withdrawal to the Hindenburg Line in early 1917 which was refused. He was promoted to General in June 1917, but he was replaced at the head of Third Army at the same time and returned to England. Lloyd George had Allenby appointed to command the Egyptian Expeditionary Force where he had to deal immediately with the death of his son. He assessed the task of capturing Jerusalem and felt he had the troops but not enough to go further and that logistics such as water supply would be a major consideration. Allenby moved the Egyptian Expeditionary Force's GHQ from the Egyptian capital city to Rafah, nearer to the front lines at Gaza, and reorganised the forces of the Egyptian Expeditionary Force into three Corps, the XX, XXI, and Desert Mounted Corps. He emphasised the importance of health and utilised irregular Arab forces under Colonel Thomas Edward Lawrence, CB, DSO. Jerusalem fell within six months and he was reinforced by three divisions from Mesopotamia though he soon had to send 60000 men to France after the German advance in 1918. He then had to wait from replacements from the Empire. With these his force beat the Turks with the Armistice of Mudros signed on 30 October 1918. Allenby was made a Field Marshal in July 1919 and created Viscount Allenby of Megiddo and of Felixstowe. After the war he served as Special High Commissioner of Egypt until 1925 when he retired. He was appointed Honorary Colonel of the Cinque Ports Fortress and made Captain of Deal Castle.

Field Marshal Julian Hedworth George Byng, 1st Viscount Byng of Vimy, GCB, GCMG, MVO, (11 September 1862 – 6 June 1935) joined the militia in 1879 as his father, the Earl of Strafford, could not afford to pay for a position in the regular army. He was offered a place in the 10th Royal Hussars by the Prince of Wales and earned the money to pay for the position by training and selling polo ponies. He joined the regiment in India in 1883 and served in the Suakin Expedition in the Sudan in 1884, while the regiment were diverted from returning to England, for which he was Mentioned in Despatches. He became a Captain in 1890 and entered the Staff College in 1892, having turned down a role as Equerry to one of the Prince of Wales' sons, wanting to be attached to infantry and artillery to gain wider experience. Prince Albert Victor died of influenza during an epidemic in 1892 and Byng commanded the pallbearers from 10th Royal Hussars at his funeral. In the 1890's he met many of the men with whom he would serve in the First World War at senior level and was promoted to Major while serving as Deputy Assistant Adjutant-General of Aldershot Command. He served in the South African Wars being promoted to Lieutenant Colonel in 1900 raising and commanding the South African Light Horse. He was twice Mentioned in Despatches and promoted to brevet Colonel in 1902. He was made a Member of the Royal Victorian Order (MVO) in 1902 and sent to command the 10th Royal Hussars as full Lieutenant Colonel at the end of the year. After a polo injury he became commander of the new Cavalry School in 1904, moving on to command 2nd Cavalry Brigade a year later. He was awarded the Order of the Bath (CB) in 1906 and took command of the 1st Cavalry Brigade. He was promoted to Major General in 1909, took command of the Territorial East Anglian Infantry Division in 1910 moving on to command British Troops in Egypt until the start of the war. He took command of the 3rd Cavalry Division in 1914 leading it until May 1915 for which he was awarded the Order of St Michael and St George (CMG). He was promoted to Lieutenant General to command the Cavalry Corps until he moved to command IX Corps at Gallipoli. His successful plan to extract all forces from the campaign gained him the Knight Commander Order of the Bath (KCB). He then commanded the Suez Canal defences before returning to the Western Front to lead the XVII Corps. By June 1916 he was in command of the Canadian Corps and led their victory at Vimy Ridge in April 1917 for which he was promoted to General. Byng took command of Britain's largest army, the Third Army, until the end of the war. He was five times Mentioned in Despatches during the war. He received the Knight Grand Cross of the Order of the Bath (GCB) and made Baron Byng of Vimy at the end of the war retiring from the army, in July 1921 he was made a Knight Grand Cross of the Order of St Michael and St George (GCMG), and in August was made Governor General of Canada where he served until 1926. In January 1928 was created Viscount Byng of Vimy.

Lieutenant General Sir Hew Dalrymple Fanshawe, KCB, KCMG, (30 October 1860 – 24 March 1957) served in the militia joining the 19th Hussars in 1882. He served in Egypt until 1884, was promoted to Captain, and then served in the Sudan with the Nile Expedition until 1885. In 1890, he was appointed as aide-de-camp to Major General Sir Evelyn Wood, VC, then commanding Aldershot Command. He returned to his regiment from 1893-97, with a promotion to Major, before he was appointed as an Assistant Military Secretary in India. He served in the South African Wars where he became a Lieutenant Colonel and was twice Mentioned in Despatches. After the South African Wars, he took command of the 2nd (Queens Bays) Dragoon

Guards until 1907 when he was promoted to Brigadier General to command the 2nd Cavalry Brigade. He moved to India in 1910 to command the Presidency Brigade and was promoted to Major General in 1913 to command the Mhow Division. He went to France at the start of the war to command the 1st Indian Cavalry Division in December 1914 before briefly commanding the Cavalry Corps and then moving to V Corps. He was removed in July 1916 for political expediency after the Actions at St Eloi Craters in March 1916. His replacement at V Corps was his elder brother Edward. He reverted to Major General, took over the 58th (2/1st London) Division on home service and in 1917 was given command of the 18th Indian Division, serving in Mesopotamia until the end of the war. He retired in 1920, with a knighthood and honorary rank of Lieutenant General.

Lieutenant General The Honourable Sir Cecil Edward Bingham, GCVO, KCMG, CB, (7 December 1861 – 31 May 1934) was commissioned into the 3rd King's Own Hussars in 1882, transferred to the 2nd Life Guards in 1886 and the 1st Life Guards in 1892. He served in the South African Wars as aide-de-camp to then Major General John French, who was commanding the Cavalry Division. He took command of the 2nd Cavalry Brigade in November 1910 and the 4th Cavalry Brigade in November 1911. He began the war with the 4th Cavalry Brigade and became commander of the 1st Cavalry Division from May 1915. In October 1915 he was given command of the Cavalry Corps in France, relinquishing command in March 1916 when it was disbanded. He then ran the Reserve Centre at England. In November 1916 he was appointed to command 73rd Division until April 1917, when he took command of the 67th (2nd Home Counties) Division until the end of the war. He was a son of the 4th Earl of Lucan.

Lieutenant General Sir Charles Toler MacMorrough Kavanagh, KCB, KCMG, CVO, DSO, (25 March 1864 – 11 October 1950) was commissioned into the 3rd Dragoon Guards in February 1884 and transferred to the 10th Royal Hussars two weeks later. He was promoted to Captain in 1891, Major in January 1900, and to brevet Lieutenant Colonel in November 1900. In June 1895 he was appointed Adjutant to the 6th Yeomanry Brigade until February 1903. He served in the South African Wars commanding the 10th Royal Hussars, where he was Mentioned in Despatches and received the Distinguished Service Order. He led the 1st Cavalry Brigade at Aldershot Command from 1909-14 when he took the 7th Cavalry Brigade to war. He was promoted to Major General to lead the 2nd Cavalry Division from May 1915 until he took command of the 5th Division in July 1915. He became a Lieutenant

General to lead I Corps from April to September 1916. He led the Cavalry Corps when it was reformed until the end of the war. He was made a Member of the Royal Victorian Order (MVO) in 1906, awarded the Order of the Bath (CB), made a Commander of the Royal Victorian Order (CVO) in 1909 and a Knight of the Order of the Bath (KCB) in 1917.

As had been traditional for years, many of the senior officers in the British Army had served in the cavalry in their path to the top. Five of the ten officers who would command the five armies on the Western Front had served in the cavalry. The two commanders of the British Expeditionary Force during the First World War, Field Marshals John French and Douglas Haig, were both cavalrymen having risen from the 19th Hussars and 7th Hussars respectively. During the war, the British cavalry provided ten Corps and 27 divisional commanders.

In addition, Field Marshal Sir William Robertson, who rose in rank from Private, served in the 3rd Dragoon Guards, became the Quartermaster General, then Chief of Staff of the British Expeditionary Force becoming the Chief of the Imperial General Staff in December 1915.

General Sir Hubert de la Poer Gough, who started the war as a brigade commander, became commander of I Corps, and later Fifth Army had served in the 16th Lancers.

Field Marshal William Riddell Birdwood, 1st Baron Birdwood, who had commanded the Australian and New Zealand Army Corps during the Gallipoli Campaign had served in 12th Lancers.

Lieutenant General Sir Charles James Briggs, served in the 1st Dragoon Guards, and went on to command the British Salonika Army.

General Sir William Eliot Peyton, commanded the Western Desert Force during the Senussi Campaign and was temporarily commander of the Fifth Army taking over command of X Corps started his career in the 15th Hussars.

Field Marshal Philip Walhouse Chetwode, 1st Baron Chetwode, 7th Baronet of Oakley, who commanded the XX Corps in Allenby's Egyptian Expeditionary Force began his career in the 19th Hussars.

Lieutenant General Sir Michael Frederic Rimington, served in the 6th Dragoons, and during the war commanded the Indian Cavalry Corps.

General Sir Henry de Beauvoir De Lisle, served in the 1st Dragoons and commanded both the XIII and XV Corps.

Composition

Division	From	To
1st Cavalry	09/10/1914	11/11/1914
2nd Cavalry	11/10/1914	14/12/1914
3rd Cavalry	24/10/1914	28/10/1914
8th	11/11/1914	14/11/1914
1st Cavalry	18/11/1914	14/12/1914
3rd Cavalry	20/11/1914	14/12/2014
2nd Cavalry	18/12/1914	26/04/1915
3rd Cavalry	18/12/1914	03/02/1915
3rd Cavalry	13/02/1915	03/05/1915
2nd Cavalry	03/05/1915	13/05/1915
3rd	04/05/1915	09/05/1915
3rd	13/05/1915	28/05/1915
1st Cavalry	16/05/1915	20/05/1915
3rd Cavalry	16/05/1915	30/05/1915
1st Cavalry	28/05/1915	08/07/1916
2nd Cavalry	30/05/1915	12/03/2016
3rd Cavalry	06/06/1915	25/06/2015
3rd Cavalry	18/07/1915	25/09/2015
3rd Cavalry	17/10/1915	12/03/1916
1st Cavalry	14/07/1916	09/08/1916
1st Cavalry	07/09/1916	20/10/1916
2nd Indian Cavalry/5th Cavalry/2nd Mounted	07/09/1916	28/09/1916
2nd Cavalry	11/09/1916	24/11/2017
1st Indian Cavalry/4th Cavalry/1st Mounted	12/09/1916	29/09/1916
3rd Cavalry	14/09/1916	30/11/1917
1st Indian Cavalry/4th Cavalry/1st Mounted	30/09/1916	06/03/1918
2nd Indian Cavalry/5th Cavalry/2nd Mounted	24/10/1916	20/03/1917

2nd Indian Cavalry/5th Cavalry/2nd Mounted	15/05/1917	06/03/1918
59th	19/05/1917	25/05/1917
34th	06/07/1917	10/07/1917
1st Cavalry	24/08/1917	07/10/1917
1st Cavalry	01/12/1917	13/03/1918
2nd Cavalry	01/12/1917	13/03/1918
24th	08/12/1917	09/03/1918
3rd Cavalry	08/12/1917	21/03/1918
1st Cavalry	25/03/1918	20/08/1918
2nd Cavalry	03/04/1918	14/07/1918
3rd Cavalry	10/04/1918	06/05/1918
3rd Cavalry	15/05/1918	11/11/1918
2nd Cavalry	25/07/1918	11/08/1918
2nd Cavalry	14/08/1918	22/08/1918
1st Cavalry	22/08/1918	07/11/1918
2nd Cavalry	24/08/1918	11/11/1918
1st Cavalry	10/11/1918	11/11/1918
1st Cavalry	18/11/2014	14/12/2014
1st Cavalry	18/12/2014	06/05/1915

Battle Honours

Battle of Messines 12 October – 2 November 1914 (1st and 2nd Cavalry Divisions; Queens Own Oxfordshire Hussars; 7th (Ferozepore) Indian Infantry Brigade; 1st Northumberland Fusiliers & 1st Lincolnshires of 3rd Division; 2nd Essex & 2nd Royal Inniskilling Fusiliers of 4th Division; 2nd Kings Own Scottish Borderers & 2nd Kings Own Yorkshire Light Infantry of 5th Division; 1/14th (London Scottish) Londons)
Second Battle of Ypres 24 April - 25 May 1915
> Battle of St Julien 24 April – 4 May 1915 (2nd Cavalry Division in Second Army to 28 April then 'Plumers Force')
> Battle of Frezenberg Ridge 8 – 13 May 1915 (1st & 3rd Cavalry Divisions in Second Army)
> Battle of Bellewarde Ridge 24 – 25 May 1915 (1st Cavalry Division, 2nd Cavalry Division with V Corps, both in Second Army)

Battle of Loos 26 – 28 September 1915 (3rd Cavalry Division with IV Corps in First Army)

Battles of the Somme 15 – 28 September 1916

> Battle of Flers-Courcelette 15 – 22 September 1916 (1st & 5th Cavalry Divisions in Reserve to XIV Corps in Fourth Army)
>
> Battle of Morval 25 – 28 September 1916 (1st, 2nd, 3rd, 4th and 5th Cavalry Division in Fourth Army)

German Retreat to the Hindenburg Line 14 March – 5 April 1917 (4th Cavalry Division in Fifth Army, 5th Cavalry Division in Fourth Army)

Battle of Arras 9 – 14 April 1917

> First Battle of the Scarpe 9 – 14 April 1917 (1st, 2nd and 3rd Cavalry Divisions in Third Army)
>
> Attack and Capture of Monchy le Preux 10 – 11 April 1917 (3rd Cavalry Division in Third Army)

Battle of Cambrai 20 November – 3 December 1917

> The Tank Attack 20 – 21 November 1917 (1st Cavalry Division with IV Corps; 2nd & 5th Cavalry Divisions under Cavalry Corps; all with Third Army)
>
> Capture of Bourlon Wood 23 – 28 November 1917 (1st & 2nd Cavalry Divisions with IV Corps in Third Army)
>
> The German Counter-Attacks 30 November – 3 December 1917 (1st, 2nd, 4th & 5th Cavalry Divisions under Cavalry Corps in Third Army)

First Battles of the Somme 21 March – 5 April 1918

> Battle of St Quentin 21 – 23 March 1918 (1st Cavalry Division with XIX Corps; 2nd & 3rd Cavalry Divisions with III Corps; in Fifth Army)
>
> Actions at the Somme Crossings 24 – 25 March 1918 (1st Cavalry Division with XIX Corps; 2nd & 3rd Cavalry Divisions with XVIII Corps; in Fifth Army)
>
> First Battle of Bapaume 25 March 1918 (1st Cavalry Division with VII Corps in Third Army)
>
> Battle of the Avre 4 – 5 April 1918 (3rd Cavalry Division with XIX Corps in Fourth Army)

Battle of the Lys 13 – 15 April 1918

> Battle of Hazebrouck 13 – 15 April 1918 (2nd Cavalry Division in Reserve to XV Corps in Second Army)

Battle of Amiens 8 – 11 August 1918 (1st, 2nd & 3rd Cavalry Division under Cavalry Corps in Fourth Army)

Second Battles of the Somme 21 August – 3 September 1918

> Battle of Albert 21 – 23 August 1918 (1st & 2nd Cavalry Divisions in Third Army)
>
> Second Battle of Bapaume 31 August – 3 September 1918 (2nd Cavalry Division in Third Army)

Battles of the Hindenburg Line 27 September – 9 October 1918

> Battle of the Canal du Nord 27 September – 1 October 1918 (3rd & 4th Cavalry Brigades of 2nd Cavalry Division in Third Army)
>
> Battle of the St Quentin Canal 29 September – 12 October 1918 (5th Cavalry Brigade of 2nd Cavalry Division in Fourth Army)
>
> Battle of the Beaurevoir Line 3 – 5 October 1918 (5th Cavalry Brigade of 2nd Cavalry Division in Fourth Army)
>
> Battle of Cambrai 8 – 9 October 1918 (1st Cavalry Division with XIII & II American Corps, 5th Cavalry Brigade of 2nd Cavalry Division & 3rd Cavalry Division all in Fourth Army; 2nd Cavalry Division (less 5th Cavalry Brigade) in Third Army)

Pursuit to the Selle 9 – 12 October 1918 (1st Cavalry Division, 5th Cavalry Brigade of 2nd Cavalry Division and part of 3rd Cavalry Division in Fourth Army; 4th Cavalry Brigade of 2nd Cavalry Division and part of 3rd Cavalry Division in Third Army; 3rd Cavalry Brigade of 2nd Cavalry Division in First Army)

The Final Advance 17 October – 11 November 1918

> Battle in Artois 2 October – 11 November 1918 (3rd Cavalry Brigade of 2nd Cavalry Division in First Army; 1st Cavalry Division with I and III Corps in Fifth Army)
>
> Advance in Picardy 17 October – 11 November 1918 (1st Cavalry Division & 5th Cavalry Brigade of 2nd Cavalry Division in Fourth Army; 4th Cavalry Brigade of 2nd Cavalry Division in Third Army)
>
> Battle of the Sambre 4 November 1918 (5th Cavalry Brigade of 2nd Cavalry Division in Fourth Army; 4th Cavalry Brigade of 2nd Cavalry Division in Third Army)
>
> Final Operations 5 – 11 November 1918 (5th Cavalry Brigade of 2nd Cavalry Division in Fourth Army)
>
> Capture of Flanders 9 – 11 November 1918 (3rd Cavalry Division in Second Army)

Capture of Mons 11 November 1918 (5th Royal Lancers and 1 Section DRHA of 2nd Cavalry Division, with 3rd Canadian Division of Canadian Corps in First Army)

Headquarters

12 October 1914	La Motte
13 October 1914	Borre
14 October 1914	Berthen
16 October 1914	Wulverghem
24 October 1914	Kemmel
30 October 1914	Wytschaete
31 October 1914	Groote Vierstraat
1 – 20 November 1914	Mont Noir or Westoutre
21 November 1914	La Motte
23 April 1915	Poperinge
24 April 1915	Westoutre
25 April 1915	Poperinge – Elverdinge Road
25 April 1915	Chateau La Lovie
2 May 1915	Houtkerque
4 May 1915	La Motte
16 May 1915	Wippenhoek
18 May 1915	Chateau La Lovie
24 May 1915	South of Vlamertinge
29 May 1915	La Motte
5 August 1915	Therouanne
25 September 1915	Noeux les Mines
25 September 1915	La Buissiere
29 September 1915	Allouagne
17 October 1915	Therouanne
19 October 1915 to 12 March 1916	Lumbres
4 September 1916	Daours
14 September 1916	South of Carnoy
28 September 1916	Daours
29 September 1916	Regniere Ecluse

6 April 1917	Duisans
11 April 1917	Arras
12 April 1917	Duisans
20 April 1917	Regniere Ecluse
18 May 1917	Villers Bretonneux
19 May 1917	Catalet
15 July 1917	Aire
20 October 1917	Beauquesne
15 November 1917	Villers Carbonnel
20 November 1917	Fins
30 November 1917	Villers Carbonnel
30 November 1917	Villers Faucon
6 December 1917	Villers Carbonnel
30 December 1917	Le Catelet
9 March 1918	Villers Carbonnel
22 March 1918	Moreuil
26 March 1918	Querrieu
7 April 1918	Rivery
10 April 1918	Auxi-le-Chateau
13 April 1918	Equierre
14 April 1918	St Andre
5 May 1918	Auxi-le-Chateau
6 August 1918	Yzeux
7 August 1918	Longeau
8 August 1918	Cachy
10 August 1918	Caix
12 August 1918	St Fuscien
16 August 1918	Auxi-le-Chateau
26 August 1918	Hautecloque
19 September 1918	Auxi-le-Chateau
27 September 1918	Bussu
2 October 1918	Bellenglise
2 October 1918	Bois de Gurlu
8 October 1918	Tumulus

8 October 1918	Estrees
9 October 1918	Serain
10 October 1918	Fayt
10 October 1918	Bertry
14 October 1918	Aizecourt le Haut

I Corps

I Corps originated in, and was formed from, pre-war Aldershot Command. (See XXIII Corps for further information on the Home Commands developed before and during the war). It was expected that any force sent to war in Europe would, at most, need six divisions, and they could be controlled from one central headquarters, not needing any Corps. However, should the need to form more than one Corps become required, then Aldershot Command would become I Corps, and the other Corps would be formed from the different Commands in the United Kingdom, up to six Corps. The need for two Corps became inevitable at the start of the war when the decision was taken that each Corps would be responsible for two divisions. Hence, I Corps went to France with 1st and 2nd Divisions. I Corps took a major role in the actions of 1914 starting at Mons and on through First Ypres. During the fighting around Ypres at the end of October 1914, General Bulfin, the commander of 2nd Brigade organised an ad hoc force of six battalions, known as 'Bulfin's Force or Detachment', and led a counterattack to hold the German advance. He was given temporary command of 1st Division following the shelling of 1st and 2nd Division headquarters at Hooge which killed or wounded many senior officers. This action won him considerable praise from the Corps commander Douglas Haig, as well as John French.

Once the era of trench warfare had set in on the Western Front, the British generally left its Corps in position for long periods, so that they became familiar with their sector, while rotating divisions as they required rest, training, or transfer to other sectors. Hence, the composition of a Corps changed, often frequently. The Corps moved as the British Army expanded and new Corps came into existence.

I Corps played a major role in the battles of 1915, at Aubers Ridge, Festubert and Loos, by which time it had been expanded with the inclusion of 47th and 1st Canadian Divisions. The commander of 47th (1/2nd London) Division, Major

General Sir Charles St Leger Barter, led a force named after him during the Battle of Festubert with his division and part of 1st Division while the commander of the 1st Canadian Division, Major General Edwin Alfred Hervey Alderson led a force named after him made up of the 51st and his divisions. During the attack at Loos a force of several battalions was placed under Lieutenant Colonel Beresford Cecil Molyneux Carter.

The Corps was less involved in 1916 and 1917 but was again heavily involved in 1918. On 25 September 1918, for the final battles, I Corps was transferred from First to Fifth Army. The Germans withdrew from 2 October 1918 so that on Armistice Day the Corps were east of the Schelde-Dendre Canal.

Commanding Officers

5 August 1914	Lieutenant General Sir Douglas Haig
26 December 1914	Lieutenant General Sir Charles Carmichael Monro
13 July 1915	Lieutenant General Hubert de la Poer Gough
1 April 1916	Lieutenant General Charles Toler MacMorrough Kavanagh
4 September 1916	Major General Havelock Hudson (acting)
30 September 1916	Lieutenant General Sir Charles Alexander Anderson
11 February 1917	Major General John Edward Capper (acting)
19 February 1917	Lieutenant General Arthur Edward Aveling Holland
19 September 1918	Major General Sir Hugh Sandham Jeudwine (acting)
4 October 1918	Lieutenant General Sir Arthur Edward Aveling Holland

Field Marshal Douglas Haig, 1st Earl Haig, KT, GCB, OM, GCVO, KCIE, (19 June 1861 – 29 January 1928) came from a family of whisky manufacturers. He was a member of the Bullingdon Club at Oxford University and a member of the university polo team also representing his country. Having lost both parents he chose to enter the army leaving Sandhurst as first in the Order of Merit to join the 7th (Queens Own) Hussars in February 1885 as a Lieutenant becoming a Captain in 1891 while serving in India. He returned to England in 1892 where he failed the entrance exam for the Staff College and went back to India. He moved again to Europe to observe French and German cavalry techniques, write books and serve on the staff of John French during which period he was recommended for entrance to the Staff College in 1896. In January 1898 he was sent to the Sudan to take part in the Mahdist War for which he joined the Egyptian Army and was promoted to brevet Major. He moved to

England in 1899 where he became Brigade Major to 1st Cavalry Brigade, promoted to Major and appointed Deputy Assistant Adjutant-General. A month later he was Assistant Adjutant General of French's force as it left for the South African Wars. He became deputy to the Assistant Adjutant General of the Cavalry Division, having expected to be given the senior role, but was soon given command of 3rd Cavalry Brigade before being made Assistant Adjutant General of the Cavalry Division until it was disbanded in 1900. He was given the temporary rank of Brigadier General with a force of 2500 men to round up the Boers. He was also given command of 17th Lancers and was four times Mentioned in Despatches during the war. At the end of the war he was awarded the Order of the Bath (CB) and promoted to Lieutenant Colonel. On returning to the United Kingdom he kept his command until 1903 but was also appointed an aide-de-camp to King Edward VII in the October 1902 South Africa Honours list, and promoted to brevet Colonel, remaining an aide-de-camp until 1904. From 1903 he was Inspector General of Cavalry in India as a Major General and from 1906 Haig was appointed Director of Military Training on the General Staff, the first of several roles at the War Office over the next few years, where he was instrumental in laying the foundations for implementing the Haldane reforms that created the Territorial Force, preparing for the British Expeditionary Force, but also for neglecting the role of artillery. For his role at the War Office he was knighted. In 1909 he became Chief of the General Staff in India where he laid plans to send an Indian army to fight in Europe if needed and was promoted to Lieutenant General a year later. He left this role to move to take command of Aldershot Command in 1912. In 1914 Haig was made aide de camp to King George V, with his wife as Lady in Waiting to the Queen, a relationship that would give Haig power in the strained relationship he was to have with Prime Minister Lloyd George later in the war. When the war began, Haig led I Corps from Aldershot Command to France and Belgium facing the Germans at Mons, during the Retreat to the Marne and in First Ypres where he mounted his white horse to encourage his men who were retreating at Gheluvelt. I Corps was reduced to 3000 men by the end of 1914 but Haig was promoted to General and given command of the newly formed First Army. He led First Army in the campaigns of 1915 at Neuve Chapelle, Festubert, Aubers Ridge and Loos until French was replaced in December 1915 and Haig was made commander of the British Expeditionary Force. He always believed the war would be won on the Western Front and preferred to see resources in France and Flanders rather than sent to the other campaigns such as Salonika and

Egypt. He is responsible for the two major offensives in 1916 and 1917, the Battles of the Somme and Third Ypres in which he lost nearly 300000 casualties in each campaign so that he become known for his policy of attrition. The losses of his plans caused the Prime Minter to want him replaced though he was made a Field Marshal in January 1917. However, his defenders will point to the fact that he was given one task, win the war, at which he was successful. Haig expected smaller German attacks in 1918 that those which happened in March and April. The threat to Amiens could have caused a retreat to the channel ports. Consequently, he was forced to sack Gough and faced his own replacement. In April the Germans threatened Hazebrouck, a town as key in logistics as Amiens to the south. Should it fall the channels ports would have again been threatened but the Germans were halted, in part due to their logistical weaknesses. German attacks continued into June with the British providing support for the French before the Allied offensives known as the Advance to Victory began on 8 August. At the end of the war Haig was offered a Viscountcy by Lloyd George, but felt it an insult as French had been made a Viscount on being stripped of command. With the King's pressure, Haig received an Earldom and was made Commander-in-Chief Home Forces in Great Britain until he retired in 1920. In retirement he was instrumental in the formation of the Royal British Legion and the annual poppy appeal. When he died he was buried in a grave with a simple CWGC headstone. He was related to Noel Coward and a senior freemason.

General Sir Charles Carmichael Monro, 1st Baronet, GCB, GCSI, GCMG, (15 June 1860 – 7 December 1929) was commissioned into the The Queen's (Royal West Surreys), at that time still the 2nd Regiment of Foot as a 2nd Lieutenant in 1879, was promoted to Lieutenant in 1881, Captain in 1889, Major in 1898 and Lieutenant Colonel in 1900. He served as Brigade Major from 1898 to his appointment as Deputy Assistant Adjutant General in 1899. He became a Colonel in 1903 and Brigadier General in 1907. He served in the South African Wars and returned to England to be commandant of the School of Musketry in 1903 and then commander of 13th Brigade in 1907. He was promoted to Major General in 1910 and took command of 2nd Division in 1912 who he took to war in 1914. Having commanded I Corps as a Lieutenant General he took command of Third Army when it was formed in July 1915. In October 1915 he moved to evaluate the Gallipoli campaign and was given command of the Mediterranean Expeditionary Force in November 1915 to oversee the withdrawal from Gallipoli. He returned to the Western Front to command First Army in 1916 and was then sent to be Commander-in-Chief in India later in the year from where he was responsible for the Mesopotamian Campaign. He was awarded the Order of the Bath (CB) in 1906, made a Knight Commander of the Order of the Bath in 1915, made a Knight Grand Cross of the Order of St Michael and St George (GCMG) in January 1916 and after the war a Baronet, awarded the Knight Grand Cross of the Order of the Bath (GCB) and made a Knight Grand Commander of the Order of the Star of India (GCSI).

General Sir Hubert de la Poer Gough, GCB, GCMG, KCVO, (12 August 1870 – 18 March 1963) was commissioned into the 16th Lancers as a 2nd Lieutenant in 1889, promoted to Lieutenant in 1890 and Captain in 1894 while serving in India. He served in the Tirah Field Force 1897–98 and on the North West Frontier. He returned to England in 1898 and entered the Staff College in 1899 leaving early to serve in the South African Wars playing a role as Brigade Intelligence Officer and encountering Winston Churchill. He was appointed unpaid Major to command a composite mounted regiment being four times Mentioned in Despatches. He was invalided home in late 1901 re-joining the Lancers as a Captain in 1902. He was promoted to Major, brevet Lieutenant Colonel and Brigade Major to the 1st Cavalry Brigade in October 1902. He was an instructor at the Staff College from 1904-06 where he was promoted to brevet Colonel. He became commander of the 16th (Queen's) Lancers in 1907, then Brigadier General to command 3rd Cavalry Brigade in January 1911 in Ireland. He was suspended for his refusal to obey orders to attack the Ulster Volunteers during the Curragh Incident in 1914 as he had relatives in Ulster, though almost immediately reinstated in the politics of the incident. At the start of the war Gough took the 3rd Cavalry Brigade to France seeing action at Mons. He was disenchanted with the division's commander, Allenby, and attached his brigade to I Corps under his friend, Haig. During a retreat of nearly 200 miles, he frequently by-passed Allenby to contact more senior officers to try to get orders he preferred to follow. By the time of the Battle of the Marne 3rd and 5th Cavalry Brigades had been formed into 'Gough's Command', an ad hoc cavalry force separate from Allenby's Cavalry Division. This became 2nd Cavalry Division in September 1914, though they were still under Allenby as he became commander of the newly formed Cavalry Corps. He was awarded the Order of the Bath (CB) for his actions during this time. 2nd Cavalry Division made good progress in northern France and Belgium in October but were ordered by Allenby to halt. Gough felt otherwise and encountered fresh German troops so had to dig in around Messines and held off a German attack on the ridge on 31 October at great cost. He was promoted to Major General at the end of October 1914. During this period Gough formed the practice of rotating units through the front lines as quickly as possible, to avoid any single unit being damaged beyond the point of effectiveness, and of holding the front lines thinly to maintain the largest possible reserve. In 1915 he led his division at Neuve Chapelle under Haig having lost his brother in February. He was appointed to command 7th Division in April 1915 and was in reserve during Second Ypres and the Battle of Aubers Ridge but led the division into attack at Festubert where they were the only division in I Corps to make any progress. He was promoted to Lieutenant General to command I Corps in July 1915 to prepare for the Battle of Loos where I corps would be given the task of taking the Hohenzollern Redoubt, north of Loos. The attack saw relatively, as felt at the time, heavy losses and this was compounded by the success of German counterattacks over the next few days. Gough acquired a reputation as ruthless in removing officers as several divisional and brigade commanders lost their posts during and after Loos. This continued during preparations for the Battle of the Somme in 1916. There is an irony in this given the way Gough was removed in April 1918. Gough was appointed to command the Reserve Corps on 4 April 1916, which was created to exploit any breakthrough achieved at the Somme. Gough spent most of the next two months supervising the training of the cavalry divisions. By mid-June he was also supervising the training of the 1st Indian Cavalry Division and 2nd Indian Cavalry Division. Reserve Corps was renamed Reserve Army on 22 May 1916 although technically still part of Rawlinson's Fourth Army. By the start of the battle Reserve Army had three infantry and three cavalry divisions and at the end of 1 July Gough also had command of VIII and X Corps, though they could not push forward due to the failure of the attacks on 1 July. Gough ordered attacks on 3 July which proved a further disaster. In the afternoon of 3 July, Reserve Army was formally made independent of Fourth Army and Gough promoted to General on 7 July. Reserve Army was responsible for the attacks by I ANZAC Corps at Pozieres and Mouquet Farm in which the Australians suffered so much, the assault on Thiepval and the Schwaben Redoubt again at high cost, and the final attacks along the Ancre, as well as assisting Fourth Army at Flers-Courcelette. Reserve Army was re-designated Fifth Army on 30 October 1916. Gough was made a Knight Commander of the Order of the Bath (KCB) in 1916 and awarded the Knight Grand Cross of the Royal Victorian Order (GCVO) in 1917 as Fifth Army moved forward to the

Hindenburg Line. Fifth Army was given the southern sector during the Battle of Arras in 1917 which included the Australians at Bullecourt where his reputation with the Australians was further damaged. On 30 April 1917, during the campaign, Gough was told that he was to command the summer offensive in Flanders, an area which he had not previously been involved, except during First Ypres in 1914, and did not know well. Plumer led the attack at Messines in June 1917 but neither he, nor Gough, were able, or wanted, to over commit before fully prepared. As such, there was a gap of seven weeks before the start of Third Ypres which gave the Germans time to develop several lines of defence. Gough had sixteen divisions for the attack on 31 July but the attack failed to reach its objectives and the campaign descended into the battles of attrition similar to the Battle of the Somme. However, the awful conditions in Flanders caused by a number of reasons, not just the weather, give us the stereotype of mud and hell that we know as Passendale. Despite some limited success on 31 July, after four days Gough's men were less than halfway to their first day objectives and had lost 30–60% of their fighting strength. Further limited gains were made in August but progress was very slow and casualties very high. At the end of the month, Second Army took the lead with Fifth Army in support. Gough had been replaced. Gough ordered more attacks in his area which further eroded morale among commanders and senior officers. Fifth Army continued to play a role in the push to take the Passendale ridge while Gough suffered declining popularity with Lloyd George and his divisional and Corps commanders. However, he still had Haig's support, though this too was on the decline. Fifth Army was moved back to the Somme in Spring 1918 and prepared for the expected German attack. When this came in March, Gough felt well prepared, but the German assault overwhelmed the British reaching a line at which key locations such as Amiens began to be threatened. On 26 March, Haig was defending Gough but one day later Gough was dismissed, probably as a scapegoat to protect Haig. Gough handed over command to Rawlinson at 4:30pm on 28 March and set up Reserve Army headquarters at Crecy on 3 April that would later form the nucleus of the reconstituted Fifth Army under Birdwood. The next day Haig received a telegram from Lord Derby ordering that Gough be dismissed altogether on the grounds of 'having lost the confidence of his troops'. After the war Gough was appointed Chief of the Allied Military Mission to the Baltic and awarded the Knight Grand Cross of St Michael and St George (GCMG) in 1919 retiring from the army as a General in 1922. He was awarded the Knight Grand Cross of the Order of the Bath

(GCB) in 1937. In May 1940 Gough joined the Home Guard and was put in command of the Chelsea Home Guard, becoming Zone Commander of Fulham & Chelsea until 1942 as his final command. He was the eldest son of General Sir Charles John Stanley Gough, VC, GCB, a nephew of General Sir Hugh Henry Gough, VC, and a brother of Brigadier General Sir John Edmund Gough, VC.

Lieutenant General Sir Charles Toler MacMorrough Kavanagh, KCB, KCMG, CVO, DSO – See Cavalry Corps

General Sir Havelock Hudson, GCB, KCIE, (22 June 1862 – 25 December 1944) was commissioned into the Northamptonshires as a Lieutenant in 1881 before transferring to the Indian Staff Corps in 1885 joining the 19th Lancers and serving on the North West Frontier. He was promoted to Captain in 1892, served during the Boxer Rebellion in China in 1900, and in the Miranzai Valley Expedition on the North-West Frontier in 1901. He was a Lieutenant Colonel commanding the 19th Lancers in 1910 before he was appointed GSO1 with the Directorate of Staff Duties and Military Training in the same year. In 1912 he was briefly appointed Commandant of the Cavalry School in India before he was promoted to Brigadier General on the General Staff of the Northern Army in India in the same year. In the war he served on Staff in the Indian Corps before being promoted to Major General to lead the 8th Division from July 1915 commanding I Corps briefly in 1916. In December 1916 he returned to India as Adjutant General until 1920. He went on to command the Eastern Army in India from 1920 to his retirement in 1924 and subsequently joined the Council of India.

Lieutenant General Sir Charles Alexander Anderson, KCB, KCIE, AM, (10 February 1857 – 20 February 1940) was commissioned into the Royal Horse Artillery in 1876, promoted to Captain in 1884, Major in 1893 and Lieutenant Colonel in 1901. He served in the Jowaki-Afridi Expedition 1877, the Second Anglo-Afghan War in 1878-80 where he was Mentioned in Despatches, the Burma Expedition in 1885-86 and on the North West Frontier in India in 1897-98 where he was three times Mentioned in Despatches. He was commander of the 1st Brigade in the Bazaar Valley Expedition in 1908, when he was promoted to Major General, and commanded the force for the Mohmand Expedition also in 1908. He led British troops in China from 1910-13. In the war he commanded the 7th (Meerut) Indian Division until September 1915 when he took command of the Indian Corps until it was disbanded in December 1915 and Anderson was instructed to form the new XV, later XVII, Corps. However, he became ill and command was given to someone else. He returned from illness to command I Corps. He returned to India to lead Southern Army, India from 1917-19, retiring in 1920. He was awarded the Order of the Bath (CB) in 1904 becoming a Knight of the Order of the Bath (KCB) in 1915. He was awarded the Knight of the Order of the Indian Empire (KCIE) in 1919. He was awarded the Albert Medal (AM) in 1906 for his actions during a fire at the Ferozepore Arsenal.

Major General Sir John Edward Capper, KCB, KCVO, (7 December 1861 – 24 May 1955) was commissioned into the Royal Engineers as a Lieutenant, promoted to Captain in 1889 while serving in India and Major in 1900. He served in the Tirah Campaign in 1897 and the South African Wars where he was promoted to brevet Lieutenant Colonel and awarded the Order of the Bath (CB). On moving to England in 1903 he found himself at the School of Aeronautics commanding the balloon section. He travelled to the USA, met the Wright brothers and played a role in the development of the army's first aeroplanes. In 1910 Capper was transferred to command the Royal School of Military Engineering where he remained until the start of the war. He was promoted to Brigadier General in 1914 as Deputy Inspector of the Lines of Communication before being given the post of Chief Engineer to III Corps. In July 1915 he was promoted to Major General and made chief engineer of the Third Army. Having lost his brother, Major General Sir Thompson Capper, during the Battle of Loos he was given command of 24th Division. In May 1917 he returned to England to run the Machine-Gun Corps Training Centre before becoming Director-General of the newly formed Tank Corps where he pushed forward the improvement and development of tanks. For this he was made a Knight Commander of the Order of the Bath (KCB). In July 1918 he was given command of 64th Division and then became Lieutenant-Governor of Guernsey in 1919. In 1921 he was awarded the Knight Commander of the Royal Victorian Order (KCVO) and retired in 1925. He served with the Home Guard in WW2 until 1943.

Lieutenant General Sir Arthur Edward Aveling Holland, KCB, KCMG, DSO, MVO, (13 April 1862 – 7 December 1927) was commissioned into the Royal Artillery in 1880, promoted to Captain in 1888 and Major in 1896. He was promoted to Colonel in 1910 when he changed his name from Butcher to Holland. He served in the Burmese Expedition, 1885-89 and from 1895-98 was Deputy Assistant Adjutant General, Royal Artillery in India. He served in the South African Wars, where he was twice Mentioned in Despatches and awarded the Distinguished Service Order. He served as Assistant Military Secretary to the Governor and Commander-in-Chief of

Malta from 1903 for which he was made a Member of the Royal Victorian Order (MVO) before moving to the War Office in 1910. In 1912 he was appointed Commandant of the Royal Military Academy, Woolwich. In September 1914 he became Brigadier General, Royal Artillery in 8th Division. He was instrumental in the development of flash-spotting, sound-ranging, and artillery survey service which were first deployed at Neuve Chapelle in 1915. He was made Brigadier General, Royal Artillery, VII Corps. He was promoted to Major General as he took command of 1st Division for the Battle of Loos but was soon moved to be Major General, Royal Artillery, Third Army. He was promoted to take command of I Corps, a role which he held to the end of the war before retiring in 1920. He was awarded the Order of the Bath (CB) in 1915, made a Knight of the Order of the Bath (KCB) in 1918, and Knight Commander of the Order of St Michael and St George (KCMG) in 1919. He was elected as Unionist Member of Parliament for Northampton in 1924 and held the seat until his death in 1927.

Lieutenant General Sir Hugh Sandham Jeudwine, KCB, KBE, (9 June 1862 – 2 December 1942) was commissioned into the Royal Artillery as a Lieutenant in 1882, was promoted to Captain in 1890, and Major in 1900. He served in the South African Wars. He was appointed Assistant Superintendent of Experiments at the School of Gunnery in 1904 and Deputy Adjutant General at Aldershot Command in 1909 before taking a post at the Staff College. He was promoted to Brigadier General to command 41st Brigade and took command of 55th Division in 1916 as a Major General. He led them at Third Ypres in 1917 and at Cambrai later that year, but their greatest success was in holding the German Sixth Army in 1918 when they filled the line after the Portuguese divisions were overrun. After the war he became Chief of General Staff at Headquarters British Army on the Rhine and then, from 1919, commanded 5th Division in Ireland. His last appointment was as Director General of the Territorial Army in 1923 before he retired in 1927.

Composition

Division	From	To
1st	20/08/1914	30/06/1915
2nd	21/08/1914	25/02/2016
1st Cavalry	05/10/1914	09/10/1914
7th	25/10/1914	07/11/1914
3rd Cavalry	28/10/1914	20/11/1914
3rd	05/11/1914	21/11/1914
1st Cavalry	11/11/1914	18/11/2014
7th (Meerut) Indian	22/12/1914	27/12/1914
47th	20/03/1915	30/06/1915
7th	10/05/1915	31/05/1915
51st	14/05/1915	18/05/1915
1st Canadian	17/05/1915	30/05/1915
9th	23/06/1915	03/10/1915
7th	30/06/1915	06/12/1915
25th	26/09/1915	30/09/1915
28th	26/09/1915	21/10/1915
12th	01/11/1915	16/06/1916
33rd	13/11/1915	02/03/1916
Dismounted Cavalry	30/12/1915	15/02/1916
16th	15/02/1916	28/08/1916
15th	02/03/1916	24/07/1916
1st	02/03/1916	05/07/1916
40th	09/06/1916	02/11/1916
8th	08/07/1916	12/10/1916
32nd	21/07/1916	17/10/1916
3rd	27/08/1916	05/10/1916
21st	07/10/1916	28/01/1917
6th	25/10/1916	30/10/1917
24th	28/10/1916	21/04/1917
37th	11/02/1917	09/03/1917

21st	12/02/1917	13/03/1917
46th	18/04/1917	28/06/1918
25th	10/09/1917	07/10/1917
2nd	15/10/1917	03/11/1917
59th	09/11/1917	17/11/1917
11th	23/11/1917	29/08/1918
25th	29/11/1917	04/12/1917
62nd	10/12/1917	18/12/1917
55th	14/12/1917	19/03/1918
42nd	20/12/1917	23/03/1918
51st	29/03/1918	08/04/1918
3rd	01/04/1918	11/04/1918
1st	07/04/1918	31/08/1918
3rd	12/04/1918	23/04/1918
55th	12/04/1918	08/10/1918
4th	13/04/1918	23/04/1918
16th	22/08/1918	11/11/1918
15th	26/08/1918	11/11/1918
47th	25/09/1918	01/10/1918
58th	14/10/1918	11/11/1918
1st Cavalry	07/11/1918	10/11/1918

Battle Honours

Battle of Mons 23 – 24 August 1914 (1st & 2nd Divisions and 5th Cavalry Brigade)
Retreat from Mons
    Landrecies 25 August 1914 (4th (Guards) Brigade of 2nd Division)
    La Grand Fayt 26 August 1914 (5th Brigade of 2nd Division)
    Etreux 27 August 1914 (1st (Guards) Brigade of 1st Division)
    Cerizy 28 August 1914 (5th Cavalry Brigade)
    Villers Cotterets 1 September 1914 (2nd Division and 3rd Cavalry Brigade)
Battle of the Marne 7 – 10 September 1914 (1st & 2nd Division)
Battle of the Aisne 12 – 15 September 1914 (1st & 2nd Division)

Actions on the Aisne Heights 20 September 1914 (1st & 2nd Divisions, 18th Brigade of 6th Division and 2nd Cavalry Brigade)

Chivy 26 September 1914 (1st Division)

First Battles of Ypres

Battle of Langemark 21 – 24 Octobber 1914 (1st & 2nd Divisions)

Battle of Gheluvelt 29 – 31 October 1914 (1st, 2nd & 7th Divisions, 2nd & 3rd Cavalry Brigades)

Battle of Nonne Bosschen 11 November 1914 (1st, 2nd, 3rd & 3rd Cavalry Divisions)

First Action at Givenchy 25 January 1915 (1st Division in First Army)

Cuinchy 29 January, 1 & 6 February 1915 (1st & 2nd Divisions in First Army)

Battle of Aubers Ridge 9 May 1915 (1st & 47th Divisions in First Army)

Battle of Festubert 15 – 25 May 1915 (2nd, 7th, 47th, 51st & 1st Canadian Divisions in First Army)

Battle of Loos 25 September – 8 October 1915 (2nd, 7th, 9th & 28th Divisions in First Army)

Hohenzollern Redoubt 13 – 19 October 1915 (2nd Division in First Army)

Hohenzollern Craters 2 – 18 March 1916 (12th Division in First Army)

Gas Attacks, Hulluch 27 – 29 April 1916 (15th & 16th Division in First Army)

Loss of the Kink 11 May 1916 (15th Division in First Army)

Battles of Arras

Battle of Vimy Ridge 9 – 14 April 1917 (24th Division in First Army)

Attack on Lievin 1 July 1917 (46th Division in First Army)

Battle of Hill 70, Lens 15 – 25 August 1917 (6th & 46th Divisions in First Army)

Battles of the Lys

Battle of Hazebrouck 12 – 15 April 1918 (3rd, 4th & 55th Divisions, 3rd Brigade of 1st Division in First Army)

Defence of Hinges Ridge 12 – 15 April 1918 (3rd & 4th Divisions in First Army)

First Defence of Givenchy 12 – 17 April 1918 (55th Division in First Army)

Battle of Bethune 18 April 1918 (1st, 3rd & 4th Divisions in First Army)

Second Defence of Givenchy 18 – 19 April 1918 (1st Division in First Army)

The Advance to Victory

The Advance in Artois and Flanders 18 August – 18 September 1918 (1st, 11th, 15th, 16th & 55th Divisions in First Army)

Capture of Givenchy Craters 24 August 1918 (55th Division in First Army)

Capture of Canteleux Trench 17 September 1918 (165th Brigade of 55th Division in First Army)

The Final Advance in Artois 2 October – 11 November 1918 (15th, 16th, 55th & 58th Divisions, part of 1st Cavalry Division in Fifth Army)

Headquarters

17 August 1914	Wassigny
21 August 1914	Marbaix
22 August 1914	Maubeuge
23 August 1914	Bonnet
24 August 1914	Vieux Mesnil
25 August 1914	Landrecies
26 August 1914	Hannappes
27 August 1914	Mont d'Origny
28 August 1914	St Gobain
30 August 1914	Vauxbain
31 August 1914	Villers Cotterets
1 September 1914	Mareuil sur Ourcq
2 September 1914	Meaux
3 September 1914	La Fringale
4 September 1914	Faremoutiers
5 September 1914	Chaumes
6 September 1914	Chaubuisson
7 September 1914	Choisy
8 September 1914	Les Jardins
9 September 1914	Charly
10 September 1914	Hautvesnes
11 September 1914	Breny
12 September 1914	Jouaignes
21 September 1914	Mont de Bas
28 September 1914	Monthuissart Farm
4 October 1914	Belleme Chateau
12 October 1914	La Crosse
18 October 1914	Cassel

19 October 1914	St Omer
20 October 1914	Poperinge
20 October 1914	Ypres
20 October 1914	St Julien
21 October 1914	Ypres
5 November 1914	Chateau de Trois Tours
21 November 1914	Hazebrouck
22 December 1914	Hinges
4 January 1915	Bethune
25 January 1915	Hinges
28 January 1915	Chocques
25 May 1915	Bethune
22 May 1915	Chicques
1 June 1915	La Buissiere
30 June 1915	Chocques
24 September 1915	Chateau Prieure St Pre
7 October 1915	Chocques
14 March 1916	La Buissiere
17 October 1918	Mazingarbe
20 October 1918	Thumeries
9 November 1918	Rongy

II Corps

II Corps originated in, and was formed from, Southern Command based at Tidworth and Salisbury. (See XXIII Corps for further information on the Home Commands developed before and during the war). It was expected that any force sent to war in Europe would, at most, need six divisions, and they could be controlled from one central headquarters, not needing any Corps. However, should the need to form more than one Corps become required, then Southern Command would become II Corps, and the other Corps, linked to different Commands, could make up to six Corps. The need for two Corps became inevitable at the start of the war when the decision was taken that each Corps would be responsible for two divisions. Hence,

II Corps went to France with 3rd and 5th Divisions, the former from Southern Command and the latter from Ireland.

II Corps went to France in August 1914 under the command of Sir James Grierson, who was from Eastern Command, but Grierson died suddenly on 17 August while on his way to the front. Sir John French wanted Sir Herbert Plumer to succeed Grierson, but the Secretary of State for War, Earl Kitchener, instead chose Sir Horace Smith-Dorrien, who was transferred from Southern Command. 3rd Division concentrated in France, south and east of the Forest or Mormal, from 11-16 August and 5th Division from 13-17 August. Smith-Dorrien caught up with his headquarters at Bavai on 21 August and the Corps moved north towards Belgium.

II Corps was first engaged two days later at the Battle of Mons, facing the heaviest weight of the German attack which continued during the fighting withdrawal including the stand at Le Cateau. It remained heavily involved on the Marne and Aisne leading counter attacks. II Corps, with its heavy casualties was effectively temporarily broken up in late October 1914 to reinforce I Corps. It played a part in Second Ypres, though parts of the Corps were given to Plumer to use in his force. During the Battle of the Somme in 1916, II Corps undertook the British attack during the Battle of Thiepval Ridge in September and the subsequent assault on St Pierre Divion during the Battle of the Ancre in November. It was also heavily involved in Third Ypres in 1917 and the final Advance to Victory in Belgium in 1918.

Commanding Officers

5 August 1914	Lieutenant General James Moncrieff Grierson
19 August 1914	Major General Sir Charles Fergusson, Bt (acting)
21 August 1914	General Horace Smith-Dorrien
1 January 1915	Lieutenant General Sir Charles Fergusson, Bt
28 May 1916	Lieutenant General Claud Jacob

Lieutenant General Sir James Moncrieff Grierson, KCB, CMG, CVO, (27 January 1859 – 17 August 1914) was commissioned into the Royal Artillery in 1877, promoted to Captain in 1886, Major in 1895 and Colonel in 1901. He served in the Egyptian War as Deputy Assistant Quartermaster General with the Indian contingent in 1882, was Deputy Assistant Adjutant and Quartermaster General for the Sudan Expedition in 1885, was Deputy Assistant Quartermaster General for 2nd Brigade during the Hazara Expedition in 1888, was appointed Deputy Assistant Adjutant General, Intelligence, at Army Headquarters in 1890 and then became Brigade Major for the

Royal Artillery at Aldershot from 1895-96 when he moved to be Military Attaché in Berlin. He served in China during the Boxer Rebellion in 1900 and in the South African Wars. Returning to England he became Assistant Quartermaster General and then Chief Staff Officer for II Corps from 1902-04 and was promoted to Brigadier General. He was promoted to Major General in 1904 to be Director of Military Operations, Army HQ, from 1904-06. He became commanding officer of 1st Division from 1906-10 and was then promoted to Lieutenant General. He was commander of Eastern Command from 1912 until August 1914 and began to take II Corps to war but died on his way to the front. He was awarded the Order of the Bath (CB) in 1900, the Order of St Michael and St George (CMG) in 1902, made a Commander of the Royal Victorian Order (CVO) in 1904 and Knight of the Order of the Bath (KCB) in 1911.

General Sir Charles Fergusson, 7th Baronet, GCB, GCMG, DSO, MVO, (17 January 1865 – 20 February 1951) was commissioned into the Grenadier Guards in 1883 as a Lieutenant, was made Adjutant in 1890, Captain in 1895, Major in 1898, brevet Lieutenant Colonel in 1900 and Colonel in 1907. He was attached to the Egyptian Army between 1895 and 1903, serving in Sudan from 1896-98. He fought in the Dongola Expedition in 1896, where he was Mentioned in Despatches, and the Nile Expedition 1897-99, where he was four times Mentioned in Despatches and wounded. He was commander of the 15th Sudanese Regiment in 1899, Omdurman District in 1900, Adjutant General of the Egyptian Army in 1901 and led 3rd Grenadier Guards from 1904-07. He was then promoted to Brigadier General in the Irish Command from 1907-09, Inspector of Infantry 1909-13 being promoted to Major General in 1908 and took command of 5th Division in 1913. When the war began he took 5th Division to France, as a Lieutenant General, and led them in the early actions in 1914 but was removed from his position in October 1914 when Corps commander Smith Dorrien asked French to have Fergusson relieved due to the latter's perceived lack of resolve. Fergusson was given command of 9th Division, then training in the United Kingdom, until the end of 1914, when he was promoted to command II Corps in Second Army headed by Smith-Dorrien who had previously asked for him to be removed from divisional command. He left II Corps to lead XVII Corps until the end of the war. After the war Fergusson was a Military Governor of Cologne before he retired in 1922 as a General. He was Governor-General and Commander-in-Chief in New Zealand between 1924 and 1930. His father and son both served in the same role. He became Baronet Fergusson of

Kilkerran in 1907. He was awarded the Distinguished Service Order in 1900, made a Member of the Royal Victorian Order (MVO) in 1906, awarded the Order of the Bath (CB) in 1911 and made a Knight Commander of the Order of the Bath (KCB) in 1915, a Knight Commander of the Order of St Michael and St George (KCMG) in 1918, Knight Grand Cross of the Order of St Michael and St George (GCMG) in 1924 and Knight Grand Cross of the Order of the Bath (GCB) in 1932.

General Sir Horace Lockwood Smith-Dorrien, GCB, GCMG, DSO, (26 May 1858 – 12 August 1930) was commissioned into the Sherwood Foresters (then the 95th Regiment of Foot) in 1877, was promoted to Captain in 1882, Major in 1892, brevet Lieutenant Colonel in 1898, brevet Colonel the same year and full Lieutenant Colonel in 1899. He became a Major General in 1901 and Lieutenant General in 1906. He was at the Battle of Isandlwana during the Anglo-Zulu War on 22 January 1879 being one of only about 50 British men who survived for which he was recommended for the Victoria Cross. He served in Egypt from 1882, where he was given command of the Mounted Infantry in Egypt, met and became a friend of Kitchener and was seconded to the Egyptian Army in 1884. He served on the Suakin Expedition in 1885 during which the British Army fought in red coats for the last time and for which he was awarded the Distinguished Service Order. He entered the Staff College in England from 1887-89 and was then posted to India where he held several Staff positions and took part in the Tirah Campaign of 1897-98. He then moved back to Egypt to take command of the 13th Sudanese Battalion, serving at the Battle of Omdurman, before taking command of the Sherwood Foresters. He served in the South African Wars being promoted to Major General to command 19th Brigade and later a division. He was three times Mentioned in Despatches. He returned to India in 1901 where he was Adjutant General to Kitchener and commanded the 4th (Quetta) Division from 1903-07. He then returned to England to head Aldershot Command, where a bitter difference with French began which continued during the First World War. From 1912 he commanded Southern Command and was promoted to General. At the start of the war he was given command of the Home Defence Army but was soon moved to II Corps by Kitchener even though he knew the problem between French and Smith-Dorrien. After the early battles of 1914 II Corps was side-lined and used to reinforce I Corps, but Smith-Dorrien was given command of the newly formed Second Army at the end of 1914. He was undermined during Second Ypres, as much of his command was handed to Plumer, so he offered to resign but was ignored and then removed from command by French on the same day to humiliate him. He was briefly appointed to command First Home Army. By the end of the year he was sent to command forces in East Africa but contracted pneumonia on route and never took up the role. He returned to England and was appointed Lieutenant of the Tower of London. He was then Governor of Gibraltar from 1918-23. He was made a Knight Commander of the Order of the Bath (KCB) in 1904, Knight Grand Cross of the Order of the Bath (GCB) in 1913 and Knight Grand Cross of the Order of St Michael and St George (GCMG) in 1915. One son was killed on active service in Italy in 1944 and another was killed in the King David Hotel bombing in Jerusalem in 1946.

Field Marshal Sir Claud William Jacob, GCB, GCSI, KCMG, (21 November 1863 – 2 June 1948) was commissioned into the Worcestershires in 1882, promoted to Captain in 1893, Major in 1901, Lieutenant Colonel in 1904 and Colonel in 1911. He moved to India in 1884 and became Adjutant of the 30th Regiment (Jacob's Rifles) Bombay Native Infantry, also known as 3rd Baluchi Regiment, in 1886 and was posted to the 24th (Baluchistan) Regiment of Bombay Infantry in 1891. He served in the Zhob Valley Expedition of 1890. He took command of the Zhob Levy Corps on the North West Frontier in 1901 and was made GSO1 of the Meerut Division in 1912. At the start of the war he went with the 7th (Meerut) Indian Division to France, where he was made a temporary Brigadier General in January 1915 and took command of the Division in September 1915 as a Major General leading them in the Battle of Loos. He was given command of 21st Division to keep him on the Western Front as the Indian Corps was moving to the Middle East. He was promoted to Lieutenant General in May 1916 to command II Corps in September 1916 and held the post until the end of the war. After the war Jacob commanded a Corps of the British Army of the Rhine, became Chief of the General Staff in India in January 1920, was promoted to General and given Northern Command in India. He became Military Secretary to the India Office and was made a Field Marshal in 1926 remaining in India until he retired in 1930. He was awarded the Order of the Bath (CB) in 1915, made a Knight of the Order of the Bath in 1917 and Knight Grand Cross of the Order of the Bath in 1926. He was made a Knight Commander of the Order of St Michael and St George in January 1919. He was made a Knight Commander of the Order of the Star of India in 1924 and Knight Grand Cross of the Order of the Star of India in 1930.

Composition

Division	From	To
3rd	20/08/1914	05/11/1914
5th	23/08/1914	14/07/1915
4th	24/08/1914	31/08/1914
2nd Cavalry	07/10/1914	11/10/1914
3rd (Lahore) Indian	23/10/1914	30/10/1914
7th	07/11/1914	13/11/1915
8th	09/11/1914	11/11/1914
3rd	21/11/1914	03/05/1915
1st Cavalry	14/12/1914	18/12/1914
2nd Cavalry	14/12/1914	18/12/1914
3rd Cavalry	14/12/1914	18/12/1914
46th	31/03/1915	24/06/1915
14th	27/05/1915	14/06/1915
28th	03/06/1915	26/09/1915
50th	23/06/1915	21/12/1915
12th	15/07/1915	29/09/1915
1st Canadian	15/07/1915	13/09/1915
37th	02/08/1915	25/08/1915
25th	30/09/1915	10/03/1916
21st	01/10/1915	30/03/1916
9th	20/12/1915	16/06/1916
17th	06/03/1916	12/06/1916
34th	24/03/1916	04/04/1916
1st Australian	08/04/1916	13/04/1916
2nd Australian	08/04/1916	13/04/1916
41st	08/05/1916	19/06/1916
3rd	21/06/1916	04/07/1916
23rd	25/06/1916	02/07/1916
38th	28/06/1916	03/07/1916
8th	03/07/1916	08/07/1916

21st	04/07/1916	10/07/1916
1st	05/07/1916	09/07/1916
33rd	09/07/1916	12/07/1916
38th	12/07/1916	14/07/1916
55th	21/07/1916	26/07/1916
48th	24/07/1916	01/08/1916
49th	24/07/1916	25/09/1916
12th	26/07/1916	16/08/1916
48th	10/08/1916	27/08/1916
25th	11/08/1916	10/09/1916
11th	03/09/1916	22/10/1916
18th	11/09/1916	18/11/1916
25th	25/09/1916	23/10/1916
39th	01/10/1916	18/11/1916
19th	17/10/1916	25/11/1916
32nd	17/10/1916	17/11/1916
4th Canadian	17/10/1916	03/12/1916
11th	15/11/1916	16/11/1916
61st	17/11/1916	01/12/1916
11th	19/11/1916	01/12/1916
51st	25/11/1916	01/12/1916
2nd	01/12/1916	09/01/1917
63rd (RN)	01/12/1916	15/01/1917
51st	15/01/1917	20/01/1917
61st	18/01/1917	04/02/1917
18th	20/01/1917	23/03/1917
2nd	20/01/1917	24/03/1917
63rd (RN)	20/01/1917	26/03/1917
17th	02/03/1917	15/03/1917
46th	24/03/1917	18/04/1917
18th	28/03/1917	26/04/1917

24th	21/04/1917	10/05/1917
30th	17/05/1917	04/08/1917
8th	12/06/1917	19/08/1917
2nd Australian	17/06/1917	04/07/1916
25th	25/06/1917	05/09/1917
18th	04/07/1917	15/08/1917
24th	05/07/1917	28/08/1917
23rd	17/07/1917	23/07/1917
56th	06/08/1917	23/07/1917
56th	06/08/1917	24/08/1917
14th	15/08/1917	29/08/1917
47th	17/08/1917	10/09/1917
23rd	24/08/1917	14/09/1917
7th	28/08/1917	03/09/1917
59th	08/10/1917	10/10/1917
50th	16/10/1917	19/10/1917
58th	01/11/1917	15/11/1917
1st	02/11/1917	27/11/1917
63rd (RN)	02/11/1917	11/11/1917
2nd	08/11/1917	23/11/1917
32nd	11/11/1917	29/03/1918
35th	14/11/1917	24/03/1918
58th	01/12/1917	06/02/1918
63rd (RN)	01/12/1917	10/12/1917
39th	18/12/1917	20/01/1918
1st	30/01/1918	07/04/1918
6th	25/03/1918	27/03/1918
30th	28/03/1918	18/04/1918
36th	28/03/1918	06/07/1918
41st	13/04/1918	24/06/1918
19th	09/05/1918	13/05/1918

33rd	12/05/1918	20/08/1918
49th	12/05/1918	23/08/1918
6th	12/05/1918	01/07/1918
34th	28/06/1918	15/07/1918
32nd	18/07/1918	07/08/1918
34th	06/08/1918	28/08/1918
14th	17/08/1918	20/09/1918
49th	28/08/1918	07/10/1918
35th	01/09/1918	15/09/1918
9th	12/09/1918	11/11/1918
29th	15/09/1918	27/10/1918
36th	20/09/1918	28/10/1918
34th	26/10/1918	11/11/1918
31st	27/10/1918	05/11/1918

Battle Honours

Battle of Mons 23-24 August 1914 (3rd & 5th Divisions)

Retreat from Mons

    Elouges 24 August 1914 (5th Division)

    Solesmes 25 August 1914 (3rd Division and 19th Brigade)

    Battle of Le Cateau 26 August (3rd, 4th, 5th & Cavalry Divisions)

    Crepy en Valois 1 September 1914 (5th Division)

Battle of the Marne 7-10 September 1914 (3rd & 5th Divisions)

Battle of the Aisne 12-15 September 1914 (3rd & 5th Divisions)

Actions on the Aisne Heights 20 September 1914 (3rd Division)

Battle of La Bassée 10 October–2 November 1914 (3rd & 5th Divisions)

Attack on Wytschaete 14 December 1914 (3rd Division)

Capture of Hill 60 17-22 April 1915 (5th Division in Second Army)

Second Battles of Ypres 1915

    Battle of Gravenstafel Ridge 22–23 April 1915 (5th Division in Second Army)

    Battle of St Julien 24 April–1 May 1915 (5th Division in Second Army)

The Battles of the Somme 1916

    Battle of Pozieres Ridge 24 July-3 September 1916 (12th, 25th, 48th & 49th Divisions in Reserve Army)

Fighting for Mouquet Farm 6 August–3 September 1916 (12th, 25th & 48th Divisions in Reserve Army)

Capture of the Wonder Work 14 September 1916 (11th Division in Reserve Army)

Battle of Flers-Courcelette 15-22 September 1916 (11th & 49th Divisions in Reserve Army)

Battle of Thiepval Ridge 26-28 September 1916 (11th & 18th Divisions in Reserve Army)

Capture of Mouquet Farm 26 September 1916 (11th Division in Reserve Army)

Battle of the Ancre Heights 1 October–11 November 1916 (18th, 19th, 25th, 39th & 4th Canadian Divisions in Reserve Army until 30 October 1916 then in Fifth Army)

Capture of Stuff Redoubt 9 October 1916 (25th Division in Reserve Army)

Capture of Schwaben Redoubt 14 October 1916 (39th Division in Reserve Army)

Capture of Regina Trench and Redoubt 21 October 1916 (18th & 25th Divisions in Reserve Army)

Capture of Stuff Trench 21 October 1916 (39th Division in Reserve Army)

Battle of the Ancre 13-18 November 1916 (18th, 19th, 39th & 4th Canadian Divisions in Fifth Army)

Operations on the Ancre 11 January–13 March 1917 (2nd, 18th & 63rd Divisions in Fifth Army)

Actions of Miraumont 17-18 February 1917 (2nd, 18th & 63rd Divisions in Fifth Army)

Capture of the Tilloys 25 February–2 March 1917 (2nd Division in Fifth Army)

Capture of Grevillers Trench 10 March 1917 (2nd Division in Fifth Army)

Capture of Irles 10 March 1917 (18th Division in Fifth Army)

The German Retreat to the Hindenburg Line 14-20 March 1917 (2nd & 18th Divisions in Fifth Army)

The Third Battles of Ypres 1917:

Battle of Pilkem 31 July–2 August 1917 (8th, 18th, 24th, 25th & 30th Divisions in Fifth Army)

Capture of Inverness Copse 10 August 1917 (18th Division in Fifth Army)

Capture of Westhoek 10 August 1917 (25th Division in Fifth Army)

Battle of Langemarck 16-18 August 1917 (8th, 14th, 18th, 24th & 56th Divisions in Fifth Army)

Fighting in front of St Julien 22 August 1917 (14th & 47th Divisions in Fifth Army)

Fighting on the Menin Road 22–23 August 1917 (14th, 23rd & 24th Divisions in Fifth Army)

Second Battle of Passchendaele 26 October–10 November 1917 (1st, 58th & 63rd Divisions in Second Army)

The Advance in Flanders 18 August–6 September 1918 (14th, 34th, 35th, 49th & 30th American Divisions in Second Army)

The Final Advance in Flanders:

Battle of Ypres 28 September-2 October 1918 (9th, 29th & 36th Divisions in Second Army)

Battle of Courtrai 14-19 October 1918 (9th, 29th & 36th Divisions in Second Army)

Ooteghem 25 October (9th & 36th Divisions in Second Army)

Tieghem 31 October (31st & 34th Divisions in Second Army)

Headquarters

17 August 1914	Landrecies
21 August 1914	Bavay
22 August 1914	Sars-la-Bruyère
24 August 1914	Hon-Hergies
24 August 1914	Bavai
25 August 1914	Croix
26 August 1914	Saint-Quentin
27 August 1914	Ham
28 August 1914	Cuts
31 August 1914	Haute-Fontaine
31 August 1914	Crépy-en-Valois
1 September 1914	Nanteuil
2 September 1914	Monthyon
3 September 1914	Couilly
3 September 1914	Maisoncelles
4 September 1914	Crecy

5 September 1914	Villepateurs
6 September 1914	Combreux
7 September 1914	Faremoutiers
8 September 1914	Coulommiers
9 September 1914	Sarcy
9 September 1914	Doue
10 September 1914	Marigny en Oroix
11 September 1914	Chezy
11 September 1914	Rozet St Albin
12 September 1914	Nampteuil
12 September 1914	Chateau Muret
4 October 1914	Verberie
7 October 1914	Abbeville
9 October 1914	Hesdin
10 October 1914	Monchy-Cayeux
11 October 1914	Lozinghem
12 October 1914	Hinges
31 October 1914	Hazebrouck
18 November 1914	Bailleul
20 June 1916	Doullens
23 June 1916	Villers-Bocage
23 July 1916	Domart
24 July 1916	Senlis
1 December 1916	Crécy-en-Ponthieu
21 January 1917	Senlis
26 March 1917	Flers
27 March 1917	Pernes
28 March 1917	Aire-sur-la-Lys
20 May 1917	Steenvoorde
24 June 1917	Hooggraaf
5 September 1917	Lillers
10 October 1917	Esquelbecq
2 November 1917	Vogeltje Convent near Poperinge
17 November 1917	La Lovie Chateau

29 April 1918	Houtkerque
30 August 1918	La Lovie Chateau
28 September 1918	Vlamertinge
16 October 1918	Noordemdhoek
18 October 1918	Zwijnskot
28 October 1918	Courtrai

III Corps

III Corps originated in, and was formed from, Irish Command. (See XXIII Corps for further information on the Home Commands developed before and during the war). It was expected that any force sent to war in Europe would, at most, need six divisions, and they could be controlled from one central headquarters, not needing any Corps. However, should the need to form more than one Corps become required, the Home Commands could form the basis for a maximum of six Corps. The need for two Corps became inevitable at the start of the war when the decision was taken that each Corps would be responsible for two divisions. Hence, I and II Corps went to France with four divisions. It soon became clear there was a need for more than two Corps and III Corps was formed in France on 31 August 1914 after the headquarters had come together in England from 5 August. The 4th and 6th Divisions should have joined III Corps headquarters in England but the losses at Mons and the Retreat from Mons meant that 4th Division went to France on 26 August to join II Corps. When III Corps moved to France 4th Division joined it, as did 19th Brigade, while 6th Division arrived on 16 September. III Corps was first engaged in the First Battle of the Marne as 6th Division supported I and II Corps before III Corps moved to take part in First Ypres.

III Corps played a minimal role in 1915 but was responsible for much of effort in the Battle of the Somme in 1916. In 1917 it fought the Battle of Cambrai and faced the onslaught of the German advance in 1918 before joining the Allied advance leading to the end of the war. During the chaotic encounters of March 1918, the Corps found Major General Antony Ernest Wentworth Harman, KCB, DSO, commanding officer of the 3rd Cavalry Division, leading 'Harman's Detachment or Force', a group of 600-700 cavalrymen remaining from 2nd and 3rd Cavalry Divisions with 600 infantry from 14th Division, eight Lewis Guns, No. 3 Balloon Company, 'O' Battery, Royal Horse Artillery and some logistical support. On 25 March, this force grew with the attachment of cavalry from 4th and 5th Cavalry Brigades and 'Reynold's Force' of about 120 men from 3rd Cavalry Brigade. The principal function of Harman's Detachment was to provide mounted reconnaissance patrols reporting to III Corps headquarters, making it vital in supplying information on the German and Allied dispositions. This force also protected the flanks and rear during the fighting retreat with one notable action involving a cavalry charge at Collezy on 24 March.

At the armistice III Corps was at Ath north of Mons. In the final few days of the advance, ad hoc units had been formed. Among these were 'Stockwell's Force' under Brigadier General Clifton Inglis Stockwell, CB, CMG, DSO, commander of 164th Brigade. On 9 November 1918 he organised a mobile column of machine guns, infantry and artillery which reached a point a mile from Enghien on the day of the armistice. It had come under command of Brigadier General D'Arcy Legard's 'Force' on 10 November as the units pushed towards Ath. Stockwell was awarded the Distinguished Service Order and Order of St Michael and St George for his actions late in this advance.

Commanding Officers

5 August 1914	Lieutenant General William Pulteney Pulteney
16 February 1918	Major General Richard Phillips Lee (acting)
26 February 1918	Lieutenant General Sir Richard Harte Keatinge Butler
11 August 1918	Lieutenant General Sir Alexander John Godley
11 September 1918	Lieutenant General Sir Richard Harte Keatinge Butler

Lieutenant General Sir William Pulteney Pulteney, GCVO, KCB, KCMG, DSO, (18 May 1861 – 14 May 1941) joined the Oxford Militia in 1878. He was commissioned into the Scots Guards in April 1881, was promoted to Lieutenant in July 1881, Captain in 1892 and Major in 1897. He served in the Anglo-Egyptian War in 1882, the Bunyoro Expedition in 1894 and the Nandi Expedition in 1895 for which he was Mentioned in Despatches and awarded the Distinguished Service Order. He served with the 1st Scots Guards in the South African Wars as a brevet Lieutenant Colonel and second in command of his unit from 1900. He was made a brevet Colonel from November 1900. He returned to England at the end of the war and took command of the 16th Brigade in Ireland from 1908 and the 6th Division in 1910. He was given command of III Corps from August 1914 to February 1918 being moved due to the failure of the campaign at Cambrai in late 1917. He took command of the XXIII Corps until 1919, with a brief interlude. He served with the British Military Mission to

Japan until his retirement in 1920. He held the office of 'Black Rod' in Parliament from 1920-41. He was created a Knight Commander of the Order of the Bath (KCB) in 1915, Knight Commander of the Order of St Michael and St George (KCMG) in 1917, and Knight Commander of the Royal Victorian Order (GCVO) in 1918.

Major General Sir Richard Phillips Lee, KCB, CMG, (4 September 1865 - 24 March 1953) became a Lieutenant Colonel in the Royal Engineers before he went to the war in September 1915 from a post in Gibraltar. He followed Sir Hubert Gough to Corps and Army level as his Chief of Engineers before being given command of 18th Division in January 1917, a post he held until the end of the war. He gained a good reputation both as an engineer and as divisional commander. He was awarded the Order of the Bath (CB) in July 1915, made a Knight Commander Order of the Bath (KCB) and the Order of St Michael and St George (CMG) in January 1919. His son, Major Richard Thomas Lee, Grenadier Guards was killed on active service in 1941.

Lieutenant General Sir Richard Harte Keatinge Butler, KCB, KCMG, (28 August 1870 – 22 April 1935) was commissioned into the Dorsetshires in 1890, was promoted to Lieutenant in 1892, Captain in 1894, brevet Major in 1900, Major in 1910 and brevet Lieutenant Colonel in 1913. He became a brevet Colonel in February 1915 while also being a temporary Brigadier General and was made a full Brigadier General three days after becoming a brevet Colonel. He was promoted to Major General in June 1916 and Lieutenant General in February 1918. In March 1896 he was appointed Adjutant of the 2nd Dorsetshires and was Brigade Major at Aldershot from 1906-10 before becoming GSO2 at Aldershot. He served in the South African Wars where he was Mentioned in Despatches. He remained after the war in command of the 10th Mounted Infantry until he returned to England to attend the Staff College. He was given command of the 2nd Lancashire Fusiliers in June 1914 but lost command in August 1914 so he could remain at Aldershot. However, he went to France in September 1914 seeing action in First Ypres commanding 3rd Brigade as a Brigadier General. In February 1915 he joined Haig's First Army as Brigadier General, General Staff (BGGS) replacing 'Johnnie' Gough, VC. When Haig became commander of the British Expeditionary Force, Butler was made Deputy Chief of Staff at GHQ but was removed during the major changes to Haig's headquarters in early 1918. At this time, he took command of III Corps just as they faced the weight of Operation Michael in March 1918. After the war he commanded 2nd Division, first in Germany and then at Aldershot until 1924 before taking charge of Western Command until he retired in 1929. He was awarded the

Order of the Bath (CB) in 1917 and made a Knight Commander of the Order of the Bath (KCB) in 1919. He was made a Knight of the Order of St Michael and St George (KCMG) in January 1918.

General Sir Alexander John Godley, GCB, KCMG, (4 February 1867 – 6 March 1957) entered the Royal Naval School but, after a few years, changed course for a career with the army. Godley attended United Services College in Devon sharing a dorm with Rudyard Kipling. He was commissioned in 1886 into the 1st Royal Dublin Fusiliers as a Lieutenant in Ireland becoming Adjutant in 1889 and Captain in 1896. He left the regiment to join the Mounted Infantry School and then served in Africa before returning to England as a brevet Major to attend the Staff College though he left to see service in the South African Wars. He was Adjutant to Colonel Baden-Powell and Chief Staff Officer to Lieutenant Colonel Herbert Plumer later commanding the Rhodesian Brigade as a Lieutenant Colonel. He transferred to the Irish Guards and then became commander of the Mounted Infantry at Aldershot and Longmoor. In 1910 he became Commandant of the New Zealand Military Forces and was promoted to Major General. He made significant reforms to the forces of New Zealand, preparing them for war, displaying his talent for organisation and was awarded the Order of Knight Commander of St Michael and St George (KCMG) in June 1914. At the start of the war he became commander of the New Zealand Expeditionary Force which he took to war and aimed for Europe. However, they were diverted to Egypt and Gallipoli where Godley was made commander of the New Zealand and Australian Division landing with them at Gallipoli on 25 April 1915. Godley continued as divisional commander for most of the campaign. When Birdwood took over command of the newly formed Dardanelles Army, Godley became commander of the Australian and New Zealand Army Corps for the final stages of the Gallipoli campaign and was promoted to temporary Lieutenant General on 25 November 1915 to undertake the withdrawal from Gallipoli, something he had advocated on the day of landing. For the success of the withdrawal he was awarded the Knight Commander of the Order of the Bath (KCB). In Egypt Godley suggested forming I and II ANZAC Corps with the reinforcements being sent from Australia and New Zealand and was given command of I ANZAC Corps made up of 1st and 2nd Australian Divisions and the New Zealand Division, but as the two Corps moved to France he took command of II ANZAC Corps, consisting of the 4th & 5th Australian Divisions and the ANZAC Mounted Division, while still commander of the New Zealand Expeditionary Force.

The Corps played an important role at Messines and Third Ypres but was suffering large numbers of casualties. Godley wanted to press on, though Plumer halted their progress after the failure of the attack on 12 October. At the end of the year II ANZAC Corps was renamed XXII Corps at the creation of the Australian Corps. Godley was temporary commander of III Corps during the early phase of the Hundred Days Offensive in August 1918 before returning to command XXII Corps. After the war, Godley became commander of IV Corps which was based in Germany as an army of occupation, and remaining as commander of the New Zealand Expeditionary Force until it was disbanded. He held several military posts until 1928 when he was made Governor of Malta and made a Knight Grand Cross of the Order of the Bath (GCB) in January 1928. In WW2 he commanded a platoon of the Home Guard. In his youth he had represented England at polo while training polo ponies to supplement his income.

Composition

Division	From	To
4th	31/08/1914	25/04/1915
6th	14/09/1914	26/05/1915
1st Canadian	15/02/1915	03/03/1915
46th	08/03/1915	31/03/1915
48th	03/04/1915	22/06/1915
1st Canadian	04/05/1915	14/05/1915
9th	17/05/1915	23/06/1915
27th	29/05/1915	18/09/1915
12th	05/06/1915	15/07/1915
3rd Cavalry	25/06/1915	18/07/2015
1st Canadian	28/06/1915	15/07/1915
8th	29/06/1915	24/03/1916
20th	26/07/1915	22/01/1916
23rd	07/09/1915	29/02/1916
34th	22/01/1916	24/03/1916
39th	06/03/1916	24/03/1916
8th	28/03/1916	03/07/1916

34th	05/05/1916	18/08/1916
19th	09/05/1916	02/08/1916
12th	16/06/1916	05/07/1916
23rd	02/07/1916	11/08/1916
1st	09/07/1916	03/10/1916
15th	03/08/1916	03/02/1917
50th	17/08/1916	26/03/1917
47th	22/08/1916	13/10/1916
23rd	11/09/1916	12/10/1916
14th	24/09/1916	04/10/1916
9th	07/10/1916	29/10/1916
1st	24/10/1916	16/05/1917
48th	23/11/1916	12/05/1917
59th	20/02/1917	19/05/2017
42nd	12/03/1917	19/05/1917
2nd Indian Cavalry/5th Cavalry/2nd Mounted	20/03/1917	07/04/1917
50th	02/04/1917	07/04/1917
59th	25/05/1917	29/05/1917
35th	02/06/1917	04/10/1917
40th	02/06/1917	11/10/1917
42nd	02/06/1917	10/07/1917
59th	02/06/1917	10/07/1917
58th	09/07/1917	10/07/1917
34th	10/07/1917	30/09/1917
56th	23/07/1917	06/08/1917
24th	24/09/1917	18/10/1917
55th	27/09/1917	18/10/1917
20th	04/10/1917	18/10/1917
40th	18/10/1917	25/10/1917
20th	29/10/1917	03/12/1917
6th	30/10/1917	01/11/1917

12th	01/11/1917	06/12/1917
40th	01/11/1917	14/11/1917
6th	15/11/1917	14/12/1917
29th	17/11/1917	05/12/1917
59th	23/11/1917	27/11/1917
2nd Cavalry	30/11/1917	01/12/1917
3rd Cavalry	30/11/1917	08/12/1917
Guards	30/11/1917	05/12/1917
61st	01/12/1917	15/12/1917
16th	03/12/1917	05/12/1917
9th	03/12/1917	09/12/1917
36th	04/12/1917	15/12/1917
59th	06/12/1917	15/12/1917
19th	08/12/1917	15/12/1917
63rd (RN)	12/12/1917	15/12/1917
47th	16/12/1917	05/01/1918
59th	25/12/1917	31/12/1917
14th	14/01/1918	28/03/1918
39th	20/01/1918	28/01/1918
30th	27/01/1918	10/02/1918
18th	04/02/1918	30/03/1918
58th	06/02/1918	03/04/1918
2nd Cavalry	13/03/1918	28/03/1918
3rd Cavalry	21/03/1918	31/03/1918
Dismounted Cavalry	22/03/1918	28/03/1918
14th	05/04/1918	10/04/1918
58th	05/04/1918	06/06/1918
5th Australian	05/04/1918	21/04/1918
18th	06/04/1918	05/05/1918
3rd Cavalry	06/04/1918	10/04/1918
8th	18/04/1918	04/05/1918

5th Australian	24/04/1918	27/04/1918
47th	05/05/1918	15/06/1918
3rd Cavalry	06/05/1918	15/05/1918
18th	25/05/1918	16/07/1918
37th	14/06/1918	21/06/1918
58th	15/06/1918	01/10/1918
47th	20/06/1918	10/09/1918
66th	22/06/1918	20/09/1918
18th	27/07/1918	01/10/1918
12th	31/07/1918	02/10/1918
63rd (RN)	12/08/1918	14/08/1918
74th	30/08/1918	27/09/1918
6th	02/09/1918	11/09/1918
46th	07/09/1918	19/09/1918
50th	28/09/1918	29/09/1918
55th	08/10/1918	11/11/1918
74th	08/10/1918	11/11/1918

Battle Honours

Retreat from Mons-Nery 1 September 1914 (Part of 10th Brigade in 4th Divisions, 19th Brigade)

Battle of the Marne 7–10 September 1914 (4th Division, 19th Brigade)

Battle of the Aisne 12–15 September 1914 (4th Division, 19th Brigade)

Battle of Armentieres 13 October–2 November 1914 (4th, 6th, 2nd Cavalry Divisions, parts of 3rd & 5th Divisions, 19th Brigade)

Capture of Meteren 13 October 1914 (10th Brigade of 4th Division)

Battles of Ypres 19 October–22 November 1914 (4th Division)

Bois Grenier 25 September 1915 (8th Division in First Army)

Battles of the Somme

    Battle of Albert 1–13 July 1916 (1st, 8th, 12th, 19th, 23rd & 34th Divisions in Fourth Army)

    Capture of La Boiselle 2–4 July 1916 (19th Division in Fourth Army)

    Capture of Contalmaison 10 July 1916 (23rd Division in Fourth Army)

Battle of Bazentin Ridge 14–17 July 1916 (1st, 5th & 34th Divisions in Fourth Army)

Attacks on High Wood 20–25 July 1916 (19th Division in Fourth Army)

Battle of Pozieres Ridge 23 July–3 September 1916 (1st, 15th, 19th, 23rd & 34th Divisions in Fourth Army)

Battle of Flers-Courcelette 15–22 September 1916 (1st, 15th, 23rd, 47th & 50th Divisions in Fourth Army)

Capture of Martinpuich 15 September 1915 (15th Division in Fourth Army)

Capture of High Wood 15 September 1916 (47th Division in Fourth Army)

Battle of Morval 25 – 28 September 1916 (1st, 23rd & 50th Divisions in Fourth Army)

Battle of the Transloy Ridges 1–18 October 1916 (9th, 15th, 23rd, 47th & 50th Divisions in Fourth Army)

Capture of Eaucourt l'Abbaye 1–3 October 1916 (47th Division in Fourth Army)

Capture of Le Sars 7 October 1916 (23rd Division in Fourth Army)

Attacks on the Butte de Warlencourt 7 October–5 November 1916 (9th, 23rd, 47th, 48th & 50th Divisions in Fourth Army)

Battle of the Ancre Heights 3–11 November 1916 (48th Division in Fourth Army)

Battle of the Ancre 13–18 November 1916 (48th Division in Fourth Army)

German Retreat to the Hindenburg Line 14 March–5 April 1917 (1st, 48th & 59th Divisions in Fourth Army)

Occupation of Peronne 18 March 1917 (48th Division in Fourth Army)

Battle of Cambrai

The Tank Attack 20–21 November 1917 (6th, 12th, 20th & 29th Divisions in Third Army)

Recapture of Noyelles 21 November 1917 (6th Division in Third Army)

Capture of Bourlon Wood 23 – 28 November 1917 (6th, 12th & 20th Divisions in Third Army)

The German Counter-Attacks 30 November–3 December 1917 (Guards, 6th, 12th, 20th, 29th, 36th, 1st Cavalry, 2nd Cavalry, 4th Cavalry & 5th Cavalry Divisions in Third Army)

Attack on Gouzeaucourt 30 November 1917 (Guards Division in Third Army)

Attack on Villers Guislain and Gauche Wood 1 December 1917 (Guards, 12th 4th Cavalry & 5th Cavalry Divisions in Third Army)

First Battles of the Somme 1918

Battle of St Quentin 21–23 March 1918 (14th, 18th, 58th, 2nd Cavalry & 3rd Cavalry Divisions in Fifth Army)

Villers Bretonneux 24–25 April 1918 (8th, 18th & 58th Divisions in Fourth Army)

The Advance to Victory

Battle of Amiens 8–11 August 1918 (12th, 18th & 58th Divisions in Fourth Army)

Battle of Albert 21–23 August 1918 (12th, 18th & 47th Divisions in Fourth Army)

Second Battle of Bapaume 31 August–3 September 1918 (18th, 47th, 58th & 74th Divisions in Fourth Army)

Battles of the Hindenburg Line

Battle of Epehy 18 September 1918 (12th, 18th, 58th & 74th Divisions in Fourth Army)

The Knoll, Ronssoy 21 September 1918 (12th & 18th Divisions in Fourth Army)

Battle of the St Quentin Canal 29 September–1 October 1918 (12th & 18th Divisions, 149th Brigade of 50th Division in Fourth Army)

The Final Advance in Artois 8 October–11 November 1918 (55th, 74th & 1st Cavalry Divisions in Fifth Army)

Headquarters

28 August 1914	Rouen
30 August 1914	Villeneuve
1 September 1914	Baron
2 September 1914	Dammartin
3 September 1914	Lagny
5 September 1914	Brie Comte Robert
7 September 1914	Maisoncelles
12 September 1914	Ecuiry
9 October 1914	Verberre
11 October 1914	St Omer
13 October 1914	Hazebrouck

16 October 1914	Bailleul
19 October 1914	Armentieres
21 October 1914	Bailleul
8 August 1915	Chateau La Motte au Bois
24 September 1915	Fort Rompu
2 October 1915	Chateau La Motte au Bois
25 March 1916	Montigny
28 July 1916	Henencourt
28 January 1917	Villers Bretonneux
29 March 1917	Foucaucourt
18 April 1917	Le Catelet
19 May 1917	Etricourt
29 October 1917	Templeux la Fosse
15 December 1917	Beauquesnes
29 January 1918	Ugny le Gay
22 March 1918	Bouchoir
23 March 1918	Noyon
25 March 1918	Ribecourt
27 March 1918	Clairoix
28 March 1918	Le Franc Port
2 April 1918	Bovelles
5 April 1918	St Fuscien
7 April 1918	Dury
28 April 1918	Long
6 May 1918	Villers Bocage
27 August 1918	Querrieu
3 September 1918	Carnoy
2 October 1918	Ferfay
7 October 1918	Chocques
18 October 1918	Le Willy
20 October 1918	Wattignies
10 November 1918	Tournoi

IV Corps

The Corps had its origin in a force operating independently in Belgium under the command of Lieutenant General Sir Henry Rawlinson. He had been sent by Sir John French on 5 October 1914, from commanding 4th Division who he had led since 23 September, to examine the developments at Antwerp. He was given command of newly arrived troops, the 7th Division, who arrived at Zeebrugge on 6 October, and the 3rd Cavalry Division, who arrived at Ostend on 7 October. Rawlinson was informed on 8 October that he had to retreat from Antwerp and that the two divisions would concentrate at Bruges. From there, on 9 October 7th Division moved to Ghent and on 10 October the cavalry moved to Thourout while the Staff officers arrived from England by 12 October.

The new formation was transferred to the British Expeditionary Force on 9 October and given the title of IV Corps. Its first task was to cover the withdrawal of the Belgian Army. Both divisions in the Corps moved to Ypres by 14 October where they linked up with the Cavalry Corps and received orders to advance but soon found they were retreating to protect Ypres where IV Corps took part in the early part of First Ypres. However, on 26 and 27 October both of its divisions were given to I Corps and Rawlinson was ordered to England to take command of 8th Division and bring them to the Western Front. On 7 November 8th Division arrived in France, linked with 7th Division and, by December, IV Corps existed once again. One week later, the Corps took over the front line at Aubers.

In 1915, it fought in all the major actions involving the British, seeing action at Neuve Chapelle, Aubers Ridge, Festubert and Loos. By the time of the battles of Aubers Ridge and Festubert, IV Corps still had 7th and 8th Divisions under command but had been reinforced by 49th Division.

Once the era of trench warfare had set in the British generally left its Corps in position for long periods, so that they became familiar with their sector, while rotating divisions. Thirteen different divisions passed through IV Corps during 1915, and only one, the 47th, stayed for longer than six months.

In 1916, commanded by Wilson, the Corps was initially holding a stretch of front line from Loos to just south of Givenchy. In March the British took over more front line from the French Tenth Army so IV Corps was moved south, to a position opposite Vimy Ridge where 47th Division conducted mining operations on 3 May and 15 May. A surprise German attack on the evening of Sunday 21 May captured a significant part of the British line. A counter-attack failed and Wilson was almost relieved of command. He then resisted pressure from Haig to conduct a limited attack and, with the Battle of the Somme taking place in which IV Corps played no part, any attack by IV Corps was postponed indefinitely. IV Corps joined the Reserve Army where it remained in reserve through the remainder of 1916, used as a holding formation rather than being deployed into the front line.

In 1917, the Corps saw more involvement as it took part in the German Retreat to the Hindenburg Line and the Battle of Cambrai. But 1918 saw a significant contribution during the retreat in March and April and the Advance to Victory leading to the end of the war. At the armistice, the Corps was east of Maubeuge in Belgium.

Commanding Officers

5 October 1914	Lieutenant General Sir Henry Seymour Rawlinson, Bt
22 December 1915	Lieutenant General Sir Henry Hughes Wilson
1 December 1916	Lieutenant General Sir Charles Louis Woollcombe
11 March 1918	Lieutenant General Sir George Montagu Harper

General Henry Seymour Rawlinson, 1st Baron Rawlinson, 2nd Baronet from 1895 to 1919, GCB, GCSI, GCVO, KCMG, (20 February 1864 – 28 March 1925), was commissioned as a Lieutenant into the King's Royal Rifle Corps in India in 1884. He was promoted to Captain in 1891, Major in January 1899, Lieutenant Colonel a day later and Colonel in 1902. He was made a Brigadier General in 1907 to command 2nd Brigade and promoted to Major General in 1909 commanding 3rd Division from 1910-14. He was promoted to Lieutenant General to command IV Corps. He served during the Third Burmese War in 1886 with Henry Wilson, transferred to the Coldstream Guards in 1889, took part in the Sudan Expedition in 1898 and the South African Wars where he was awarded the Order of the Bath (CB). He returned to England where he was made Commandant of the Staff College in 1903. He was on leave at the start of the war but made Director of Recruiting at the War Office, then given command of 4th Division in September 1914. He led IV Corps through all the campaigns of 1915 and was promoted to brevet General at the end of the year, taking command of Fourth Army at the start of 1916 responsible for, and playing a major role in, the Battle of the Somme. In January 1917, Rawlinson was promoted to full General 'for distinguished service in the field'. For a period in 1917–18, he also commanded the Second Army. In February 1918 he was appointed British Permanent Military Representative to the inter-Allied Supreme War Council at Versailles. On 28 March 1918 he took command of Fifth Army as Gough was removed and it was renamed Fourth Army a few days later. He was given responsibility for the attack on 11 August 1918 that began the Advance to Victory, though this attack was much better prepared than the first day of the Battle of the Somme. Rawlinson had four Canadian, five Australian, five British and one American divisions and all Allied armour at his control. In the Hundred Days Campaign Rawlinson's men gained 85 miles, taking 80000 prisoners and 1100 guns. In 1919 he organised the evacuation of Allied troops from Russia and then took charge of Aldershot Command. In 1920 he was made Commander in Chief, India where he dealt with the consequences of the Amritsar Massacre, the Moplah Uprising in 1921 and the attack on the police station at Chauri Chaura in 1922 which ended the campaign led by Ghandi. He was appointed to be Chief of the Imperial General Staff in 1925 but died in India after a brief illness before he could return to England to take up the post. He was made a Knight Grand Cross of the Royal Victorian Order (GCVO) in 1917 and appointed a Knight Commander of the Order of St Michael and St George (KCMG) in 1918. In August 1919 Parliament passed a vote of thanks to him and awarded him £30000 as he was also made Baron Rawlinson of Trent in Dorset and appointed a Knight Grand Cross of the Order of the Bath (GCB). In 1924, Rawlinson was appointed a Knight Grand Commander of the Order of the Star of India (GCSI).

Field Marshal Sir Henry Hughes Wilson, 1st Baronet, GCB, DSO, (5 May 1864 – 22 June 1922), was born and grew up in Ireland, spoke with an Irish accent, joined the Longford Militia, also the 6th (Militia) Rifle Brigade in 1882 and was then commissioned into the Royal Irish in 1884 before transferring back to the Rifle Brigade. He was promoted to Captain in 1893, Major in 1901, brevet Lieutenant Colonel in 1902, Colonel and Brigadier General in 1907 and Major General in 1913. He went to India in 1885 taking part in the Third Burmese War in 1886 and was wounded in 1887 which left a significant scar on his face, returning to Ireland to recover through 1888. He joined the 2nd Rifle Brigade in 1889 and entered the Staff College from 1891-93. He went out of his way to avoid overseas postings to India and Hong Kong, joining the War Office in 1894 soon becoming Staff Captain in the Intelligence Section. He then tried to get postings to expeditions in Africa but it was not until he became Brigade Major to 3rd Brigade in 1899, as it went to take part in the South African Wars, that he went overseas moving in 1900 to work with

Rawlinson as Deputy Assistant Adjutant-General and Assistant Military Secretary to Roberts. He returned to the War Office during the South African Wars and was awarded the Distinguished Service Order. He was given command of 9th Rifle Brigade in 1902-03 before joining the War Office again as an Assistant Adjutant-General. He was persistent in developing political links and was put in charge of the new department which managed the Staff College, the Royal Military Academy at Woolwich, the Royal Military College at Sandhurst and officers' promotion examinations which gave him a wide responsibility across the country. He became Commandant of the Staff College from 1907-10 before being moved to be Director of Military Operations at the War Office where he began planning for the war he expected to come. His perceived involvement in the Curragh Incident in 1914 caused him problems and held him back from promotion during the early part of the war as politicians did not want to see him in senior roles. At the start of the war he became Sub Chief of Staff going to France with the British Expeditionary Force on French's staff. Wilson temporarily acted as Chief of Staff for the British Expeditionary Force in October. When Robertson became Chief of Staff in January 1915 Wilson was removed from his position and appointed Principal Liaison Officer with the French as a temporary Lieutenant General. He was known to keep relations smooth by mis-translating, but also continued to 'politic' opposing Gallipoli as he believed the war would be won on the Western Front, until his liaison role was again undermined in late 1915 as he attended the Anglo-French Chantilly Conference in December. However, the new coalition government improved his potential career opportunities. With French's removal, Wilson tried to resign, not wanting to serve under Haig or Robertson, but he was persuaded this was unacceptable. Despite not having commanded a brigade or division he was given command of IV Corps under Rawlinson, though he wanted XIV Corps under Allenby. He was nearly removed due to a failed counterattack in May 1916. By October the Corps had no divisions and Wilson went on leave. Yet again political developments were to help his career over the opposition of senior officers. Lloyd George became Prime Minister and took Wilson to a conference in preference to Haig. Wilson was sent as Senior Military Representative, as Robertson had refused to go, on a British mission to Russia in January 1917 after leaving command of IV Corps. Wilson was appointed Chief of British Mission to the French Army on 17 March, with a promotion to full Lieutenant General which Robertson had blocked in November 1916 but his dislike of Petain led to the French commander dealing directly with

Haig. Once again Wilson was side-lined though the post theoretically continued to exist through 1917 as he toured the French front where it became clear his skills were being wasted. Lloyd George suggested an inter-Allied body of three Prime Ministers and three soldiers be set up over all the national Staffs with Wilson as the British military representative. At the same time, Wilson took on Eastern Command with headquarters in Pall Mall near to Parliament where he was close to the Prime Minster and regularly providing advice to the Cabinet. He also recommended taking advantage of the stalemate on the Western Front to develop the campaigns in the Middle East. Lloyd George made Wilson the British Military Representative on the Supreme War Council and he was promoted to General. In February 1918 Wilson was appointed Chief of the Imperial General Staff where he radically increased the role of tanks and removed the Corps commanders involved in the Battle of Cambrai. He held this role until he retired in 1922 and was also Britain's chief military adviser at the Paris Peace Conference at the end of which he was promoted to Field Marshal and made a baronet. After the war he wanted to reduce the commitments in the Middle East, Russia, Germany and Transcaucasia, and bring the army home to face the socialist threat and the independence campaign in Ireland. When he retired, he became Member of Parliament for North Down but was assassinated outside his London home in June 1922. Wilson was awarded the Order of the Bath (CB) in 1908, made a Knight Commander of the Order of the Bath (KCB) in June 1915 and Knight Grand Cross of the Order of the Bath (GCB) in December 1918.

Lieutenant General Sir Charles Louis Woollcombe, KCB, KCMG, (23 March 1857 – 6 May 1934) served with the 1st Devon Militia, before being commissioned in the Duke of Cornwall's Light Infantry, then the 46th (South Devonshire) Regiment of Foot, in 1876. A year later he transferred to the King's Own Scottish Borderers, then the 25th Regiment of Foot. He served in India in the Peshawar Valley Expedition and in Afghanistan between 1878-80 and in the Chin Lushai Expedition in Burma between 1889-90. He was Deputy Assistant Adjutant General for Musketry in Bengal from 1890, Brigade Major for the Chitral Relief Force in 1895, served on the North West Frontier as Assistant Adjutant General of the Mohmand Field Force in 1897, the Tirah Expedition from 1897-98 and then became Assistant Adjutant General in India in 1899. He served in the South African Wars and then became Assistant Adjutant General for Musketry in India from 1901-06. He was commander of the Allahabad Brigade in India from 1906 and of the Garhwal Brigade from 1907-10. He was made a Major General in 1908 and he commanded the Highland

Division, later 51st Division, in 1911. He served in the war as commander of Eastern Command from 1914 and 2nd Army, Central Force until given command of 11th Division in July 1916, despite holding the rank of Lieutenant General, and of IV Corps in December 1916. He took Eastern Command again in 1918, having been sacked from IV Corps for the failure of the Battle of Cambrai, until he retired in 1920. He was made a Knight Commander of the Order of the Bath (KCB) in 1916 and Knight Commander of the Order of St Michael and St George (KCMG) in October 1919.

Lieutenant General Sir George Montague Harper, KCB, DSO, (11 January 1865 – 15 December 1922) was commissioned as a Lieutenant into the Royal Engineers in 1884, promoted to Captain in 1892, Major in 1901 and Lieutenant Colonel in 1907. He served in the South African Wars where he was awarded the Distinguished Service Order. He returned to England to enter the Staff College in 1901 and served on staff at the college from 1908-10. He served at the war Office 1903-1908 where he was developing plans for mobilization in case of war. He became Deputy Director of Military Operations at the War Office in 1911 where he continued to develop the plans for moving the British Expeditionary Force to France in the event of war. When the war began he oversaw mobilisation and moved to Staff with the British Expeditionary Force in France but did not get on with the Chief of Staff which caused significant problems so he was removed in November 1914, but also promoted to Brigadier General. In February 1915 he was given command of 17th Brigade, was soon made Director of Military Operations and then promoted to Major General to command the 51st (Highland) Division in September 1915 leading them in the Battles of the Somme in 1916 and Battle of Arras in 1917. The division took part in some of Third Ypres, all the time getting the division and Harper a good reputation, and taking part in the Battle of Cambrai in November 1917. Harper has been blamed for the failure of his division to succeed at Cambrai due to his inability to properly understand how to use infantry with tanks, but this has been shown to be wrong. He was promoted to Lieutenant General to command IV Corps in March 1918, a position he held until the end of the war. After the war he took charge of Southern Command until he died in a car accident in 1922. He was awarded the Order of the Bath (CB) in February 1915 and made a Knight Commander of the Order of the Bath (KCB) in January 1918.

Composition

Division	From	To
3rd Cavalry	06/10/1914	22/10/1914
7th	07/10/1914	25/10/1914
63rd (RN)	08/10/1914	11/10/1914
7th	13/11/1914	10/05/1915
8th	14/11/1914	31/05/1915
1st Canadian	03/03/1915	12/04/1915
49th	14/04/1915	31/05/1915
1st Canadian	30/05/1915	28/06/1915
51st	31/05/1915	26/06/1915
7th	31/05/1915	30/06/1915
48th	22/06/1915	18/07/1915
1st	30/06/1915	02/03/1916
47th	30/06/1915	30/07/1916
15th	17/07/1915	02/03/1916
3rd Cavalry	25/09/1915	17/10/1915
16th	18/12/1915	15/02/1916
2nd	25/02/1916	21/07/2016
23rd	29/02/1916	25/06/1916
63rd (RN)	05/06/1916	04/10/1916
37th	16/07/1916	14/10/1916
15th	24/07/1916	27/07/1916
9th	25/07/1916	07/10/1916
24th	20/09/1916	14/10/1916
2nd Canadian	12/10/1916	21/10/1916
1st Cavalry	20/10/1916	08/11/1916
11th	22/10/1916	15/11/1916
25th	23/10/1916	29/10/1916
40th	02/11/1916	15/11/1916
46th	11/11/1916	01/12/1916
61st	15/11/1916	17/11/1916

18th	18/11/1916	01/12/1916
63rd (RN)	18/11/1916	01/12/1916
2nd	19/11/1916	01/12/1916
19th	25/11/1916	30/11/1916
32nd	25/11/1916	01/12/1916
11th	01/12/1916	06/02/1917
51st	01/12/1916	15/01/1917
61st	01/12/1916	18/01/1917
2nd	11/01/1917	20/01/1917
51st	20/01/1917	08/02/1917
61st	04/02/1917	21/05/1917
35th	12/02/1917	23/05/1917
32nd	16/02/1917	20/05/1917
2nd Indian Cavalry/5th Cavalry/2nd Mounted	07/04/1917	15/05/1917
48th	25/05/1917	05/07/1917
20th	26/05/1917	20/07/1917
5th Australian	26/05/1917	17/06/1917
2nd Australian	17/06/1917	28/07/1917
62nd	24/06/1917	29/06/1917
3rd	26/06/1917	17/09/1917
58th	04/07/1917	09/07/1917
58th	10/07/1917	31/07/1917
59th	10/07/1917	01/09/1917
9th	31/07/1917	30/08/1917
36th	25/08/1917	29/11/1917
56th	31/08/1917	24/11/1917
24th	20/09/1917	24/09/1917
55th	25/09/1917	27/09/1917
62nd	13/10/1917	30/10/1917
40th	14/11/1917	15/11/1917
62nd	15/11/1917	04/12/1917

51st	17/11/1917	30/11/1917
1st Cavalry	20/11/1917	30/11/1917
40th	21/11/1917	23/11/1917
Guards	23/11/1917	30/11/1917
2nd Cavalry	24/11/1917	30/11/1917
2nd	25/11/1917	01/12/1917
47th	27/11/1917	01/12/1917
59th	27/11/1917	01/12/1917
61st	30/11/1917	01/12/1917
20th	03/12/1917	06/12/1917
29th	05/12/1917	18/12/1917
12th	06/12/1917	08/12/1917
25th	15/12/1917	30/03/1918
51st	15/12/1917	29/03/1918
6th	01/01/1918	25/03/1918
41st	09/03/1918	04/04/1918
2nd Canadian	14/03/1918	26/03/1918
19th	21/03/1918	29/03/1918
42nd	24/03/1918	11/11/1918
NZ Division	24/03/1918	11/11/1918
37th	25/03/1918	29/03/1918
62nd	25/03/1918	14/07/1918
37th	30/03/1918	05/06/1918
57th	09/04/1918	12/04/1918
57th	13/04/1918	29/07/1918
37th	21/06/1918	11/11/1918
63rd (RN)	29/07/1918	05/08/1918
62nd	06/08/1918	19/08/1918
63rd (RN)	14/08/1918	31/08/1918
5th	18/08/1918	24/08/1918
62nd	22/08/1918	23/08/1918

5th	26/08/1918	11/11/1918

Battle Honours

Antwerp Operations 9–10 October 1914 (7th & 3rd Cavalry Divisions)

First Battles Ypres 1914

      Battle of Langemark 21-24 October 1914 (7th & 3rd Cavalry Divisions)

Neuve Chapelle Moated Grange Attack 18 December 1914 (8th Division)

Rouges Bancs Well Farm Attack 18 December 1914 (7th Division)

Battle of Neuve Chapelle 10-13 March 1915 (7th & 8th Divisions in First Army)

Battle of Aubers 9 May 1915 (7th, 8th & 49th Divisions in First Army)

Attack at Fromelles 9 May 1915 (7th, 8th & 49th Divisions in First Army)

Second Action of Givenchy 15-16 June 1915 (7th, 51st & 1st Canadian Divisions in First Army)

Battle of Loos 25 September–8 October 1915 (1st, 15th, 47th & 3rd Cavalry Divisions in First Army)

Hohenzollern Redoubt 13-19 October 1915 (1st & 47th Divisions in First Army)

German attack on Vimy Ridge 21 May 1916 (47th Division in First Army)

Operations on the Ancre 11 January–13 March 1917 (2nd, 11th & 61st Divisions in Fifth Army)

German Retreat to the Hindenburg Line 14 March–5 April 1917 (32nd, 35th & 61st Divisions in Fourth Army)

Actions on the Hindenburg Line 20 May-16 June 1917 (20th Division in Fifth Army to 31 May then Third Army)

Battle of Cambrai 1917

      The Tank Attack 20-21 November 1917 (36th, 51st, 56th, 62nd & 1st Cavalry Divisions in Third Army)

      Capture of Cantaing 21 November 1917 (51st Division in Third Army)

      Capture of Tadpole Copse 21 November 1917 (56th Division in Third Army)

      The Capture of Bourlon Wood 23-28 November 1917 (Guards, 2nd, 36th, 40th, 47th, 51st, 56th, 59th, 62nd, 1st Cavalry & 2nd Cavalry Divisions in Third Army)

      The German Counter-Attacks 30 November–1 December 1917 (2nd, 47th & 59th Divisions in Third Army)

First Battles of the Somme 1918

      Battle of St. Quentin 21-23 March 1918 (6th, 19th, 25th, 41st & 51st Divisions in Third Army)

Counter Attack at Beugny 22 March 1918 (19th Division in Third Army)

First Battle of Bapaume 24-25 March 1918 (19th, 25th, 41st, 51st & 62nd Divisions in Third Army)

First Battle of Arras 28 March 1918 (41st, 42nd, 62nd & New Zealand Divisions, 4th Australian Brigade of 4th Australian Division in Third Army)

Battle of the Ancre 5 April 1918 (37th, 42nd & New Zealand Divisions, 4th Australian Brigade of 4th Australian Division in Third Army)

Bucquoy 22-23 June 1918 (part of 5th Kings Own Yorkshire Light Infantry, 62nd Division in Third Army)

Second Battles of the Somme 1918

Battle of Albert 21-23 August 1918 (5th, 37th, 42nd, 63rd & New Zealand Divisions in Third Army)

Second Battle of Bapaume 31 August–3 September 1918 (5th, 42nd & New Zealand Divisions in Third Army)

Battles of the Hindenburg Line

Battle of Havrincourt 12 September 1918 (37th & New Zealand Divisions in Third Army)

Battle of Épehy 18 September 1918 (5th Division in Third Army)

Battle of the Canal du Nord 27 September–1 October 1918 (5th, 37th, 42nd & New Zealand Divisions in Third Army)

Battle of Cambrai 8-9 October 1918 (37th & New Zealand Divisions in Third Army)

Pursuit to the Selle 9-12 October 1918 (5th, 37th, 42nd & New Zealand Divisions in Third Army)

Final advance in Picardy

Battle of the Selle 17-25 October 1918 (5th, 37th, 42nd & New Zealand Divisions in Third Army)

Capture of Grand Champ Ridge 23 October 1918 (5th Division in Third Army)

Battle of the Sambre 4 November 1918 (37th & New Zealand Divisions in Third Army)

Capture of Le Quesnoy 4 November 1918 (New Zealand Division in Third Army)

Headquarters

8 October 1914	Bruges
8 October 1914	Ostende
12 October 1914	General Staff to Chateau Wynendaele near Torhout, Admin Staff to Nieuport
13 October 1914	General Staff to Roeselare
14 October 1914	General Staff to Ypres, Administrative Staff to Rosendael near Dunkirk
15 October 1914	Poperinge
19-23 October 1914	Ypres & Poperinge (alternating)
25 – 27 October 1914	Ypres & Hooge (alternating)
27 October 1914	Ypres
1 November 1914	Steenvoorde
2 November 1914	Arcques
3 November 1914	Boulogne
7 November 1914	Merville
31 May 1915	Hinges
1 June 1915	Merville
1 June 1915	Hinges
30 June 1915	Labuissière
26 September 1915	Vaudricourt
4 October 1915	Labuissière
12 March 1916	Ranchicourt
15 October 1916	Contay
18 October 1916	Domart-en-Ponthieu
10 November 1916	Beauval
1 December 1916	Senlis
20 January 1917	Crécy-en-Ponthieu
8 February 1917	Moreuil
18 March 1917	Beaucourt
29 March 1917	Nesle
20 May 1917	Querrieu
26 May 1917	Grévillers
17 July 1917	Etricourt

20 October 1917	Villers-au-Flos
1 December 1917	Beauquesne
15 December 1917	Grévillers
23 March 1918	Mailly Maillet
25 March 1918	Marieux
4 September 1918	Grévillers
9 October 1918	Havrincourt Wood
12 October 1918	Ligny-en-Cambrésis
8 November 1918	Le Quesnoy

V Corps

V Corps was organised within Second Army of the British Expeditionary Force. The headquarters began to form in England on 27 December 1914 while the rest of the Corps formed in France in January where both parts came together on 10 January. On 18 February 1915 it came under command of Sir Herbert Plumer, who had been commanding Northern Command in England. It comprised 27th and 28th Divisions, both composed of 'Regular' army battalions brought back from the Empire.

The two divisions took over French trenches in front of the Messines-Wytschaete Ridge, in the south of the Ypres Salient. These were poor quality low-lying trenches which were often wet and flooded. As the men had returned from the Empire, they had equipment that was not designed for cold and wet winters in northern Europe. V Corps played a small part in the Battle of Neuve Chapelle, and 27th Division took part in the Action at St Eloi, both in March 1915. But their main challenge was Second Ypres in April and May 1915. The Germans launched their gas attack on 22 April which destroyed the French troops holding the line north and east of Ypres. The Germans then pushed the British line, with the French section now thinly held by Canadians, back towards the town but V Corps held the advance. Plumer was given extra divisions, including cavalry, to become 'Plumers Force' which was ordered to organise a withdrawal to the 'Frezenberg Line'. As a consequence of the creation of 'Plumer's Force', Second Army was reduced to a single Corps and its commander, Smith-Dorrien, resigned. Plumer was appointed to succeed him, and V Corps reverted to Second Army control, with Allenby transferred from Cavalry Corps to take command. Among the desperate fighting to hold the German advance in April, four battalions of the 28th Division were placed under Lieutenant Colonel Augustus David Geddes on 23 April as 'Geddes Detachment' and used as a mobile force to plug gaps where needed. Added during the next few days were two battalions from 27th Division. As Plumer's Force was being formed at the end of the month, it was decided to disband Geddes Detachment. Geddes was killed on 28 April. Following the large contribution in April and May 1915, the Corps took part in further actions at Ypres later in 1915 including a diversionary attack at the time of the Battle of Loos in September.

As 1916 began the Corps still held the line at Ypres and found itself involved in a number of actions in the first half of the year. Several things are worthy of note. First, the recapture of the Bluff in March was based on innovative artillery techniques pioneered by V Corps' artillery commander Brigadier General Herbert Crofton Campbell Uniacke, later knighted and promoted to Major General. On 4 April, the Canadian Corps changed places with V Corps, the first time that a whole Corps of the British Expeditionary Force relieved another. On 4 July, Hew Fanshawe was relieved from command of V Corps and was replaced by his elder brother, Edward Fanshawe.

In August 1916, V Corps was transferred from Second Army to Reserve Army, later Fifth Army, and moved south take over the sector on the River Ancre, where little or no progress had been made during the Somme Offensive. They began to attack in September and continued to make very limited progress through to November.

Action in this area continued into 1917 as the Germans moved to the Hindenburg Line. The Corps played a part in the Arras Offensive at the south end of the line being responsible for attacks at Bullecourt with the Australians. After Bullecourt, Fifth Army moved north to prepare for Third Ypres. V Corps was initially held in reserve but moved into the line in September. It did not take part in the attack on the Passendale Ridge and was moved to Third Army for the Battle of Cambrai relieving IV Corps in the line in time to face the German counter attacks.

The Corps was holding the line to which it had retreated at Cambrai, a salient in front of Flesquieres, when the German offensive began on 21 March 1918. Third Army's commander, Byng, ordered V Corps to hold its line, allowing a withdrawal of 4000m, unaware of how extensive the German attack was and the movement of Fifth Army under Gough. V Corps was nearly surrounded and had to mount a hasty retreat which caused a gap between Third and Fifth Armies. By the end of March the Corps was back on the battlefields of 1916 at the Ancre as Fanshawe was relieved of command. Subsequently, V Corps took part in the Advance to Victory. Finding that the German trenches did not exist, there was no barbed wire, and the Germans were withdrawing at pace, the Corps commander, Shute, ordered open warfare, no artillery barrages, with the artillery moving up behind the infantry in support and a series of night attacks which took objectives with few casualties. As a result, V Corps gained more ground than formations that made conventional set piece attacks behind a barrage. On the day of the armistice, V Corps was within a mile or two of the Franco-Belgian border, having established a line south-east of Maubeuge.

Commanding Officers

8 January 1915	Lieutenant General Sir Herbert Charles Onslow Plumer
8 May 1915	Lieutenant General Sir Edmund Henry Hynman Allenby
23 October 1915	Lieutenant General Hew Dalrymple Fanshawe
5 July 1916	Lieutenant General Edward Arthur Fanshawe
11 August 1916	Major General Oliver Stewart Wood Nugent (acting)
17 August 1916	Lieutenant General Edward Arthur Fanshawe
28 April 1918	Lieutenant General Cameron Dinsdale Deane Shute

Field Marshal Herbert Charles Onslow Plumer, 1st Viscount Plumer, GCB, GCMG, GCVO, GBE, (13 March 1857 – 16 July 1932) was commissioned as a Lieutenant into the Yorks and Lancasters, then the 65th Regiment of Foot in 1876, was promoted to Captain in 1882, Major in 1893, Lieutenant Colonel and Colonel in 1900. He went to India in 1879 where he became Adjutant and then moved to Africa where he served in the Nile Expedition in the Sudan in 1884 being Mentioned in Despatches. He attended the Staff College in England from 1886-87 and then became Deputy-Assistant Adjutant-General in Jersey in 1890. He was made Assistant Military Secretary to the Commanding Officer of Cape Colony in December 1895 taking part in actions in Rhodesia in 1896-97 commanding the Relief Force during the Second Matabele War. He became Deputy Assistant Adjutant-General at Aldershot in 1897. He took part in the South African Wars commanding a mixed force and was Mentioned in Despatches. He was promoted to Major General in 1902 to command 4th Brigade and then 10th Division in 1903 taking Eastern Command in the same year. He became Quartermaster-General to the Forces in February 1904, took command of 7th Division in 1906, 5th Division within Irish Command in 1907, was promoted to Lieutenant General in 1908, and took charge of Northern Command in 1911. Plumer formed V Corps in France in January 1915. During Second Ypres he led an enlarged Corps with divisions from other Corps, a formation known as 'Plumer's Force', to successfully defend the city. Consequently, he was given command of Second Army as a full General. He led Second Army to a great success at Messines in June 1917 but at Third Ypres it became bogged down. He was given command of the forces sent to Italy in late 1917 returning to command Second Army in 1918 during the advance that ended the war. After the war he commanded the army of occupation in Germany, was promoted to Field Marshal, created Baron Plumer of Messines and of Bilton in 1919 and became Governor of Malta in May 1919. In 1925 he became High Commissioner of the British Mandate for Palestine. He became Viscount Plumer in 1929. He was awarded the Order of the Bath (CB) in 1901, made a Knight Commander of the Order of the Bath (KCB) in 1906 and Knight Grand Cross of the Order of the Bath (GCB) in January 1918, a Knight Grand Cross of the Order of St Michael and St George (GCMG) in January 1916, Knight Grand Cross of the Royal Victorian Order (GCVO) in 1917 and Knight Grand Cross of the Order of the British Empire (GBE) in 1924.

Field Marshal Edmund Henry Hynman Allenby, 1st Viscount Allenby, GCB, GCMG, GCVO – See Cavalry Corps

Lieutenant General Sir Hew Dalrymple Fanshawe, KCB, KCMG – See Cavalry Corps

Lieutenant General Sir Edward Arthur Fanshawe, KCB, (4 April 1859 – 13 November 1952) was commissioned as a Lieutenant in the Royal Artillery in 1878, was promoted to Captain in 1886, Major in 1896, Lieutenant Colonel in 1903 and Colonel in 1908. He served in the Second Anglo-Afghan War in 1878-80, the Sudan Expedition of 1885, the South African Wars and in India before moving to command 6th Division's artillery in Ireland. In 1913, he was transferred to command the divisional artillery in the 43rd (Wessex) Division. He was about to take them to India at the start of the war when he was transferred to command the artillery of 1st Division in September 1914 as a Brigadier General. He was promoted to Major General and moved to England to command the newly formed 31st Division but was transferred in August 1915 to command the 11th (Northern) Division at Gallipoli. He remained with the division, moving with it to France in 1916 until he was promoted to Lieutenant General to command V Corps replacing his younger brother. He led the Corps from Ypres to the Somme and into 1917 where it fought in Third Ypres. He also faced the German advance in 1918 following which he was removed from command. He retired in 1923 and was the eldest of three brothers who rose to senior ranks in the army in the war. He was made a Knight Commander of the Order of the Bath (KCB) in March 1915.

Major General Sir Oliver Stewart Wood Nugent, KCB, DSO, (9 November 1860 – 31 May 1926) was commissioned into the Royal Munster Fusiliers as a Lieutenant in 1882 transferring to the King's Royal Rifle Corps a year later. He was promoted to Captain in 1890, Major in 1899 and Lieutenant Colonel in 1906. He served in the Hazara Expedition of 1888, Miranzai Expedition of 1891, where he was Mentioned in Despatches, and the Chitral Expedition of 1895 where he was again Mentioned in Despatches and awarded the Distinguished Service Order. He served in the South African Wars, where he was wounded, before returning to the United Kingdom to become Deputy Assistant Quartermaster General to III Corps in Ireland in 1902. He was aide de camp to King George V from 1909-16. He was promoted to Brigadier General to command 41st Brigade at the start of the war and took command of the 36th (Ulster) Division in September 1915 being promoted to Major General in January 1916. The division saw some limited success on the first day of the Battle of the Somme but had to withdraw due to failure by the divisions on either flank to make progress. He remained in command until May 1918. He commanded the Meerut Division in India from August 1918 to 1920 and retired in 1920. He was awarded the Order of the Bath (CB) in 1917 and made a Knight Commander of the Order of the Bath (KCB) in 1922.

General Sir Cameron Dinsdale Deane Shute, KCB, KCMG, (15 March 1866 – 25 January 1936) was commissioned into the Welsh Regiment in 1885, moved to the Rifle Brigade in 1895 and took part in the Nile Expedition in 1898. He served as Deputy Assistant Adjutant General in Malta from 1899 and as a Staff Officer at Scottish Coast Defences from 1905. He was promoted to Lieutenant Colonel to command the 2nd Rifle Brigade in 1910 and then became a Staff Officer at Aldershot Command just before the start of the war. He became a Brigadier General commanding 59th Brigade in 1915 and was then promoted to Major General to command the 63rd (Royal Naval) Division in October 1916. As an army officer he never quite fitted in with the naval traditions of 63rd Division. He moved to command 32nd Division from February 1917 until April 1918 though he and Major General the Honourable Alan Richard Montagu-Stuart-Wortley of 19th Division changed positions for a month around the time of the Battle of Messines in 1917. He was the last commander of V Corps. After the war he led the 4th Division and then Northern Command from 1927 to his retirement in 1931.

Composition

Division	From	To
27th	31/12/1914	29/05/1915
28th	16/01/1915	03/06/1915
3rd Cavalry	03/02/1915	06/02/1915
1st Canadian	12/04/1915	04/05/1915
50th	23/04/1915	23/06/1915
3rd (Lahore) Indian	24/04/1915	03/05/1915
4th	25/04/1915	31/05/1915
2nd Cavalry	26/04/1915	03/05/1915
3rd	03/05/1915	04/05/1915
3rd Cavalry	03/05/1915	16/05/1915
1st Cavalry	06/05/1915	16/05/1915
3rd	09/05/1915	13/05/1915
2nd Cavalry	13/05/1915	30/05/1915
1st Cavalry	20/05/1915	28/05/1915
1st Indian Cavalry/4th Cavalry/1st Mounted	23/05/1915	14/06/1915
14th	25/05/1915	27/05/1915
6th	26/05/1915	31/05/1915
3rd	28/05/1915	18/06/1916
3rd Cavalry	30/05/1915	06/06/1915
14th	14/06/1915	23/07/1915
46th	24/06/1915	01/10/1915
5th	14/07/1915	04/08/1915
17th	19/07/1915	06/03/1916
14th	16/09/1915	28/09/1915
24th	01/10/1915	22/03/1916
9th	03/10/1915	20/12/1915
50th	21/12/1915	03/04/1916
3rd Canadian	22/03/1916	04/04/1916
1st Canadian	03/04/1916	04/04/1916

24th	03/04/1916	03/07/1916
2nd Canadian	03/04/1916	04/04/1916
50th	04/04/1916	11/08/1916
41st	19/06/1916	03/07/1916
24th	16/07/1916	26/07/1916
41st	16/07/1916	16/08/1916
20th	19/07/1916	21/07/1916
36th	22/07/1916	16/08/1916
18th	24/07/1916	26/07/1916
19th	04/08/1916	14/08/1916
23rd	12/08/1916	15/08/1916
20th	14/08/1916	15/08/1916
55th	14/08/1916	19/08/1916
2nd	16/08/1916	19/11/1916
6th	16/08/1916	17/08/1916
Guards	16/08/1916	25/08/1916
39th	24/08/1916	01/10/1916
48th	27/08/1916	18/09/1916
51st	01/10/1916	02/10/1916
63rd (RN)	04/10/1916	18/11/1916
3rd	05/10/1916	15/11/1916
37th	22/10/1916	13/12/1916
11th	16/11/1916	19/11/1916
32nd	17/11/1916	25/11/1916
3rd	22/11/1916	29/11/1916
7th	23/11/1916	29/11/1916
19th	30/11/1916	10/03/1917
18th	01/12/1916	20/01/1917
32nd	01/12/1916	16/02/1917
46th	01/12/1916	06/12/1916
7th	12/01/1917	07/07/1917

62nd	18/01/1917	24/06/1917
31st	22/02/1917	25/03/1917
11th	23/02/1917	19/04/1917
46th	07/03/1917	24/03/1917
18th	23/03/1917	28/03/1917
2nd	24/03/1917	26/03/1917
58th	06/04/1917	04/07/1917
62nd	29/06/1917	07/07/1917
56th	23/07/1917	06/08/1917
23rd	08/08/1917	24/08/1917
56th	24/08/1917	31/08/1917
18th	30/08/1917	07/09/1917
9th	05/09/1917	01/10/1917
42nd	07/09/1917	22/09/1917
59th	07/09/1917	28/09/1917
61st	07/09/1917	15/09/1917
55th	15/09/1917	25/09/1917
3rd	17/09/1917	28/09/1917
1st Cavalry	07/10/1917	20/11/2017
59th	10/10/1917	09/11/1917
1st Canadian	12/10/1917	21/10/1917
2nd Canadian	12/10/1917	18/10/1917
48th	12/10/1917	09/11/1917
11th	16/10/1917	23/11/1917
40th	15/11/1917	16/11/1917
59th	17/11/1917	17/11/1917
Guards	17/11/1917	23/11/1917
2nd	23/11/1917	25/11/1917
40th	23/11/1917	28/11/1917
47th	24/11/1917	27/11/1917
2nd	01/12/1917	04/04/1918

47th	01/12/1917	16/12/1917
59th	01/12/1917	02/12/1917
51st	03/12/1917	15/12/1917
25th	06/12/1917	08/12/1917
63rd (RN)	10/12/1917	12/12/1917
17th	12/12/1917	13/08/1918
19th	15/12/1917	21/03/1918
36th	15/12/1917	26/12/1917
59th	15/12/1917	25/12/1917
61st	15/12/1917	23/12/1917
63rd (RN)	15/12/1917	15/06/1918
47th	05/01/1918	12/04/1918
12th	25/03/1918	06/06/1918
38th	02/04/1918	11/11/1918
35th	06/04/1918	30/06/1918
63rd (RN)	19/06/1918	29/07/1918
21st	01/07/1918	11/11/1918
63rd (RN)	05/08/1918	12/08/1918
17th	18/08/1918	11/11/1918
33rd	15/09/1918	11/11/1918
12th	16/06/2018	14/07/1918

Battles Honours

Action of St. Eloi 14-15 March 1915 (27th Division in Second Army)

Second Battles of Ypres 1915

> Battle of Gravenstafel 22-23 April 1915 (27th, 28th & 1st Canadian Divisions, Geddes Detachment, 13th Brigade of 5th Division in Second Army)
>
> The Gas Attack 22 April 1915 (1st Canadian Division and part of 28th Division in Second Army)
>
> Battle of St. Julien 24 April–4 May 1915(4th, 27th, 28th, 50th, 3rd (Lahore) Indian, 2nd Cavalry & 1st Canadian Divisions, Geddes Detachment, 13th Brigade of 5th Division in Second Army to 28 April then as 'Plumer's Force')

Battle of Frezenberg Ridge 8-13 May 1915 (4th, 27th, 28th, 50th, 1st Cavalry & 3rd Cavalry Divisions in Second Army)

Battle of Bellewaarde Ridge 24-25 May 1915 (4th, 27th, 28th, 50th, 1st Cavalry & 2nd Cavalry Divisions in Second Army)

First Attack on Bellewaarde 16 June 1915 (3rd Division in Second Army)

Actions of Hooge 19 and 30 July and 9 August 1915(3rd Division in Second Army)

Second Attack on Bellewaarde 25-26 September 1915(46th Division in Second Army)

Loss of the Bluff 14-15 February (17th Division in Second Army)

Recapture of the Bluff 2 March 1916 (3rd & 17th Divisions in Second Army)

Capture of St. Eloi Craters 27 March–4 April 1916 (3rd Division in Second Army)

Wulvergem Gas Attack 30 April 1916 (3rd & 24th Divisions in Second Army)

Battles of the Somme 1916

Fighting on the Ancre 3 September 1916 (39th Division in Reserve Army)

Battle of Thiepval Ridge 26-28 September 1916 (39th Division in Reserve Army)

Battle of the Ancre Heights 1–5 October 1916 (39th Division in Reserve Army)

Battle of the Ancre 13-18 November 1916 (2nd, 3rd, 32nd, 37th, 51st & 63rd Divisions in Fifth Army)

Capture of Beaumont Hamel 13 November 1916 (51st Division in Fifth Army)

Capture of Beaucourt 14 November 1916 (63rd Division in Fifth Army)

Operations on the Ancre 11 January–13 March 1917 (7th, 31st, 32nd, 46th & 62nd Divisions in Fifth Army)

Attack on Rettemoy Graben 12 March 1917 (46th Division in Fifth Army)

German retreat to the Hindenburg Line 14 March–5 April 1917 (7th, 46th & 62nd Divisions in Fifth Army)

First Attack on Bullecourt 11 April 1917 (62nd Division in Fifth Army)

German attack on Lagnicourt 15 April 1917 (62nd Division in Fifth Army)

Battle of Bullecourt 3-17 May 1917 (7th, 58th & 62nd Divisions in Fifth Army)

Actions on the Hindenburg Line 20 May–16 June 1917 (58th & 62nd Divisions in Fifth Army)

Third Battles of Ypres 1917

Battle of the Menin Road 20-25 September 1917 (3rd, 9th, 55th & 59th Divisions in Fifth Army)

Battle of Polygon Wood 26 September–3 October 1917 (3rd & 59th Divisions in Fifth Army)

Battle of Cambrai 1917

The German Counter-Attacks 30 November–3 December 1917 (2nd, 47th & 59th Divisions, 51st Division from VI Corps in Third Army)

Welsh Ridge 30 December 1917 (63rd Division in Third Army)

First Battles of the Somme 1918

Battle of St. Quentin 21-23 March 1918 (2nd, 17th, 47th & 63rd Divisions in Third Army)

First Battle of Bapaume 24-25 March 1918 (2nd, 12th, 17th, 47th & 63rd Divisions in Third Army)

First Battle of Arras 28 March 1918 (2nd & 12th Divisions in Third Army)

Battle of the Ancre 5 April 1918 (12th, 38th, 47th & 63rd Divisions in Third Army)

Second Battles of the Somme 1918

Battle of Albert 21-23 August 1918 (17th, 21st & 38th Divisions in Third Army)

Second Battle of Bapaume 31 August–3 September 1918 (17th, 21st & 38th Divisions in Third Army)

Battles of the Hindenburg Line

Battle of Havrincourt 12 September 1918 (38th Division in Third Army)

Battle of Épehy 18 September 1918 (17th, 21st, 33rd & 38th Divisions in Third Army)

Battle of the St. Quentin Canal 29 September–2 October 1918 (21st & 33rd Divisions in Third Army)

Battle of the Beaurevoir Line 3-5 October 1918 (33rd & 38th Divisions in Third Army)

Battle of Cambrai 8-9 October 1918 (17th, 21st, 33rd & 38th Divisions in Third Army)

Capture of Villers Outreaux 8 October 1918 (38th Division in Third Army)

Pursuit to the Selle 9-12 October 1918 (17th & 33rd Divisions in Third Army)

The Final Advance in Picardy

Battle of the Selle 17-25 October 1918 (17th, 21st, 33rd & 38th Divisions in Third Army)

Crossing of the Selle 20 October 1918 (17th & 33rd Divisions in Third Army)

Attack on Forest and Ovillers 23 October 1918 (21st & 33rd Divisions in Third Army)

Battle of the Sambre 4 November 1918 (17th & 38th Divisions in Third Army)

Headquarters

11 January 1915	Abbeville
13 January 1915	Hazebrouck
4 February 1915	Poperinge
26 April 1915	Abeele
4 April 1916	Bailleul
16 August 1916	Marieux
2 October 1916	Acheux
29 November 1916	Doullens
12 January 1917	Acheux
2 April 1917	Bihucourt
7 July 1917	Duisans
16 July 1917	Givenchy Chateau near Eperlecques
7 September 1917	Ten Elms Camp near Poperinge
28 September 1917	Esquelbecq
10 October 1917	Lillers
12 October 1917	Camblain l'Abbaye
14 November 1917	Querrieu
20 November 1917	Grévillers
1 December 1917	Villers-au-Flos
23 March 1918	Méaulte
24 March 1918	Toutencourt
27 March 1918	Talmas
27 March 1918	Naours
28 August 1918	Senlis
24 September 1918	Manancourt
12 October 1918	Selvigny
5 November 1918	Poix-du-Nord

VI Corps

VI Corps headquarters began to form at the end of May 1915 and the Corps took control of a section of line at Ypres in June when it was made up of 4th and 6th Divisions as part of Plumer's Second Army. It played a small part in the final actions of Second Ypres and then took part in further actions in the Salient in 1915 including diversionary attacks to support the Battle of Loos. Finally, in December it suffered the first use of phosgene gas in an attack by the German XXVI Reserve Corps in which the British lost over 1000 men, mostly from the 49th Division.

In 1916 the Corps, now part of Third Army, played little part in the offensives on the Somme and the commanding officer found himself removed from command. He was replaced by Haldane who became the second and last commanding officer of the Corps.

The Corps played a much larger part in the last two years of the war. In 1917 it was involved in the Battles of Arras and Cambrai. In 1918 it faced the brunt of the German Offensive in March before being involved in the push that led to victory during the second part of the year. In the final weeks of the war this became a rush to push the Germans back as far as possible and the Corps became the advance spearhead for Third Army. On Armistice Day the Corps, in the form of 62nd and Guards Divisions, was on the south bank of the River Sambre and about 8km east of Maubeuge.

Commanding Officers

| 27 May 1915 | Lieutenant General John Lindesay Keir |
| 8 August 1916 | Lieutenant General James Aylmer Lowthorpe Haldane |

Lieutenant General Sir John Lindesay Keir, KCB, (6 July 1856 – 3 May 1937) was commissioned into the Royal Artillery in February 1876 and served in India for six years before transferring to the Royal Horse Artillery and then the Royal Field Artillery. He was promoted to Captain in 1884, Major in 1892, Lieutenant Colonel in 1901, brevet Colonel in 1902 while in South Africa, and Colonel on his return from the South African Wars. He attended the Staff College in England in 1892, re-joined the Royal Horse Artillery, served in the South African Wars commanding the 1st Imperial Yeomanry and then the Royal Artillery Mounted Rifles from the end of 1901 and was Mentioned in Despatches. He returned to England in 1902 joining the Royal Horse Artillery, soon becoming Assistant Adjutant-General. He was given command of a Brigade in India in 1907 as a Brigadier General, promoted to Major General in 1909, returned to England in 1911 and took command of the South Midland Division in 1912. In 1914 he was given command of 6th Division taking it to France in September 1914 and into action at the Battle of the Aisne remaining in command until given the newly formed VI Corps. He led the Corps into a series of actions in 1915 but they saw little formal action in 1916. This may have been due to a dispute between Keir and the head of Third Army, Allenby. Haig supported Allenby and Keir was removed from command remaining in England for the rest of the war. He retired in July 1918. He was awarded the Order of the Bath (CB) in 1908, made a Knight of the Order of the Bath (KCB) in 1915 and knighted after the war.

General Sir James Aylmer Lowthorpe Haldane, GCMG, KCB, DSO, (17 November 1862 – 19 April 1950) was commissioned in the Gordon Highlanders in 1882, was promoted to Lieutenant in 1886, Captain in 1892, Major and brevet Lieutenant Colonel in 1902 and Colonel in 1906. He served in India, taking part in the Chitral Expedition 1894-95 as part of the Waziristan Field Force, the Tirah Campaign 1897-98 for which he was awarded the Distinguished Service Order, and became aide-de-camp to the Commander-in-Chief East Indies in 1898. He served in the South African Wars being taken prisoner and helping Churchill to escape. In 1901 he was appointed a Staff Captain in the Intelligence Section at the War Office. He was military attaché with the Imperial Japanese Army from 1904-05 during the Russo-Japanese War and accompanied Japanese forces into Manchuria. He was Assistant Director of Military Intelligence from 1906-09 and promoted to Brigadier General in 1910 to command 10th Brigade who he took to France in 1914. He led the 3rd Division from November 1914 until taking command of VI Corps, a position he held until the end of the war. After the war he took command of forces in Mesopotamia from 1920-22 and retired in 1925 as a General. He was cousin to 1st Viscount Haldane, Secretary of State for War from 1905–1912, responsible for the Haldane Reforms. He was awarded the Order of the Bath (CB) in 1906 made Knight Commander of the Order of the Bath (KCB) in 1918 and Knight Grand Cross of the Order of St Michael and St George (GCMG) in 1922.

Composition

Division	From	To
4th	31/05/1915	13/07/1915
6th	31/05/1915	01/02/1916
49th	28/06/1915	05/02/1916
14th	23/07/1915	16/09/1915
14th	28/09/1915	03/02/1916
20th	22/01/1916	04/02/1916
56th	21/02/1916	05/05/1916
14th	22/02/1916	01/08/1916
5th	23/02/1916	17/07/1916
55th	06/05/1916	21/07/1916
11th	07/07/1916	03/09/1916
21st	18/07/1916	21/09/1916
12th	16/08/1916	30/09/1916
35th	30/08/1916	12/02/1917
14th	04/10/1916	08/01/1917
12th	23/10/1916	14/04/1917
9th	29/10/1916	14/01/1917
3rd	08/02/1917	19/05/1917
15th	18/02/1917	06/05/1917
37th	09/03/1917	12/04/1917
17th	12/04/1917	26/04/1917
29th	12/04/1917	26/04/1917
12th	23/04/1917	24/05/1917
56th	26/04/1917	02/07/1917
29th	03/05/1917	04/06/1917
37th	19/05/1917	03/06/1917
61st	24/05/1917	26/07/1917
3rd	31/05/1917	26/06/1917
12th	07/06/1917	01/07/1917
62nd	07/07/1917	13/10/1917

7th	07/07/1917	28/08/1917
42nd	10/07/1917	23/08/1917
21st	07/08/1917	30/08/1917
50th	07/08/1917	16/10/1917
16th	28/08/1917	03/12/1917
9th	30/08/1917	05/09/1917
4th	08/09/1917	20/09/1917
51st	29/09/1917	02/11/1917
34th	30/09/1917	07/10/1917
3rd	02/10/1917	01/04/1918
29th	16/10/1917	17/11/1917
34th	02/11/1917	28/03/1918
Guards	11/11/1917	17/11/1917
62nd	14/11/1917	15/11/1917
40th	17/11/1917	21/11/1917
59th	19/11/1917	23/11/1917
56th	24/11/1917	03/12/1917
40th	28/11/1917	29/03/1918
51st	30/11/1917	03/12/1917
59th	02/12/1917	06/12/1917
25th	04/12/1917	06/12/1917
19th	06/12/1917	08/12/1917
25th	08/12/1917	15/12/1917
6th	14/12/1917	01/01/1918
59th	31/12/1917	01/04/1918
31st	22/03/1918	02/04/1918
Guards	22/03/1918	11/11/1918
42nd	23/03/1918	24/03/1918
2nd Canadian	28/03/1918	01/07/1918
32nd	29/03/1918	18/07/1918
57th	02/04/1918	09/04/1918

33rd	08/04/1918	10/04/1918
5th	08/04/1918	12/04/1918
2nd	13/04/1918	11/11/1918
3rd Canadian	26/06/1918	25/07/1918
59th	26/07/1918	25/08/1918
57th	29/07/1918	29/07/1918
5th	15/08/1918	18/08/1918
3rd	17/08/1918	11/11/1918
62nd	19/08/1918	22/08/1918
3rd Canadian	20/08/1918	23/08/1918
52nd	21/08/1918	25/08/1918
56th	21/08/1918	25/08/1918
57th	21/08/1918	25/08/1918
2nd Cavalry	22/08/1918	24/08/1918
62nd	23/08/1918	11/11/1918
5th	24/08/1918	26/08/1918

Battle Honours

German Liquid Fire Attack, Hooge 30-31 July 1915 (14th Division in Second Army)
Hooge 9 August 1915 (6th Division in Second Army)
Second Attack on Bellewaarde 25 September 1915 (14th Division in Second Army)
First Phosgene Gas Attack 19 December 1915 (49th Division in Second Army)
Battles of Arras 1917

> First Battle of the Scarpe 9-14 April 1917 (3rd, 12th, 15th, 17th, 29th & 37th Divisions in third Army)
>
> Capture of Monchy le Preux 11 April 1917 (37th & 3rd Cavalry Divisions in Third Army)
>
> Second Battle of the Scarpe 23-24 April 1917 (3rd, 15th, 17th & 29th Divisions in Third Army)
>
> Capture of Guemappe 23 April 1917 (15th Division in Third Army)
>
> Battle of Arleux 28-29 April 1917 (3rd & 12th Divisions in Third Army)
>
> Third Battle of the Scarpe 3-4 May 1917 (3rd, 12th, 29th & 56th Divisions in Third Army)
>
> Attack on Devil's Trench 12 May 1917 (12th Division in Third Army)

Capture of Roeux 13-14 May 1917 (3rd Division in Third Army)
Battle of Cambrai 1917
>Attack at Bullecourt 20 November 1917 (3rd & 16th Divisions in Third Army)
>Capture of Bourlon Wood 25-28 November 1917 (56th Division in Third Army)
>German Counter-Attacks 30 November–3 December 1917 (3rd, 51st & 56th Divisions in Third Army)

First Battles of the Somme 1918
>Battle of St. Quentin 21-23 March 1918 (Guard, 3rd, 31st, 34th, 40th & 59th Divisions in Third Army)
>First Battle of Bapaume 24-25 March 1918 (Guards, 3rd, 31st, 40th, 42nd & 59th Divisions in Third Army)
>First Battle of Arras 1918 28 March 1918 (Guards, 3rd, 31st, 97th Brigade of 32nd & 2nd Canadian Divisions in Third Army)
>Battle of the Ancre 5 April 1918 (32nd Division in Third Army)

Second Battles of the Somme 1918
>Battle of Albert 21-23 August 1918 (Guards, 2nd, 3rd, 52nd, 56th & 59th Divisions in Third Army)
>Capture of Mory Copse 24 August 1918 (99th Brigade of 2nd Division in Third Army)
>Capture of Behagnies and Sapignies 25 August 1918 (5th Brigade of 2nd Division in Third Army)
>Second Battle of Bapaume 31 August–3 September 1918 (Guards, 2nd, 3rd & 62nd Divisions in Third Army)

Second Battles of Arras 1918
>Battle of the Scarpe 26-30 August 1918 (Guards & 62nd Divisions in Third Army)
>Assault of the Drocourt-Queant Line 3 September 1918 (2nd Division in Third Army)

Battles of the Hindenburg Line:
>Battle of Havrincourt 12 September 1918 (Guards, 2nd & 62nd Divisions in Third Army)
>Battle of the Canal du Nord 27 September–1 October 1918 (Guards, 2nd, 3rd & 62nd Divisions in Third Army)
>Capture of Mont sur l'Oeuvre 1 October 1918 (2nd Division in Third Army)

Battle of Cambrai 8-9 October 1918 (Guards, 2nd & 3rd Divisions in Third Army)

Capture of Forenville 8 October 1918 (2nd Division in Third Army)

Pursuit to the Selle 9-12 October 1918 (Guards Division in Third Army)

Final Advance in Picardy:

Battle of the Selle 17-25 October 1918 (Guards, 2nd, 3rd & 62nd Divisions in Third Army)

Capture of Solesmes 20 October 1918 (62nd Division in Third Army)

Battle of the Sambre 4 November 1918 (Guards & 62nd Divisions in Third Army)

Passage of the Grand Honnelle 5-7 November 1918 (Guards & 62nd Divisions in Third Army)

Occupation of Maubeuge 9 November 1918 (Guards Division in Third Army)

Headquarters

27 May 1915	Godewaersvelde
31 May 1915	Chateau La Lovie
5 February 1916	Toutencourt
2 March 1916	Avesnes les Comte
14 March 1916	Noyelle Vion
19 April 1917	Duisans
7 July 1917	Bihucourt
17 September 1917	Bretencourt
22 March 1918	Humbercamps
25 March 1918	Pas-en-Artois
26 March 1918	Tincques
27 March 1918	Noyelle Vion
12 August 1918	Lucheux
25 August 1918	Las Bazeque Wood
3 September 1918	Ervillers
30 September 1918	Hermies
13 October 1918	Estourmel
4 November 1918	Solesmes
9 November 1918	Gommegnies

VII Corps

VII Corps formed in France on 14 July 1915 as part of Third Army with 4th and 48th Divisions. It held the left of the British front, reaching south to the boundary with the French forces at Hebuterne an area in which it remained until the Battle of the Somme. It was not involved in any of the major actions of 1915 which is not to say it did not take part in minor operations, trench raids and artillery duels. In 1916 it took part in its first battle leading the diversionary attack at Gommecourt at the end of the British line on the first day of the Battle of the Somme. The 46th Division suffered 2455 casualties, and 56th Division 4313, for no gain.

In 1917 the Corps played a part in following the German Retreat to the Hindenburg Line. Third Army and VII Corps continued to be active in 1917 as it was involved in the Battles of Arras and Cambrai. In 1918 it was badly affected during the German advance in March and April. As a consequence, its commander was removed, and the Corps was taken out of the line on 7 April to become a training unit in the rear. First, at Bernaville and then in the St Omer area, the Corps took over the battle training of divisions which were resting and recovering in preparation to return to the front line. The Corps was also used for creating new defensive lines in the rear and became unofficially part of the Labour Corps. Consequently, after a period under a temporary commanding officer, it had no need for a GOC after June 1918. At the Armistice Day it was in the Fruges area of northern France.

Commanding Officers

15 July 1915	Lieutenant General Sir Thomas D'Oyly Snow
3 January 1918	Lieutenant General Sir Walter Norris Congreve, VC
13 April – 19 June 1918	Major General Sir Robert Dundas Whigham
28 October 1918	Colonel Lord Henry Francis Montagu-Douglas Scott
4 November 1918	Brigadier General Charles Johnstone Armstrong

Lieutenant General Sir Thomas D'Oyly Snow, KCB, KCMG, (5 May 1858 – 30 August 1940) was commissioned into the Somerset Light Infantry, then the 13th Regiment of Foot, in 1879 taking part in the Anglo-Zulu War the same year. In 1884–85, having transferred to the Mounted Infantry Regiment of the Camel Corps, Snow served in the Nile Expedition during the Mahdist War and was severely wounded at the Battle of El Gubat in January 1885. He became a Captain in 1887, Brigade Major at Aldershot in 1895 and Major in the Royal Inniskilling Fusiliers in 1897. He served in the Nile Campaign of 1898 where he was twice Mentioned in Despatches. He became a brevet Lieutenant Colonel, second in command of the 2nd Northamptonshires in India from 1899 to 1903 when he returned to the United Kingdom as a full Lieutenant Colonel. In June 1903 he was promoted to Colonel and appointed Assistant Quartermaster-General of IV Corps, which later became Eastern Command, having never led a battalion. He was promoted to Assistant Adjutant-General in 1905, Brigadier General in 1906 and took command of the 11th Brigade in 1909. He was awarded the Order of the Bath (CB) in the 1907 Birthday Honours List. Snow was promoted to Major General in March 1910 to command the 4th Division and was still there at the outbreak of war as the division was deployed for home defence on the eastern coast, but they were sent to France later in August joining II Corps in the Retreat from Mons and fighting at Le Cateau. He was wounded in September 1914 when his horse fell on him, so he was invalided until November. He then took command of 27th Division at Winchester as it formed with men returning from overseas. He led them during Second Ypres in 1915 for which he received the Knight Commander of the Order of the Bath (KCB). He was soon promoted to command VII Corps. The Corps was responsible for the diversionary attack at Gommecourt on the first day of the Battle of the Somme in 1916. In 1917 Snow led the Corps in the offensives at the Battle of Arras in the Spring and the Battle of Cambrai in November. He, and several other Corps commanders, were replaced after Cambrai, which did not go well, and he was moved to England in January 1918 where he took charge of Western Command. He was promoted to Lieutenant General and appointed a Knight Commander of the Order of St Michael and St George (KCMG) in recognition of his services on the Western Front. He had also been six times Mentioned in Despatches, appointed a Commander of the Legion of Honour by the French Government, and made a Grand Cross of the Order of Leopold from Belgium. He held command of XXIII Corps on a temporary basis due to the absence of Pulteney. He retired in 1919 holding positions as Colonels of two regiments and undertaking charitable work. Snow is the grandfather of British broadcasters Peter Snow and Jon Snow and great grandfather of historian and TV presenter, Dan Snow.

General Sir Walter Norris Congreve, VC, KCB, MVO, (20 November 1862 – 28 February 1927) was commissioned as a Lieutenant in the Rifle Brigade in 1885, promoted to Captain in 1893, Major in 1901 and brevet Lieutenant Colonel the next day. He served in the South African Wars where he was awarded the Victoria Cross for his actions at the Battle of Colenso in December 1899. Captain Congreve, with two other officers, The Honourable Frederick Hugh Sherston Roberts (whose father had won the Victoria Cross) and Harry Norton Schofield, and Corporal George Edward Nurse retrieved artillery pieces under fire. All four received the Victoria Cross for this action. Then, although wounded himself, seeing one of the officers fall, Congreve went out with Major William Babtie, Royal Army Medical Corps, who also received the Victoria Cross for this action, and brought in the wounded man. Congreve's citation reads 'At Colenso on the 15th December, 1899, the detachments serving the guns of the 14th and 66th Batteries, Royal Field Artillery, had all been either killed, wounded, or driven from their guns by Infantry fire at close range, and the guns were deserted. About 500 yards behind the guns was a donga in which some of the few horses and drivers left alive were sheltered. The intervening space was swept with shell and rifle fire. Captain Congreve, Rifle Brigade, who was in the donga, assisted to hook a team into a limber, went out; and assisted to limber up a gun. Being wounded, he took shelter; but, seeing Lieutenant Roberts fall, badly wounded, he went out again and brought him in. Captain Congreve was shot through the leg, through the toe of his boot, grazed on the elbow and the shoulder, and his horse shot in three places.' He was also twice Mentioned in Despatches and served on Staff as Private Secretary to Kitchener. In December 1902, he became Assistant Military Secretary and aide de camp to the Duke of Connaught in Ireland, being made a Member of the Royal Victorian Order (MVO) in 1903. By the start of the war he was a Brigadier General commanding 18th Brigade who he took to France where they were involved in the Battle of the Aisne and some of the units took part in the Christmas Truce. He became Major General in 1915 to command 6th Division and took command of XIII Corps in November 1915 leading them into the Battle of the Somme. XIII Corps succeeded in securing Delville Wood, but it was one of the bloodiest confrontations of the Somme, with both sides suffering large casualties. In June 1917 he was wounded by German shellfire near Vimy Ridge, which cost him his arm and his command. He was made a Knight of the Order of the Bath (KCB) in 1917. After a period of convalescence in England, Congreve returned to France in January 1918 to command VII Corps as a Lieutenant General and, from April 1918, X Corps. However, the German offensive caused major losses to both Corps such that, on 15 May, he was ordered home. Haig, with whom he had shared rooms at Sandhurst, refused to see him before his departure. He played no further role in the war. After the war he was knighted and made commander of the Egyptian Expeditionary Forces from 1919-23, commander of Southern Command from 1923-24 and Governor of Malta until his death in 1927. He was father of Major William La Touche Congreve, VC – they are one of only three father and son pairs to win a Victoria Cross. William Congreve was killed on 20 July 1916 while serving as Brigade Major of 76th Brigade during the Battle of the Somme. He was the first officer during the war to be awarded a Victoria Cross having already been awarded the Distinguished Service Order and a Military Cross.

General Sir Robert Dundas Whigham, GCB, KCMG, DSO, (5 August 1865 – 23 June 1950) was commissioned into the 1st Royal Warwickshires as a Lieutenant in 1885, was promoted to Captain in 1892, to Major in 1900, Lieutenant Colonel in 1908 and Colonel in 1911. He was Adjutant for the Royal Warwickshires in 1892 and moved to the Egyptian Army in 1897-98 where he served in the Nile Expedition in 1898 for which he was Mentioned in Despatches. He served in the South African Wars as Deputy Assistant Adjutant General at Army Headquarters from 1900-02 for which he was awarded the Distinguished Service Order and Mentioned in Despatches. He moved to England in 1902 to become Brigade Major to II Corps and was then Deputy Assistant Adjutant General 1906-09 and GSO1 at the War Office from 1912 to September 1914. He served as GSO1 to 2nd Division from September to December 1914 when he was promoted to a Brigadier General to serve on staff at I Corps. He was then made Sub-Chief of the General Staff in France from July to December 1915, promoted to Major General in January 1916, and moved to the War Office to be Deputy Chief of the Imperial General Staff from December 1915 to April 1918. After his brief holding role at VII Corps, after which the Corps had no commanding officer, he was given command of 59th Division and then 62nd Division until the end of the war. After the war he was commanding officer of the Light Division in the British Army of the Rhine and commanding officer of 3rd Division from 1919-22, Adjutant-General to the Forces from 1923-27 and led Eastern Command from 1927 until he retired in 1931. He was awarded the Order of the Bath (CB) in 1915 and Knight Commander of the Order of St Michael and St George (KCMG) in 1919. His father represented the MCC at cricket, his sister and brother were successful golfers. His son, Flying Officer Robert George Murray Whigham was shot down near Brest in the attack the Gneisenau on 24 July 1941 aged 38 years.

Colonel Lord Henry Francis Montagu-Douglas Scott (15 January 1868 – 19 April 1945) arrived as the Labour Corps Commandant for the remnants of VII Corps on 28 October 1918. He was commissioned into the Royal Scots (Lothian Regiment) as a 2nd Lieutenant, was promoted to Lieutenant in 1888, Captain in 1890, Major in 1901 and Lieutenant Colonel and Colonel in 1905. He served in the South African Wars. He commanded the 18th (1st Public Schools) Royal Fusiliers in the war. The battalion landed in France in November 1915 as part of 19th Brigade in 33rd Division. They transferred to GHQ Troops in February 1916 and disbanded in April 1916. He then commanded the 8th Bedfordshires until April 1917 when he was posted to GHQ. Toward the end of the war, he was transferred to the Labour Corps. He was five times Mentioned in Despatches. After the war he was a deputy governor of the Bank of Scotland. He was the fourth son of the 6th Duke of Buccleuch. He made one first class cricket appearance in 1891.

Finally, on 4 November 1918 Brigadier General Charles Johnstone Armstrong, CMG, CB, (27 August 1872 – 1933) briefly took command until 1919 as the labourers in VII Corps were tasked with repair and reconstruction of all canals in France and Belgium devastated by the war. He was from Canada and was commissioned into the Militia in 1894 serving in the South African Wars with the 2nd Royal Canadian Regiment of Infantry. When the war in South Africa ended, he became divisional engineer of the Central South African Railways until he returned to Canada in 1910. At the start of the war he was appointed to command the Canadian Engineers and was commissioned as a Lieutenant Colonel leaving Canada in September 1914 and arriving in France with the 1st Canadian Division in April 1915. When the Canadian Corps was formed, he was promoted to command the engineers as a Brigadier General. He was Mentioned in Despatches in June 1915 and awarded the Order of St Michael and St George (CMG) in January 1916. He was involved in a railway accident in February 1916 and due to complications from the accident, did not return to the front until January 1918. During the German advance in March 1918 he helped to put together an ad hoc force which included his Canadian engineers to support Fifth Army. For his later work he was twice Mentioned in Despatches and awarded the Order of the Bath (CB) in 1919. He returned to Canada to work in the Department of Militia and Defence, later the Department of National Defence, before becoming the district officer commanding Military District No. 1. He retired in 1933 as a Major General.

Composition

Division	From	To
4th	13/07/1915	07/05/1916
48th	18/07/1915	06/03/1916
37th	25/08/1915	16/07/1916
36th	09/10/1915	18/11/1915
36th	30/01/1916	07/02/1916
55th	09/02/1916	06/05/1916
56th	05/05/1916	23/08/1916
46th	07/05/1916	11/11/1916
17th	21/08/1916	23/10/1916
33rd	04/09/1916	18/10/1916
49th	25/09/1916	24/01/1917
48th	30/09/1916	23/11/1916
23rd	14/10/1916	15/10/1916
30th	26/10/1916	12/04/1917
46th	06/12/1916	24/01/1917
14th	08/01/1917	12/04/1917
46th	20/02/1917	01/03/1917
56th	08/03/1917	26/04/1917
21st	13/03/1917	07/08/1917
58th	19/03/1917	01/04/1917
17th	23/03/1917	04/04/1917
50th	11/04/1917	26/04/1917
33rd	12/04/1917	05/07/1917
30th	19/04/1917	30/04/1917
14th	24/04/1917	12/07/1917
18th	26/04/1917	04/07/1917
50th	02/05/1917	04/05/1917
50th	19/05/1917	23/05/1917

50th	26/05/1917	07/08/1917
56th	02/07/1917	23/07/1917
48th	05/07/1917	23/07/1917
17th	25/09/1917	04/10/1917
40th	11/10/1917	18/10/1917
20th	18/10/1917	29/10/1917
24th	18/10/1917	08/12/1917
55th	18/10/1917	08/12/1917
40th	25/10/1917	01/11/1916
1st Cavalry	30/11/1917	01/12/1917
Dismounted Cavalry	30/11/1917	04/12/1917
21st	01/12/1917	01/04/1918
16th	05/12/1917	25/03/1918
9th	09/12/1917	01/04/1918
14th	07/01/1918	14/01/1918
39th	28/01/1918	25/03/1918
12th	24/03/1918	25/03/1918
1st Cavalry	24/03/1918	25/03/1918
35th	24/03/1918	06/04/1918
3rd Australian	27/03/1918	06/04/1918
4th Australian	27/03/1918	06/04/1918
37th	29/03/1918	30/03/1918
18th	30/03/1918	04/04/1918
1st Australian	05/04/1918	06/04/1918
39th	02/05/1918	06/04/1918
40th	02/05/1918	22/06/1918
59th	06/05/1918	08/05/1918
34th	05/06/1918	18/06/1918
39th	05/06/1918	16/08/1918
41st	24/06/1918	30/06/1918
30th	27/06/1918	08/07/1918

35th	30/06/1918	02/07/1918
14th	03/07/1918	17/08/1918
50th	03/07/1918	03/07/1918
33rd	20/08/1918	27/08/1918
49th	23/08/1918	28/08/1918

Battle Honours

The Battles of the Somme 1916

Attack on the Gommecourt Salient 1 July 1916 (46th & 56th Divisions in Third Army)

German Retreat to the Hindenburg Line 14 March–5 April 1917 (14th, 21st, 30th, 56th & 58th Divisions in Third Army)

The Battles of Arras 1917

First Battle of the Scarpe 9-14 April 1917 (14th, 21st, 30th, 33rd, 50th & 56th Divisions in Third Army)

Capture of Wancourt 11 April 1917 (14th Division in Third Army)

Capture of Wancourt Ridge 13-15 April 1917 (50th Division in Third Army)

Second Battle of the Scarpe 23-24 April 1917 (30th, 33rd & 50th Divisions in Third Army)

Third Battle of the Scarpe 3-4 May 1917 (14th, 18th & 21st Divisions in Third Army)

Actions on the Hindenburg Line 20 May–16 June 1917 (21st & 33rd Divisions in Third Army)

The Battle of Cambrai 1917

The Tank Attack 20-21 November 1917 (55th Division in Third Army)

The German Counter-Attacks 30 November–3 December 1917 (21st, 24th & 55th Divisions in Third Army)

Welsh Ridge 30 December 1917 (26th Brigade of 9th Division in Fifth Army)

The First Battles of the Somme 1918

Battle of St. Quentin 21-23 March 1918 (9th, 16th, 21st & 39th Divisions in Fifth Army)

Actions at the Somme Crossings 24-25 March 1918 (39th Division in Third Army)

First Battle of Bapaume 24-25 March 1918 (9th, 12th, 21st, 35th, 116th Brigade of 39th Division & 1st Cavalry Divisions in Fifth Army)

The Battle of the Ancre 5 April 1918 (35th Division, 10th and 11th Brigades of 3rd Australian Division, 12th and 13th Brigades of 4th Australian Divisions in Third Army)

Headquarters

14 July 1915	St Omer
19 July 1915	Marieux
24 February 1916	Pas-en-Artois
14 January 1917	Fosseux
16 April 1917	Bretencourt
8 August 1917	St. Pol-sur-Ternoise
18 October 1917	Templeux-la-Fosse
29 October 1917	Le Catelet
29 December 1917	Templeux-la-Fosse
19 February 1918	Haut Allaines
20 February 1918	Templeux-la-Fosse
22 March 1918	Cléry-sur-Somme
23 March 1918	Maricourt
23 March 1918	Corbie
26 March 1918	Montigny
6 April 1918	Bernaville
2 May 1918	Houlle
26 September 1918	Fruges

VIII Corps

VIII Corps was formed at Gallipoli. At the start of the invasion in April the forces of 29th and Royal Naval Divisions fought under the Mediterranean Expeditionary Force. From this came the British Army Corps Gallipoli but, as the battle became protracted, British divisions arrived as reinforcements. British Army Corps headquarters formed at Helles on 24 May 1915 becoming VIII Corps on 5 June. At the time of the formation of VIII Corps, IX Corps began to form, and British Army Corps was disbanded.

The Corps' battle front was at Cape Helles on the tip of the Gallipoli peninsula but, despite a year of battle, gains were limited, and losses were great. Hence, the Allies evacuated the peninsula in January 1916 moving the divisions to Mudros and then Egypt. Corps headquarters arrived in Alexandria on 17 January 1916 though the Corps was disbanded on 27 January at Cairo with some divisions being sent to other theatres.

VIII Corps began to reform in France at Marieux on 7 March 1916. Its original commanding officer returned to prepare the Corps for the Battle of the Somme. The Corps was responsible for the area attacked at Serre, the Redan Ridge and what is now Newfoundland Park although the Corps had developed a bad reputation with Haig's headquarters in the month leading up to the attack. The Corps was a combination of 'regular', 4th & 29th, territorial, 48th, and New Army, 31st, Divisions. No progress was made on the first day of the battle at significant loss but some of the more remembered stories of the first day took place from the Corps' area, such as the Newfoundlanders above Beaumont Hamel, the Public Schools Battalion at Hawthorn Crater, the Accrington, Sheffield, Bradford and Leeds pals at Serre, and the loss of Brigadier General Bertie Prowse from 11th Brigade. Poor preparation, a limited scope of the plan, the German defences, and accommodating sideshows like the early explosion of the mine at Hawthorn Crater to get footage for a film, all led to the Corps seeing some of the worst casualties on the day. Artillery fire was weaker here and the Germans had the advantage of high ground. VIII corps suffered 14581 casualties on 1 July 1916. Any very small gains were abandoned within a day or two. Of the three Corps which tried a creeping barrage, only VIII Corps was completely unsuccessful.

At the end of July 1916, the Corps moved to the Ypres sector but was not involved in any significant battles throughout the remainder of 1916 and 1917 though it did hold sections of the line for most of that period. It was in Fourth Army for the start of the Battle of the Somme, Reserve Army from 4 July, Second Army from the end of July 1916, Fourth Army from December 1917 and Second Army again from 14 April 1918 when it was moved from the front line at Ypres to hold positions in the rear in Belgium until 15 June 1918. On 22 June 1918 the Corps commander was transferred to command XVIII Corps in First Army and two days later VIII headquarters was disbanded. On 2 July XVIII was renamed VIII Corps with Hunter-Weston in command and XVIII Corps ceased to exist.

The new VIII Corps took part in the Advance to Victory campaign as part of First Army. On Armistice Day the Corps was located on the Nimy-Turbise road north of Mons.

Commanding Officers

24 May 1915	Lieutenant General Sir Aylmer Gould Hunter-Weston
17 July 1915	Lieutenant General the Honourable Sir Frederick William Stopford (temp)
24 July 1915	Major General William Douglas (acting)
8 August 1915 – 27 January 1916	Lieutenant General Sir Francis John 'Joey' Davies
18 March 1916	Lieutenant General Sir Aylmer Gould Hunter-Weston

Lieutenant General Sir Aylmer Gould Hunter-Weston, KCB, DSO, GCStJ, (23 September 1864 – 18 March 1940) was commissioned into the Royal Engineers in 1884, promoted to Captain in 1892, Major in 1895, Lieutenant Colonel in 1900 and Colonel in 1908. He served on the Indian North West Frontier being on the Miranzai Expedition of 1891 and the Waziristan Expedition of 1894–95 when he was wounded. He served on staff during the Nile Expedition of 1896 and then attended the Staff College from 1898-99. He served in the South African Wars, first as a Staff Officer, then in command of the Mounted Engineers followed by command of the Royal Engineer Cavalry Division. He became Deputy Assistant Adjutant-General and then Chief of Staff to French's Cavalry Division before he commanded a cavalry column. He was awarded the Distinguished Service Order and Mentioned in Despatches. He returned to England in 1902 to join the staff of the Royal Engineers followed by a position at Eastern Command from 1904-08 and Scottish Command from 1908-11. In 1911 Hunter-Weston was appointed Assistant Director of military training. In February 1914 he became a Brigadier General to command 11th Brigade and took them to France in 4th Division serving at Le Cateau and on the Aisne where he gained a good reputation. In October 1914 he was promoted to Major General and given command of 29th Division to take them to Gallipoli. He was sceptical of the possibility of a successful landing at Helles on the tip of the peninsula which he expected would be heavily defended by the Turks but thought careful planning focusing on V, W and X Beaches would help. Nonetheless, his management of the initial landing period was not considered to be the best and by 4 May the division had suffered about 40% casualties. As the campaign proceeded and more reinforcements were dispatched to Helles, on 24 May he was promoted to Lieutenant General and placed in command of VIII Corps with 29th Division, the Royal Naval Division, 42nd Division and the 49th Indian Infantry Brigade. It was at this time still called the British Army Corps becoming VIII Corps in June. By now his reputation had diminished and he was criticised in the diaries of several senior officers. Some had even begun to refuse his orders. Hunter-Weston was relieved of command on 23 July, officially invalided due to sunstroke or enteric fever and dysentery. He returned to England to recover where he was knighted and returned to command the Corps in March 1916 to prepare for the Battle of the Somme. The Corps was responsible for the northern end of the line and suffered high casualties failing to capture any of their objectives. He encouraged his officers to believe that the artillery bombardment would do its task of destroying the German defences, and to prepare the men to walk across no-man's land to occupy the empty German front line on 1 July 1916. He ordered them to stick to the very prescriptive elements of his plan. The Corps was moved to the Reserve Army under Gough and Hunter-Weston's reputation was permanently damaged. But the shortage of good officers probably explained why he kept his job, though the Corps was moved to the rear. He was elected to parliament in October 1916 representing North Ayrshire as a Unionist and was the first MP to also command a Corps, though they were not involved in any actions. He suggested a role for the Corps carrying out a diversionary attack for the Battle of Messines in June 1917, but this was vetoed by Plumer. Hence, its only role at Ypres in 1917 was in December holding the ground gained, though Hunter-Weston raised concerns about this task. He played an active role leading his corps in the Hundred Days Offensive. He became the 27th Laird of Hunterston in 1908, was awarded the Order of the Bath (CB) and made a Knight Commander of the Order of the Bath (KCB) in August 1915. He remained in politics after the war moving to the constituency of Bute and Northern Ayrshire in 1918 which he represented until 1935.

Lieutenant General Sir Frederick William Stopford, KCB, KCMG, KCVO, (2 February 1854 – 4 May 1929) was commissioned into the Grenadier Guards in 1871. He served in the Egyptian Expeditionary Force in 1882 and the Suakin Expedition in 1885 before he was made Brigade Major to the Brigade of Guards which had been posted to Egypt. He became Brigade Major to 2nd Brigade at Aldershot in 1886, Deputy Assistant Adjutant General at Horseguards in 1892, and Deputy Assistant Adjutant General at Aldershot in 1894. He served in the Fourth Anglo-Ashanti War in 1895-96 before becoming Assistant Adjutant General at Horseguards in 1897. He served in the South African Wars for which he was knighted and appointed a Knight Commander of the Order of St Michael and St George (KCMG) in 1900. He returned to England to be Deputy Adjutant General at Aldershot in 1901, became chief staff officer for I Corps as a Brigadier General in 1902 and was appointed Director of Military Training at the War Office in 1904. He was promoted to Major General to command the Brigade of Guards in 1904 and became commander of London District in 1906. By 1914 he was commander of the Tower of London and the Home Forces Second Army, destined for retirement but was sent by Kitchener to take command of the newly formed IX Corps having never led a division. He briefly led VIII Corps in the absence of Hunter-Weston before IX Corps formed. During this week in command he learned of the plan for IX Corps to attack Suvla Bay in August with the four divisions it had brought from England. Lacking energy and suffering from ill-health, he was an elderly and inexperienced General. His long-distance command from an off-shore battleship, HMS Jonquil, proved he was unsuitable for the post of leading a Corps, notably as he was asleep during the landings at Suvla Bay. Further, he was blamed for the failure to attack following the landings. After a month he was removed from IX Corps and sent home returning to his post at the Tower of London until 1917 until he retired in 1920. He was a younger son of the 4th Earl of Courtown. He was made a Knight Commander of the Royal Victorian Order (KCVO) in June 1909 and was made a Knight Commander of the Order of the Bath (KCB) in June 1921.

Major General Sir William Douglas, KCMG, CB, DSO, (13 August 1858-1920) was commissioned in to the 1st Royal Scots in 1878, promoted to Lieutenant in the same year, Captain in 1885, Major in 1895, Lieutenant Colonel in 1900 and Colonel in 1906. He was Adjutant to the 1st Royal Scots from 1880-87 and 1893-94, and the

3rd Royal Scots from 1888-93. He served in the Bechuanaland Expedition from 1884-85 and attended the Staff College from 1896-97. He served in the South African Wars commanding the 1st Royal Scots and then a column for which he was Mentioned in Despatches and awarded the Distinguished Service Order. He served on Staff in the 6th and 8th Divisions until promoted to Brigadier General to command 14th Brigade from 1909-12. He was promoted to Major General commanding 42nd (East Lancashire) Division in May 1913, remaining with the division until March 1917. They went to Egypt in 1914 and were sent to Gallipoli to reinforce the British Army Corps on 1 May 1915. He was asked to command VIII Corps during the absence of Hunter-Weston, and as Stopford was required to command XI Corps. He commanded the Desert Column in 1916 and the Western Reserve Centre after leaving 42nd Division. He was four times Mentioned in Despatches during the war. He was awarded the Order of the Bath (CB) in 1908 and made a Knight Commander of the Order of St Michael and St George (KCMG) in November 1915.

General Sir Francis John 'Joey' Davies, KCB, KCMG, KCVO, (3 July 1864 – 18 March 1948) was commissioned into the Worcestershire Militia in 1881 and transferred to the Grenadier Guards as a Lieutenant in 1884, was promoted to Captain in 1895, Major in 1899 and Lieutenant Colonel in 1900. He became Adjutant to the 2nd Grenadier Guards in 1893 and moved to South Africa in 1897 where he was Deputy Assistant Adjutant General for the Cape of Good Hope before serving in the South African War as Deputy Assistant Adjutant General responsible for Intelligence. He returned to England after the war to be Deputy Assistant Quartermaster General at the War Office from 1902-04, Assistant Director of Military Operations 1904-07 and Assistant Quartermaster General for Western Command in 1907-09. He took command of 1st (Guards) Brigade as a Brigadier General in 1909 and returned to the War Office in 1913. He took command of the newly formed 8th Division in September 1914 leading them at the Battles of Neuve Chapelle and Aubers Ridge before being sent to Gallipoli to take command of VIII Corps. In January 1916, when the Corps moved to Egypt and was temporarily disbanded, he returned to England to serve as Military Secretary, responsible for personnel, at the War Office. He was given Scottish Command in 1919 before he retired in 1923. He was son of Lieutenant General Henry Fanshawe Davies, grandson of General Francis John Davies and great-grandson of Admiral of the Fleet Sir Thomas Byam Martin. His younger brother was Major General Henry Rodolph Davies who commanded the 11th (Northern) Division.

Composition

British Army Corps Gallipoli

Division	From	To
29th	25/04/1915	24/05/1915
63rd (RN)	25/04/1915	24/05/1915
42nd	09/05/1915	24/05/1915

VIII Corps

Division	From	To
29th	24/05/1915	19/08/1915
42nd	24/05/1915	28/01/1916
63rd (RN)	24/05/1915	09/01/1916
52nd	06/06/1915	10/01/1916
29th	20/12/1915	13/01/1916
13th	28/12/1915	10/01/1916
31st	07/03/1916	10/07/1916
36th	07/03/1916	30/03/1916
29th	15/03/1916	28/07/1916
48th	30/03/1916	15/07/1916
4th	07/05/1916	22/07/1916
35th	06/07/1916	12/07/1916
12th	10/07/1916	26/07/1916
38th	14/07/1916	12/06/1917
25th	18/07/1916	31/07/1916
29th	29/07/1916	08/10/1916
4th	30/07/1916	25/08/1917
4th	03/09/1916	17/09/1916
55th	02/10/1916	12/06/1917
39th	18/11/1916	23/02/1917
21st	28/01/1917	12/02/1917

23rd	19/03/1917	04/04/1917
39th	16/04/1917	13/06/1917
61st	26/07/1917	15/08/1917
18th	15/08/1917	30/08/1917
14th	02/09/1917	05/10/1917
8th	02/09/1917	22/03/1918
30th	22/09/1917	22/11/1917
33rd	06/10/1917	02/04/1918
14th	13/11/1917	03/01/1918
39th	22/11/1917	10/12/1917
50th	01/12/1917	21/03/1918
29th	04/01/1918	09/04/1918
59th	01/04/1918	12/04/1918
41st	04/04/1918	13/04/1918
39th	17/04/1918	02/05/1918
40th	17/04/1918	02/05/1918
59th	19/04/1918	06/05/1918
33rd	20/04/1918	01/05/1918
66th	21/04/1918	02/05/1918
19th	24/04/1918	26/04/1918
25th	25/04/1918	25/04/1918
34th	25/04/1918	12/05/1918
30th	27/04/1918	12/05/1918
19th	13/05/1918	04/06/1918
74th	18/05/1918	23/05/1918
21st	18/06/1918	22/06/1918
8th	18/06/1918	23/06/1918
20th	01/07/1918	30/10/1918
24th	01/07/1918	06/10/1918
52nd	01/07/1918	23/07/1918
8th	20/07/1918	11/11/1918

51st	02/08/1918	14/08/1918
4th	03/09/1918	17/09/1918
66th	20/09/1918	26/09/1918
58th	01/10/1918	14/10/1918
12th	02/10/1918	11/11/1918
52nd	07/10/1918	11/11/1918
63rd (RN)	11/10/1918	05/11/1918
49th	04/11/1918	11/11/1918

Battles Honours

Battles of Helles 24 May-6 June 1915

Third Battle of Krithia 4 June 1915 (29th, 42nd & Royal Naval Divisions, 29th Indian Brigade)

Gully Ravine 28 June–2 July 1915 (29th Division, 156th Brigade of 52nd Division, 29th Indian Brigade)

Achi Baba Nullah 12-13 July 1915 (52nd Division)

Krithia Vineyard 6-13 August 1915 (29th & 42nd Divisions)

Krithia Nullahs 29 December 1915 (52nd Division)

The Last Turkish Attacks 7 January 1916 (13th Division)

Evacuation of Helles 8-9 January 1916 (13th, 29th, 52nd & Royal Naval Division)

Battles of the Somme 1916

Battle of Albert 1-13 July 1916 (4th, 29th, 31st & 48th Divisions in Fourth Army)

Second Battles of Arras 1918

Battle of the Scarpe 26-30 August 1918 (8th Division in First Army)

Final Advance in Artois

Final Advance 2 October–11 November 1918 (8th, 12th, 20th, 52nd & 58th Divisions, 3rd Cavalry Brigade of 2nd Cavalry Division in First Army)

Forcing the Rouvroy-Fresnes Line 7-8 October 1918 (8th Division in First Army)

Capture of Douai 17 October 1918 (8th Division in First Army)

Headquarters

24 May 1915	Helles
17 January 1916	Alexandria
18-27 January 1916	Cairo
7 March 1916	Marieux
29 July 1916	Chateau La Lovie
30 May 1917	Vogeltje Convent near Poperinge
13 June 1917	Esquelbecq
2 September 1917	Flêtre
15 November 1917	Hooggraaf
18 November 1917	Vogeltje Convent near Poperinge
14 April 1918	Cassel
5 May 1918	Merckeghem
15 May 1918	Châlons-sur-Marne
16 June 1918	Long
2 July 1917	Camblain-l'Abbé
19 October 1918	Petit Cuincy
23 October 1918	Orchies

Mediterranean Expeditionary Force

The Mediterranean Expeditionary Force commanded Allied forces at Gallipoli and Salonika. Its headquarters was formed in March 1915 under General Sir Ian Hamilton until he was dismissed due to the failure of the 29th Division at Gallipoli. Command briefly passed to General William Birdwood, commander of the Australian and New Zealand Army Corps, but for the remainder of the Gallipoli campaign it was led by General Sir Charles Monro.

While the Gallipoli theatre was the only active Mediterranean theatre, the Mediterranean Expeditionary Force was used to refer to the forces at Gallipoli. With the opening of the Salonika campaign in October 1915, the forces at Gallipoli were referred to as the Dardanelles Army and the Salonika contingent became the Salonika Army on the Macedonian Front.

At the end of 1915 when the Gallipoli campaign ended the Mediterranean Expeditionary Force was commanded by General Archibald Murray who was based in Egypt. The defence of the Suez Canal warranted a new command headquarters so the Egyptian Expeditionary Force was set up in March 1915, though nominally still under the Mediterranean Expeditionary Force.

Mediterranean Expeditionary Force

Division	From	To
42nd	25/09/1914	09/05/1915
10th Indian	24/12/1914	07/01/1916
2nd Mounted	19/04/1915	18/08/1915
53rd	29/07/1915	09/08/1915
10th	02/10/1915	01/11/1915
53rd	15/12/1915	01/04/1916
54th	18/12/1915	02/04/1916
2nd Mounted	01/01/1916	21/01/1916
13th	10/01/1916	22/01/1916
52nd	10/01/1916	27/01/1916
11th	12/01/1916	01/02/1916

Indian Expeditionary Force G

In April 1915, Indian Expeditionary Force F, made up of the 28th, 29th and 30th Brigades, was sent to the Middle East where 29th Brigade was used as Indian Expeditionary Force G to reinforce the Gallipoli Campaign. It was attached to the British 29th Division and played a part in the Third Battle of Krithia. The Brigade was also involved in the Battle of Gully Ravine and the Battle of Sari Bair after which it was withdrawn from the peninsula. It re-joined the other two brigades who were being used in Egypt. 29th Brigade was broken up in June 1917 and its battalions posted to 75th Division.

IX Corps

In June 1915 it was decided to send reinforcements to the British Army Corps, part of the Mediterranean Expeditionary Force, in Gallipoli. The aim was to achieve a substantial victory on the peninsula and accomplish a victory damaging the Turkish contribution to the war. The Corps was formed on 16 June at the Tower of London in England as the man chosen to be commander, Lieutenant General the Honourable Sir Frederick William Stopford, was Lieutenant of the Tower of London. It left England on 22 June and arrived at Mudros on 9 July where it spent a month in preparation for landings at Suvla Bay. The landings were handled so badly that Stopford was removed from command nine days after the first landing, having proved out if his depth, though this had been his first senior position in battle. The Corps made little progress at Gallipoli and was withdrawn on 20 December 1915. The divisions in the Corps went to Imbros or Mudros and thence to other campaigns in the area or France. Headquarters moved to Egypt on 1 January 1916 taking responsibility for the Suez Canal defences until April 1916.

The Corps transferred to France and was reformed under new leadership. On 3 July 1916 it moved to Second Army, on 16 July 1916 to Fourth Army, on 1 August 1916 to Reserve Army and on 14 August to Second Army. It remained out of major battles in 1916 but was used for the Battle of Messines and Third Ypres in 1917.

In 1918 it faced Operation Georgette, or the Battles of the Lys, in Belgium and French Flanders. During this German offensive, several ad hoc forces fought within the Corps. 'James's Force', 2000 men of 59th Division under Brigadier General Cyril Henry Leigh James, CB commanding officer of 177th Brigade, fought with 49th Division from 16-19 April. 'Wyatt's Force' of 1400 men under Brigadier General Louis John Watt, DSO commanding officer of 116th Brigade in 39th Division was formed on 13 April. Of note is that in 1920 he was given the task of choosing the body of the 'Unknown Warrior' who was finally laid to rest in Westminster Abbey. After severe losses during the Battle of the Lys in April 1918 the Corps was moved south to a quiet sector to reform. However, this quiet sector became the focus of the next German attack so IX Corps also took part in the Battle of the Aisne where it suffered heavy casualties. 'Gater's Force' of several composite battalions from 21st Division formed on 31 May under Brigadier General Sir George Henry Gater, GCMG, KCB, DSO, & Bar commander of 62nd Brigade, and fought until 19 June.

The Corps went on to play a significant part in the Advance to Victory. On 9 November it was ordered by Fourth Army to halt on the La Capelle-Avesnes-Maubeuge road on the right of the advance.

Commanding officers

17 June 1915	Lieutenant General the Honourable Sir Frederick William Stopford
16 August 1915	Major General Henry de Beauvoir De Lisle (temp)
24 August 1915	Lieutenant General the Honourable Sir Julian Hedworth George Byng
8 February 1916 – 22 April 1916	Lieutenant General Sir Francis John 'Joey' Davies
20 June 1916	Lieutenant General Alexander Hamilton Gordon
16 July 1918	Major General Sir Robert Dundas Whigham (temp)
22 July 1918	Major General Harold Whitla Higginson (temp)
30 July 1918	Lieutenant General Sir Alexander Hamilton Gordon
10 September 1918	Major General Edward Peter Strickland (temp)
13 September 1918	Lieutenant General Sir Walter Pipon Braithwaite

Lieutenant General Sir Aylmer Gould Hunter-Weston, KCB, DSO – See VIII Corps

General Sir Henry de Beauvoir De Lisle, KCB, KCMG, DSO, (27 July 1864 – 16 July 1955) was commissioned into the 2nd Durham Light Infantry in 1883, was promoted to Captain in 1891, Major in 1902 and brevet Lieutenant Colonel a day later becoming a full Lieutenant Colonel and brevet Colonel in 1906. He was a full Colonel in 1910. He served with the Mounted Infantry in Egypt from 1885-86 for which he was awarded the Distinguished Service Order, was Adjutant of the 2nd Durham Light Infantry in India from 1892-96, attended Staff College in 1899 and then took part in the South African Wars commanding a mobile column during which he was wounded, three times Mentioned in Despatches and awarded the Order of the Bath (CB). On returning to England in 1902 he joined the 5th (Princess Charlotte of Wales's) Dragoon Guards as a Major. He moved as second in command to the 1st (Royal) Dragoons in 1903, taking command in 1906. He served on Staff at Aldershot from 1910-11, briefly commanded 4th Cavalry Brigade in 1911, and then took charge of 2nd Brigade as a Brigadier General in 1911 leading them to France in 1914. He was soon promoted to command 1st Cavalry Division as a Major General. He was sent to lead 29th Division at Gallipoli from June 1915, with brief temporary command of the Corps, returning to France in January 1916 in charge of 29th Division. He was given command of XIII Corps in March 1918 as a Lieutenant General and XV Corps in April 1918. After the war he oversaw Western Command until 1923, retiring in 1926 as a full General. He was made a Knight Commander of the Order of the Bath (KCB) in 1917 and Knight Commander of the Order of St Michael and St George (KCMG) in 1919.

Field Marshal Julian Hedworth George Byng, 1st Viscount Byng of Vimy, GCB, GCMG, MVO – See Cavalry Corps

General Sir Francis John 'Joey' Davies, KCB, KCMG, KCVO – See VIII Corps

Lieutenant General Sir Alexander Hamilton-Gordon, KCB, (6 July 1859 – 13 February 1939) was commissioned into the Royal Artillery in 1880. He served in the Second Afghan War in 1880 and South African Wars where he was Deputy Assistant Adjutant General for Intelligence from 1901. Returning to England he was appointed a Deputy Assistant Quarter-Master-General at Aldershot in October 1901. From 1910-14 he became Director of Military Operations in India returning to England at the start of the war as commanding officer of Aldershot Command where he remained until 1916. He was given command of IX Corps, though he had never commanded a division and spent much of his time in administrative roles, as it reformed in France after its time at Gallipoli and Egypt. He was relieved of command in 1918 and retired in 1920. He was appointed Knight Commander of the Order of the Bath (KCB) in 1918. His paternal grandfather was the 4th Earl of Aberdeen, Prime Minister of the United Kingdom from 1852-55. He was grandson and great grandson of the astronomers John and William Herschel.

General Sir Robert Dundas Whigham, GCB, KCMG, DSO – See VII Corps

Major General Harold Whitla Higginson CB, DSO & Bar (10 November 1873 – 30 October 1954) was commissioned into the Royal Dublin Fusiliers in 1894, was promoted to Lieutenant in 1896, Captain in 1899 and Major in 1913. He served in the Lapai Expedition in West Africa in 1897-98, the South African Wars where he was Mentioned in Despatches, operations in Aden in 1903 and was Adjutant of the 4th Royal Dublin Fusiliers from 1904-07. He served in Egypt in 1908. He was Adjutant of the 2nd Royal Dublin Fusiliers in England from 1911 until he moved to become Brigade Major at the Warwickshire Brigade in the South Midland Division in May 1914. He went with them to France in May 1915 but soon left to take command of the 2nd Royal Dublin Fusiliers a month later as a Lieutenant Colonel, part of the 10th Brigade in 4th Division. He was promoted to Brigadier General in

May 1916 to command 53rd Brigade in the 18th (Eastern) Division. His new brigade performed well on 1 July 1916, the first day of the Battle of the Somme, at Montauban, one of the few successes of the day. He led his brigade to a series of successes during the Battle of the Somme in 1916 and during the German Retreat to the Hindenburg Line in early 1917. However, like all units it struggled during Third Ypres and the German Advance in 1918. Even so, as the brigade did achieve some notable counter-attacks and held the German advance in places, he was promoted to command 12th Division in April 1918 and led the Corps for a week. After the war he was given 17th Brigade in Ireland and 2nd Brigade at Aldershot in 1922. He commanded British troops in Ceylon (Sri Lanka) from 1924-28 and 55th Division from 1928-32 when he retired. He was awarded the Distinguished Service Order in January 1916 and a Bar in September 1918. He was awarded the Order of the Bath (CB) in 1919.

Lieutenant General Sir Edward Peter Strickland, KCB, KBE, CMG, DSO, (3 August 1869 – 24 June 1951) was commissioned into the Norfolk Regiment in 1888, was promoted to Lieutenant in 1891, Captain and brevet Major in 1899, full Major in 1908 and Lieutenant Colonel in 1909. He served in Burma from 1888-89, with the Egyptian Army 1893-1903, on the Dongola expedition in 1896 and on the Nile Expedition of 1899 for which he was awarded the Distinguished Service Order. He served in the West African Frontier Force from 1906-13 and commanded the North Nigeria Regiment in 1909. He was made a full Lieutenant Colonel to command the 1st Manchesters in India in June 1914 taking them to France at the start of the war as part of the Jullundur Brigade in the 3rd (Lahore) Indian Division. He was promoted to Brigadier General to command the Jullundur Brigade in January 1915 and moved to 98th Brigade in 33rd Division in November 1915. He was promoted to Major General to command the 1st Division in June 1916 leading the division until the end of the war, with a very brief time temporarily in command of IX Corps. After the war he was given command of a division in the British Army of the Rhine, took command of 6th Division in Ireland in 1919, survived an assassination attempt and was appointed military governor for the counties of Munster, Kilkenny and Wexford in January 1921. He led 2nd Division from 1923-27 and commanded British Troops in Egypt from 1927 to his retirement in 1931. He was awarded the Order of St Michael and St George (CMG) in 1913, the Order of the Bath (CB) in 1917 and made a Knight of the Order of the Bath (KCB) in 1919. He was created a Knight of the British Empire (KBE) in 1923 and promoted to Lieutenant General in 1926.

General Sir Walter Pipon Braithwaite, GCB, (11 November 1865 – 7 September 1945) was commissioned as a Lieutenant in the Somerset Light Infantry in 1886, was promoted to Captain in 1894, Major in 1900, Lieutenant Colonel in 1907 and Colonel in 1909. He served in the South African Wars where he was three times Mentioned in Despatches. He returned to England in 1902 to become Deputy Assistant Quartermaster-General of Southern Command and II Corps. He transferred to the Loyal North Lancashires in 1906 and moved to India to be Commandant of the Indian Army Staff College in 1909. He returned to England to join the War Office at the start of the war. In 1915 he was appointed Chief of Staff for the Mediterranean Expeditionary Force but was recalled to London after Gallipoli and given command of 62nd Division who he took to France in January 1917 and led them until he was given command of IX Corps in September 1918. After the war he produced a report for Haig on the performance of the British Staff officers that was generally supportive of the officers. He became Commander-in-Chief of Western Command in India in 1920, Scottish Command in 1923, Eastern Command in 1926 and Adjutant-General to the Forces in 1927. He retired in 1931 and became a commissioner of the Commonwealth War Graves Commission from 1927-31 when he moved to be Governor of the Royal Hospital Chelsea from 1931-38. In 1928 he oversaw arranging Douglas Haig's funeral. His son died on the first day of the Battle of the Somme in 1916.

Composition

Division	From	To
11th	16/07/1915	12/01/1916
10th	17/07/1915	02/10/1915
54th	04/08/1915	18/12/1915
53rd	09/08/1915	15/12/1915
2nd Mounted	18/08/1915	20/12/1915
29th	19/08/1915	20/12/1915
13th	28/08/1915	28/12/1915
10th Indian	07/01/1916	07/03/1916
29th	13/01/1916	07/03/1916
42nd	28/01/1916	22/04/1916
11th	01/02/1916	08/02/1916

54th	02/04/1916	01/06/1916
24th	03/07/1916	16/07/1916
2nd Australian	04/07/1916	26/10/1916
17th	11/07/1916	23/07/1916
36th	15/07/1916	19/07/1916
18th	21/07/1916	24/07/1916
7th	21/07/1916	01/08/1916
9th	23/07/1916	25/07/1916
24th	26/07/1916	01/08/1916
14th	01/08/1916	07/08/1916
48th	01/08/1916	10/08/1916
50th	11/08/1916	15/08/1916
19th	14/08/1916	06/10/1916
23rd	15/08/1916	11/09/1916
36th	16/08/1916	07/07/1917
41st	16/08/1916	24/08/1916
4th Canadian	28/08/1916	05/10/1916
7th	18/09/1916	19/11/1916
16th	21/09/1916	20/06/1917
25th	29/10/1916	21/03/1917
19th	10/03/1917	29/04/1917
19th	08/05/1917	06/12/1917
11th	19/05/1917	22/06/1917
37th	25/06/1917	30/01/1918
14th	12/07/1917	15/08/1917
30th	04/08/1917	22/09/1917
39th	27/09/1917	16/10/1917
39th	12/11/1917	22/11/1917
30th	22/11/1917	07/01/1918
4th Australian	09/01/1918	12/01/1918
7th	22/02/1918	24/03/1918

1st Australian	03/04/1918	05/04/1918
21st	03/04/1918	06/04/1918
25th	03/04/1918	25/04/1918
9th	04/04/1918	11/04/1918
19th	08/04/1918	24/04/1918
33rd	10/04/1918	20/04/1918
49th	10/04/1918	20/04/1918
34th	12/04/1918	25/04/1918
59th	12/04/1918	19/04/1918
50th	26/04/1918	03/07/1918
8th	04/05/1918	13/06/1918
25th	08/05/1918	26/06/1918
21st	14/05/1918	14/06/1918
19th	04/06/1918	04/07/1918
50th	14/07/1918	15/09/1918
8th	14/07/1918	20/07/1918
12th	16/07/1918	28/07/1918
18th	16/07/1918	27/07/1918
2nd Canadian	29/07/1918	01/08/1918
1st	11/09/1918	11/11/1918
32nd	11/09/1918	11/11/1918
6th	11/09/1918	11/11/1918
46th	19/09/1918	11/11/1918
20th	11/12/1918	30/01/1918

Battle Honours

Battle of Suvla

> The Landing at Suvla 6-15 August 1915 (10th, 11th, 53rd & 54th Divisions)
> Capture of Karakol Dagh 7 August 1915 (34th Brigade of 11th Division)
> Capture of Chocolate Hill 7-8 August 1915 (Hill's Force, 31st & 30th Brigades of 10th Division)
> Battle of Scimitar Hill 21 August 1915 (11, 29th & 2nd Mounted Divisions)
> Attack on 'W' Hills 21 August 1915 (11th & 2nd Mounted Divisions)

Evacuation of Suvla 19-20 December 1915 (11th, 13th & 2nd Mounted Divisions, 88th Brigade of 29th Division, 29th Indian Infantry Brigade)

Battle of Messines 7-14 June 1917 (11th, 16th, 19th & 36th Divisions in Second Army)

Capture of Wytschaete 7 June 1917 (16th & 36th Divisions in Second Army)

Third Battles of Ypres

> Battle of Pilckem Ridge 31 July–2 August 1917 (37th Division in Second Army)
> Battle of the Menin Road 20-25 September 1917 (19th & 37th Divisions in Second Army)
> Battle of Polygon Wood 26 September–3 October 1917 (19th & 37th Divisions in Second Army)
> Battle of Broodseinde 4 October 1917 (19th & 37th Divisions in Second Army)
> Battle of Poelcapelle 9 October 1917 (19th & 37th Divisions in Second Army)
> First Battle of Passchendaele 12 October 1917 (19th & 37th Divisions in Second Army)
> Second Battle of Passchendaele 26 October–10 November 1917 (19th Division in Second Army)

Battles of the Lys:

> Battle of Messines 10-11 April 1918 (9th, 19th, 21st, 25th, 29th, 36th, 33rd & 49th Divisions in Second Army)
> Loss of Hill 63 (7th Brigade of 25th Division in Second Army)
> Battle of Hazebrouck 12-15 April 1918 (33rd Division in Second Army)
> Battle of Bailleul 13-15 April 1918 (6th, 9th, 19th, 25th, 29th, 33rd, 34th, 36th, 49th & 59th Divisions in Second Army)
> Defence of Neuve Eglise 13-14 April 1918 (33rd & 49th Divisions in Second Army)

First Battle of Kemmel Ridge 17-19 April 1918 (6th, 19th, 25th, 30th, 33rd, 34th, 36th, 49th & 59th Divisions, 'James's Force, 'Wyatt's Force' in Second Army)

German Offensive in Champagne

Battle of the Aisne, 1918 27 May–6 June 1918 (8th, 19th, 21st, 25th & 50th Divisions, 'Gater's Force' in French Sixth Army to 29 May then in French Fifth Army)

Battles of the Hindenburg Line

Battle of Épehy 18 September 1918 (1st & 6th Divisions in Fourth Army)

Attack on the Quadrilateral and Fresnoy 24 September 1918 (1st & 6th Divisions in Fourth Army)

Battle of the St. Quentin Canal 29 September–2 October 1918 (1st, 6th, 32nd & 46th Divisions in Fourth Army)

Passage of Bellenglise 29 September 1918 (46th Division in Fourth Army)

Battle of the Beaurevoir Line 3-5 October 1918 (1st, 6th, 32nd & 46th Divisions in Fourth Army)

Battle of Cambrai 8-9 October 1918 (6th & 46th Divisions in Fourth Army)

Pursuit to the Selle 9-12 October 1918 (6th & 46th Divisions in Fourth Army)

Final Advance in Picardy

Battle of the Selle 17-25 October 1918 (1st, 6th & 46th Divisions in Fourth Army)

Attack South West of Landrecies 2 November 1918 (96th Brigade of 32nd Division in Fourth Army)

Battle of the Sambre 4 November 1918 (1st & 32nd Divisions in Fourth Army)

Passage of the Sambre-Oise Canal 4 November 1918 (1st & 32nd Divisions in Fourth Army)

Final Operations 5-11 November 1918 (1st, 32nd, 46th Divisions & 5th Cavalry Brigade of 2nd Cavalry Division in Fourth Army)

Headquarters

17 June 1915	Tower of London
9 July 1915	Mudros
25 July 1915	Imbros
7 August 1915	Suvla
1 January 1916	Cairo

6 January 1916	Alexandria
14 January -1 June 1916	Port Tewfik Suez
12 June 1916	Bailleul
5 July 1916	Mont Noir
16 July 1916	Talmas
23 July 1916	Villers-Bocage
1 August 1916	Domart-en-Ponthieu
14 August 1916	Bailleul
31 March 1917	Mont Noir
12 February 1918	Noyon
23 March 1918	Montdidier
24 March 1918	Bernaville
3 April 1918	Flêtre
12 April 1918	St. Sylvestre-Cappel
13 April 1918	Godewaersvelde
21 April 1918	Houtkerque
27 April 1918	Fère-en-Tardenois
8 May 1918	Montigny
21 May 1918	Jonchery
27 May 1918	Romigny
28 May 1918	Châtillon
30 May 1918	Vertus
9 June 1918	Fère-Champenoise
6 July 1918	Oisemont
16 July 1918	Molliens-Vidame
30 July 1918	Huppy
8 September 1918	Villers-Carbonnel
2 October 1918	Poeuilly
21 October 1918	Brancoucourt
24 October 1918	Busigny

X Corps

X Corps was formed in France in July 1915 joining Third Army. It took no part in any major actions in 1915 but was part of the move that relieved the French Tenth Army by taking over the line south of Loos to the Somme. By now part of Fourth Army, the first battle in which it took part was the Battle of the Somme where its 36th (Ulster) Division captured the Schwaben Redoubt on the first day of the battle and held it for a short time. But as no progress was made by the 32nd Division at Thiepval, having lost many 'pals' on the ridge, the 36th had to withdraw as best as possible to its start line. On 4 July the Corps was transferred, while in the line, to the new Reserve Army where it remained for the rest of the Battle of the Somme in 1916 but was moved away from the front, handing over to II Corps on 24 July.

In 1917, X Corps formed a part of the Second Army which prepared for the for the operations in Belgium in the summer. A significant breakthrough was anticipated after the disaster of the Somme the previous year, but Third Ypres became another battle of attrition, this time in the mud of the Ypres Salient. At the end of Third Ypres, X Corps was withdrawn from the front line and remained in the rear until July 1918.

In 1918, the Corps spent much of the first few months with no divisions under its control having responsibility for just some Corps troops. On 24 March it passed from Second Army to GHQ Reserve and took over several Australian divisions. However, the German advance saw the divisions allotted to the Corps moved on to front line Corps and X Corps move to Third Army. During the period of the German offensives in March to June 1918, the Corps played no active part. Its role was to oversee movements of units and train or manage troops behind the lines. The Corps, part of First Army from May, moved forward in July 1918 taking part of the Second Army front and relieving the French XVI Corps.

It was part of the Advance to Victory. By 8 November the Corps held the bank of the River Schelde, crossing it on 9 November 1918 and capturing Renaix. On Armistice Day the Corps were about 20km north of Mons at Lessines.

Commanding Officers

15 July 1915	Lieutenant General Sir Thomas Lethbridge Napier Morland
15 April 1918	Lieutenant General Sir Walter Norris Congreve, VC (temp)
24 May 1918	Lieutenant General Sir William Eliot Peyton
3 July 1918	Lieutenant General Sir Reginald Byng Stephens

General Sir Thomas Lethbridge Napier Morland, KCB, KCMG, DSO, (9 August 1865 – 21 May 1925) was commissioned into the King's Royal Rifle Corps in 1884, promoted to Captain in 1893, brevet Major in 1899 and full Major in 1901, brevet Lieutenant Colonel in 1900, brevet Colonel in 1903 and full Colonel in 1905. He served in Malta from 1895-98, moved to the West African Frontier Force in 1898 and became the commanding officer of the Force in 1900 leading the Kaduna Expedition in 1900 and the Kano Sokoto Campaign in 1903. He was wounded, Mentioned in Despatches and awarded the Distinguished Service Order for his service in West Africa. From 1905-09, he was Inspector-General of the West African Field Force. In 1910, Morland returned to England and was promoted to Brigadier General to command 2nd Brigade, a position he held until 1913 when he was promoted to Major General. He was in turn given command of 47th from August-September 1914, 14th from September-October 1914 and 5th from October 1914– July 1915) Divisions. He was promoted to Lieutenant General to command X Corps when it was formed. He left X Corps to command XIII Corps in April 1918 and remained until the end of the war. He was made commander of the British Army of the Rhine in 1920 and in 1922 took Aldershot Command. He was promoted to General and retired in 1923. He was awarded the Order of the Bath (CB) in 1903, made a Knight Commander of the Order of the Bath (KBE) in 1915 and a Knight of the Order of St Michael and St George (KCMG) in 1917. His younger brother, Colonel Charles Bernard Morland is buried in Ypres Town Cemetery having been killed on 31 October 1914 commanding 2nd Welsh.

Lieutenant General Sir Walter Norris Congreve, VC – See VII Corps

General Sir William Eliot Peyton, KCB, KCVO, DSO, (7 May 1866 – 14 November 1931) failed to pass the entrance examination for Sandhurst so he enlisted in the ranks of his father's regiment, the 7th (The Princess Royal's) Dragoon Guards, in 1885, where he rapidly rose to be a Sergeant before gaining a commission as a 2nd Lieutenant in 1887. He was promoted to Lieutenant in 1890, Captain in 1896, Major and brevet Lieutenant Colonel in 1900 and brevet Colonel in 1905. He was the regiment's Adjutant from 1892-96 when he transferred to the 15th Hussars. He was soon seconded to the Egyptian Army and served in the Dongola Expedition in 1896 for which he was Mentioned in Despatches. He served in the Sudan in 1897-98 for which he was again Mentioned in Despatches and awarded the Distinguished Service Order. He served in the South African Wars from 1899-1900 and then entered Staff College in England in 1901. He commanded the 15th Hussars from 1903-07 when he went to India to become Assistant Quartermaster-General. He was promoted to Brigadier General to command the Meerut Cavalry Brigade from 1908-12. He became Military Secretary to the Commander-in-Chief, India in 1912. He returned to England at the start of the war as Adjutant General of 1st Mounted Division. He was promoted to Major General in August 1914 to command 2nd Mounted Division at Gallipoli until January 1916. He then commanded the Western Frontier Force in Egypt in 1916, leading an expedition against the Senussi and re-occupying Sidi Barrani and Sollum, again being Mentioned in Despatches. The Force, in the form of armoured cars led by the 2nd Duke of Westminster, rescued the shipwrecked British prisoners of HMS Tara for which Peyton was Mentioned in Despatches. In May 1916 he became Haig's Military Secretary until March 1918. After Gough's removal in 1918 during the German advance, Peyton was given command of Fifth Army. But there was no substantive army and it was a nominal role for a potential reserve formation. When Fifth Army was reformed, Peyton was given X Corps and promoted to Lieutenant General, though again he was not involved in action. He was given command of 40th Division when X Corps were moved back to the front leading the Division in the advance of late 1918. After the war, Peyton moved to India to command the United Provinces District and the 3rd Indian Division at Meerut between 1920-22. He was Military Secretary to the Secretary of State for War from 1922-26 and led Scottish Command from 1926 to his retirement in 1930 as a General. He was made a Member of the Royal Victorian Order (MVO) after the Delhi Durbar in 1911. He was knighted and made a Knight Commander of the Royal Victorian Order (KCVO) in 1917. He was awarded the Order of the Bath (CB) in 1913 and made a Knight Commander of the Order of the Bath (KCB) in 1917

General Sir Reginald Byng Stephens, KCB, CMG, (10 October 1869 – 6 April 1955) was commissioned into the Rifle Brigade as a 2nd Lieutenant in 1890, was promoted to Lieutenant in 1892, Captain in 1897, brevet Major in 1900 and brevet Colonel in 1914. He served in the Second Matabele War in 1896-97 and in the Nile

Expedition of 1898. He served in the South African Wars 1899–1902, during which he was severely wounded and was three times Mentioned in Despatches. After the war he was sent to Egypt with his battalion and by 1914 was commanding the battalion. In 1915 he was promoted to Brigadier General to command 25th Brigade and was promoted to Major General in 1916 to command 5th Division in Italy. He was made a temporary Lieutenant General in 1918 to take command of X Corps leading them until the end of the war. After the war he reverted to Major General and was Commandant of Sandhurst from 1919-23, led 4th Division from 1923-26 and was Director-General of the Territorial Army from 1927-31. He was promoted to full Lieutenant General in 1925 and General in 1930 retiring in 1931. He was awarded the Order of St Michael and St George (CMG) in 1916, the Order of the Bath (CB) in 1918 and made a Knight Commander of the Order of the Bath (KCB) in 1919.

Composition

Division	From	To
18th	21/07/1915	02/03/1916
51st	21/07/1915	02/01/1916
5th	01/08/1915	23/02/1916
22nd	06/09/1915	25/10/1915
27th	23/10/1915	15/11/1915
32nd	26/11/1915	21/07/1916
30th	08/01/1916	05/02/1916
49th	05/02/1916	24/07/1916
36th	01/03/1916	07/03/1916
48th	06/03/1916	30/03/1916
36th	30/03/1916	15/07/1916
25th	20/06/1916	18/07/1916
12th	05/07/1916	10/07/1916
48th	15/07/1916	24/07/1916
15th	27/07/1916	03/08/1916
47th	30/07/1916	22/08/1916
7th	01/08/1916	07/08/1916

19th	02/08/1916	04/08/1916
51st	06/08/1916	11/08/1916
5th	06/08/1916	07/08/1916
2nd Indian Cavalry/5th Cavalry/2nd Mounted	08/08/1916	07/09/1916
1st Cavalry	09/08/1916	07/09/1916
23rd	11/08/1916	12/08/1916
2nd	13/08/1916	16/08/1916
35th	13/08/1916	15/08/1916
50th	15/08/1916	17/08/1916
34th	18/08/1916	20/08/1916
20th	19/08/1916	20/08/1916
55th	19/08/1916	30/08/1916
NZ Division	20/08/1916	08/09/1916
3rd	23/08/1916	27/08/1916
56th	23/08/1916	04/09/1916
41st	24/08/1916	07/09/1916
6th	29/08/1916	07/09/1916
14th	31/08/1916	12/09/1916
24th	04/09/1916	20/09/1916
7th	10/09/1916	18/09/1916
16th	17/09/1916	21/09/1916
4th	17/09/1916	25/09/1916
30th	21/09/1916	04/10/1916
2nd Indian Cavalry/5th Cavalry/2nd Mounted	28/09/1916	24/10/1916
5th	28/09/1916	01/10/1916
1st Indian Cavalry/4th Cavalry/1st Mounted	29/09/1916	30/09/1916
55th	30/09/1916	02/10/1916
Guards	01/10/1916	24/10/1916
21st	02/10/1916	07/10/1916
1st	03/10/1916	24/10/1916

NZ Division	06/10/1916	11/10/1916
56th	11/10/1916	23/10/1916
23rd	12/10/1916	14/10/1916
8th	12/10/1916	17/10/1916
47th	13/10/1916	16/10/1916
41st	16/10/1916	20/10/1916
5th Australian	18/10/1916	19/10/1916
1st Australian	20/10/1916	23/10/1916
20th	20/10/1916	31/10/1916
23rd	24/10/1916	27/02/1917
41st	24/10/1916	26/09/1917
47th	24/10/1916	17/08/1917
39th	23/02/1917	16/04/1917
23rd	04/04/1917	17/07/1917
19th	29/04/1917	08/05/1917
24th	10/05/1917	05/07/1917
39th	07/08/1917	27/09/1917
24th	28/08/1917	20/09/1917
33rd	01/09/1917	06/10/1917
23rd	14/09/1917	02/11/1917
21st	15/09/1917	18/11/1917
7th	25/09/1917	02/11/1917
5th	28/09/1917	27/11/1917
14th	05/10/1917	13/11/1917
39th	16/10/1917	12/11/1917
9th	18/11/1917	03/12/1917
20th	06/12/1917	11/12/1917
39th	10/12/1917	18/12/1917
29th	18/12/1917	04/01/1918
1st Canadian	26/03/1918	28/03/1918
2nd Canadian	26/03/1918	28/03/1918

5th Australian	27/03/1918	05/04/1918
38th	01/04/1918	02/04/1918
33rd	02/04/1918	06/04/1918
2nd Australian	03/04/1918	06/04/1918
2nd	04/04/1918	13/04/1918
47th	12/04/1918	29/04/1918
57th	12/04/1918	13/04/1918
59th	08/05/1918	03/07/1918
14th	02/06/1918	03/07/1918
34th	18/06/1918	28/06/1918
25th	26/06/1918	30/06/1918
36th	06/07/1918	20/09/1918
30th	08/07/1918	11/11/1918
35th	14/07/1918	01/09/1918
29th	22/07/1918	01/08/1918
34th	23/09/1918	26/10/1918
36th	28/10/1918	09/11/1918
29th	07/11/1918	11/11/1918

Battle Honours

Battles of the Somme 1916

The Battle of Albert 1-13 July 1916 (12th, 25th, 32nd, 36th & 49th Divisions in Fourth Army)

Battle of Bazentin Ridge 14-17 July 1916 (25th, 32nd, 48th & 49th Divisions in Reserve Army)

Capture of Ovillers 17 July 1916 (48th Division in Reserve Army)

Battle of Pozières Ridge 15 July–3 September 1916 (48th & 49th Divisions in Reserve Army)

Battle of Messines 7-14 June 1917 (23rd, 24th, 41st & 47th Divisions in Second Army)

Third Battles of Ypres

Battle of Pilkem Ridge 31 July–2 August 1917 (41st & 47th Divisions in Second Army)

Battle of Langemarck 16-18 August 1917 (39th Division in Second Army)

Battle of the Menin Road 20-25 September 1917 (23rd, 33rd, 39th & 41st Divisions in Second Army)

Battle of Polygon Wood 26 September–3 October 1917 (5th, 7th, 21st, 23rd, 33rd & 39th Divisions in Second Army)

Battle of Broodseinde 4 October 1917 (5th, 7th & 21st Divisions in Second Army)

Battle of Poelcapelle 9 October 1917 (5th & 7th Divisions in Second Army)

First Battle of Passchendaele 12 October 1917 (23rd Division in Second Army)

Second Battle of Passchendaele 26 October–10 November 1917 (5th, 7th, 21st & 29th Divisions in Second Army)

Advance to Victory

Advance in Flanders 18 August–6 September 1918 (30th & 36th Divisions in Second Army)

Capture of Neuve Eglise 1 September 1918 (89th Brigade of 30th Division in Second Army)

Capture of Wulvergem 2 September 1918 (21st Brigade of 30th Division in Second Army)

Final Advance in Flanders (29th, 30th & 34th Divisions in Second Army)

The Battle of Ypres, 1918 28 September-2 October 1918 (30th & 34th Divisions in Second Army)

The Battle of Courtrai 14-19 October 1918 (30th & 34th Divisions in Second Army)

Action of Ooteghem 25 October 1918 (34th Division in Second Army)

Headquarters

14 July 1915	St Omer
19 July 1915	Querrieu
11 August 1915	Hénencourt
30 August 1915	Querrieu
23 February 1916	Baizieux
4 March 1916	Toutencourt
28 June 1916	Senlis-le-Sec
24 July 1916	Domart-en-Ponthieu
1 August 1916	Villers-Bocage

119

7 August 1916	Long
25 October 1916	Steenvoorde
26 October 1916	Abeele
15 November 1917	Fruges
11 December 1917	Esquelbecq
24 March 1918	Frévent
26 March 1918	Hauteclocque
3 July 1918	Esquelbecq
7 July 1918	Zuytpeene
1 September 1918	Terdeghem
2 October 1918	Mont Noir
21 October 1918	Triere des Prêtres north of Tourcoing

XI Corps

XI Corps was formed in France on 29 August 1915. It played a role in the Battle of Loos in 1915 but spent much of its time in northern France acting as a Corps that accepted divisions new to trench warfare preparing them with experience in trench life and then moving them on to other Corps.

Its only major engagement in 1916 was the Battle of Fromelles on 19-20 July, a diversion to the Somme offensive in which two untried divisions, one an Australian division newly formed and poorly equipped, were launched into an ill-planned subsidiary attack. It achieved nothing but cost thousands of casualties causing great resentment in Australia.

It was still a 'line holding' Corps in 1917 until XI Corps was one of two Corps moved to Italy on 16 November 1917 arriving on 1 December. However, its time in Italy was short lived as it returned to France on 10 March 1918 when it returned to the sector it had held before its move to Italy.

The Corps was in place to face Operation Georgette, or the Battle of the Lys, in April 1918. It also played a role in the Advance to Victory at the end of the year having transferred from First Army to Fifth Army on 1 July 1918. After the capture of Lille and a ceremonial march through the city in late October 1918, the XI Corps flag was sent to the Governor of Paris to display. On Armistice Day the Corps was holding a line south of Lessines and north of Mons.

Commanding Officers

29 August 1915	Major General Frederick Rudolph Lambart, the 10th Earl of Cavan (temp)
4 September 1915	Lieutenant General Richard Cyril Byrne Haking
13 August 1916	Lieutenant General Sir Charles Alexander Anderson (temp)
30 September 1916	Lieutenant General Sir Richard Cyril Byrne Haking

Field Marshal Frederick Rudolph Lambart, 10th Earl of Cavan from 1900, KP, GCB, GCMG, GCVO, GBE, (16 October 1865–28 August 1946), known as Viscount Kilcoursie from 1887-1900, was commissioned into the Grenadier Guards in 1885, promoted to Captain in 1897, Major in 1902, Lieutenant Colonel in 1908 and Colonel in 1911. He was Adjutant of his regiment from 1897-1900. He served in the South African Wars where he was Mentioned in Despatches. He became second in command of his regiment in 1905, took command in 1908 and retired in 1913. When the war began, he returned to service and was promoted to Brigadier General to command 4th (Guards) Brigade. He took them to France and Flanders seeing action at First Ypres and the Battle of Festubert. He was promoted to Major General to command the 50th Division in June 1915 moving to the Guards Division in September 1915 having briefly led the XI Corps. He was promoted to Lieutenant General to lead XIV Corps in January 1916 on its formation leading them in the Battle of the Somme and Third Ypres before taking the Corps to Italy in October 1917. He was made commander in chief of British troops in Italy in March 1918. After the war he was appointed to be Lieutenant of the Tower of London, aide de camp to King George V and took charge of Aldershot Command in 1920 before being promoted to General in 1921. He was appointed Chief of the Imperial General Staff in February 1922 before he retired in 1926. He was made a member of the Royal Victorian Order (MVO) in 1910 and was awarded the Order of the Bath (CB) in February 1915. He was elected a representative peer from Ireland on 24 September 1915 and, as such, was one of the last to be so elected before the creation of the Irish Free State. He was appointed a Knight of the Order of St Patrick (KP) in November 1916, a Knight Commander of the Order of the Bath (KCB) in January 1918, Knight Grand Cross of the Order of St Michael and St George (GCMG) in 1919, Knight Grand Cross of the Royal Victorian Order (GCVO) in 1922, Knight Grand Cross of the Order of the Bath (GCB) in 1926, Knight Grand Cross of the Order of the British Empire (GBE) in 1927 and was promoted to Field Marshal in 1932. He commanded troops at the coronation of King George VI and commanded the Hertfordshire Local Defence Volunteers in WW2.

General Sir Richard Cyril Byrne Haking, GBE, KCB, KCMG, (24 January 1862 – 9 June 1945) was commissioned in 1881 into the Hampshires, became a Captain in 1889, Major in 1899, Lieutenant Colonel in 1903, Colonel in 1905 and Brigadier General in 1908. He served in Burma from 1885-87, Ireland, the South African Wars and then at the Staff College. He became GSO1 for 3rd Division from 1906-08 and then Southern Command before taking command of 5th Brigade in 1911. His book 'Company Training' published in 1913, partly inspired by Haig's 1909 'Field Service Regulations', focused on morale and leadership as the key elements to success in war. He took his brigade to war in 1914, seeing action at Mons, on the Aisne and Marne before being wounded in September and returning to England. He was sent back to France in December 1914 to command 1st Division as a Major General. He led them at the Battle of Aubers Ridge in May 1915 where his attacking brigades lost over 50% of their fighting strength in little over an hour but he pressed for further attacks. He took command of XI Corps in preparation for the Battle of Loos. The late release of Haking's XI Corps on the first day of the battle was believed to have lost the opportunity of a breakthrough. Arguments over the role of XI Corps were important in leading to the resignation of French as Commander-in-Chief. Haking was secure in his position and received no blame for the failure of the attack once Haig, who had been Haking's commander, became Commander in Chief. XI Corps were involved in several unsuccessful attacks in 1916 including Boars Head and Fromelles. Haking claimed in May 1916 that no division could be considered a fighting unit until they had carried out a successful trench raid. Haking acquired a reputation as a 'butcher' and was one of the few First World War Generals to have gained this label while the fighting was still taking place. Haking's skills of personnel management and his views in part explain why he did not receive further promotion. The Corps were not involved on the Somme and went to Italy in late 1917. It returned to France in time for the German Offensive in northern France in April 1918. After being part of the defensive action, Haking's reputation improved in 1918. He became chief of the British section of the Armistice Commission in 1918-19, commander of the British military mission to Russia and the Baltic Provinces in 1919 and commander of Allied troops in the plebiscite area of East Prussia and Danzig in 1920, before becoming High Commissioner to the League of

Nations in Danzig in 1921–23. He became commander of the British Troops in Egypt from 1923–27 and was promoted to General in 1925 retiring in 1927. He was awarded the Order of the Bath (CB) in 1910, became a Knight of the Order of the Bath (KCB) in 1916, Knight of the Order of St Michael and St George (KCMG) in 1918 and Knight Grand Cross of the Order of the British Empire (GBE) in 1921.

Lieutenant General Sir Charles Alexander Anderson – See I Corps

Composition

Division	From	To
23rd	29/08/1915	07/09/1915
24th	29/08/1915	01/10/1915
Guards	29/08/1915	17/02/1916
21st	13/09/1915	01/10/1915
12th	29/09/1915	01/11/1915
46th	01/10/1915	19/12/1915
19th	03/11/1915	07/05/1916
38th	04/12/1915	15/06/1916
35th	08/02/1916	06/07/1916
33rd	02/03/1916	09/07/1916
39th	24/03/1916	12/08/1916
8th	24/03/1916	28/03/1916
61st	22/05/1916	15/11/1916
31st	10/07/1916	10/10/1916
5th Australian	16/07/1916	21/07/1916
30th	02/08/1916	18/09/1916
5th	01/10/1916	27/03/1917
56th	23/10/1916	08/03/1917
37th	13/12/1916	11/02/1917
49th	04/03/1917	12/07/1917
66th	15/03/1917	24/06/1917
57th	20/05/1917	11/10/1917
2nd	23/06/1917	15/10/1917
38th	14/09/1917	22/11/1917

25th	07/10/1917	23/11/1917
42nd	19/11/1917	22/11/1917
48th	04/12/1917	09/03/1918
5th	05/12/1917	09/03/1918
55th	19/03/1918	12/04/1918
50th	04/04/1918	08/04/1918
51st	08/04/1918	06/05/1918
61st	10/04/1918	22/07/1918
3rd	11/04/1918	12/04/1918
50th	12/04/1918	26/04/1918
5th	12/04/1918	15/08/1918
52nd	24/04/1918	06/05/1918
14th	03/05/1918	02/06/1918
16th	04/05/1918	16/05/1918
31st	26/06/1918	02/07/1918
74th	26/06/1918	30/06/1918
74th	02/07/1918	30/08/1918
61st	01/08/1918	06/10/1918
59th	25/08/1918	11/11/1918
19th	25/09/1918	04/10/1918
74th	30/09/1918	08/10/1918
47th	01/10/1918	11/11/1918
57th	14/10/1918	11/11/1918

Battle Honours

The Battle of Loos 25 September–8 October 1915 (Guards, 12th, 21st & 24th Divisions in First Army)

Actions of the Hohenzollern Redoubt and Hulluch Quarries 13-19 October 1915 (Guards, 12th & 46th Divisions in First Army)

Attack at Fromelles 19-20 July 1916 (61st & 5th Australian Divisions in First Army)

Battles of the Lys

Battle of Estaires 9-11 April 1918 (3rd, 51st, 55th & 61st Divisions, 2nd Brigade of 1st Division, 1st & 2nd Portuguese Divisions in First Army)

First Defence of Givenchy 9-12 April 1918 (55th Division in First army)

Battle of Hazebrouck 12-15 April 1918 (5th, 50th, 51st & 61st Divisions in First Army)

Defence of Hinges Ridge 12-15 April 1918 (51st Division in First Army)

Defence of Nieppe Forest 12-15 April 1918 (5th Division in First Army)

Battle of Béthune 18 April 1918 (61st Division in First Army)

Action of La Becque 28 June 1918 (5th & 31st Divisions in First Army)

The Advance in Flanders 18 August–6 September 1918 (59th, 61st & 74th Divisions in Fifth Army)

The Final Advance in Artois 2 October–11 November 1918 (47th, 57th, 59th & 74th Divisions in Fifth Army)

Occupation of Lille 17 October 1918 (57th Division in Fifth Army)

Official Entry into Lille 28 October 1918 (47th Division in Fifth Army)

Headquarters

29 August 1915	St Omer
7 September 1915	Tilques
22 September 1915	Allouagne
25 September 1915	Noeux-les-Mines
3 October 1915	Vaudricourt
10 November 1915	Merville
5 March 1916	Hinges
22 November 1917	Béthune
24 November 1917	Busnes
28 November 1917	Lillers
1 December 1917	Mantua
3 December 1917	Padova
6 December 1917	Camposampiero
27 January 1918 – 11 March 1918	Merlengo
13 March 1918	Air sur la Lys
16 March 1918	Hinges
9 April 1918	Robecq
10 April 1918	Norrent-Fontes
20 April 1918	Roquetoire
7 September 1918	Busnes

125

18 October 1918	Fromelles
19 October 1918	La Madeleine, Lille

XII Corps

XII Corps was formed at Doullens in France on 8 September 1915 joining Third Army with three divisions. It was involved with supporting artillery in the Battle of Loos. In October 1915, the Corps was sent from France taking two divisions to reinforce Allied forces on the Macedonian front. Corps headquarters arrived at Salonika on 12 November 1915 where it became part of the British Salonika Army or Force.

On 28 December 1915 XII Corps headquarters reformed at Lembet Camp and was fully established by January 1916 with a third division under command. The Corps held a position around Salonika for most of 1916 until it moved north, to replace French units, taking part in some actions in August and September 1916.

Its first major action was the Battle of Dojran in April-May 1917 when it attacked the Bulgarian positions west of Lake Doiran. The Corps commander developed an ambitious plan that the Army commander felt was too much, notably due to the terrain of hills and narrow ravines. An artillery bombardment warned the Bulgarians of the coming attack leading to the Corps suffering high casualties for almost no gains. A repeat attack three weeks later in May again cost high casualties with little gains.

The Corps took time to recover so did not launch another attack until September 1918. Again, it had limited success except to draw Bulgarian attention away from the French attack which broke the Bulgarian defences and led to the end of the conflict in the Balkans. The Corps made progress through Bulgarian territory towards the Turkish border planning to attack the Turks from the north, but the Turks signed an armistice on 30 September 1918 before the Corps was in position. At the end of the war the Corps occupied parts of European Turkey and Wilson was appointed commander of Allied Forces at Gallipoli and Bosporus.

Commanding Officers

5 September 1915	Lieutenant General Sir Henry Fuller Maitland Wilson
4 January 1917	Major General Edward Charles William MacKenzie-Kennedy (temp)
11 January 1917	Lieutenant General Sir Henry Fuller Maitland Wilson

Lieutenant General Sir Henry Fuller Maitland Wilson, KCB, KCMG, (18 February 1859 – 16 November 1941) was commissioned as a 2nd Lieutenant into the Rifle Brigade in 1878, promoted to Captain in 1884, Major in 1895, brevet Lieutenant Colonel in 1900, full Lieutenant Colonel in 1902, brevet Colonel in 1904 and full Colonel in 1907. He served in India with the 4th Rifle Brigade from 1878 seeing action in the Second Anglo-Afghan War 1878–79 and becoming Adjutant in 1884. He returned to England in 1889 to be Adjutant of the 5th (Militia) Rifle Brigade in London. He served in the South African Wars with 1st Rifle Brigade where he was twice Mentioned in Despatches. He became second-in-command of 4th Rifle Brigade in Dublin before returning to South Africa for the end of the war and was again Mentioned in Despatches. He took command of 2nd Rifle Brigade in 1902 serving in Egypt, Aden, and India until 1907 and was then made Adjutant General of the South Army in India. He was promoted to Brigadier General in 1911 to command 12th Brigade who he took to France in 1914 with 4th Division fighting at Le Cateau covering the British retreat. He took temporary command of 4th Division at the Aisne in September and was promoted to Major General in October 1914 during First Ypres. During Second Ypres in 1915, his division was used to send reinforcements forward in piecemeal detachments to join six divisions but not as a whole division. It reformed in May. Wilson was promoted to Lieutenant General in September 1915 to command the newly formed XII Corps. He took them to Salonika at the end of 1915 where he remained until the end of the war. He became commander of Allied Forces Gallipoli and Bosporus at the end of the war and from February 1919 Commander, Allied Forces Turkey in Europe, British Salonika Army, and British Army of the Black Sea, which combined posts he held until 18 November 1920. He retired in 1929. He was awarded the Order of the Bath (CB) in 1910, was made a Knight Commander of the Order of the Bath (KCB) in June 1915, and Knight Commander of the Order of St Michael and St George (KCMG) in 1918.

Major General Edward Charles William MacKenzie-Kennedy, KBE, CB, (1860- 4 September 1932) was commissioned in 1879 and transferred to the Indian Army in 1882. He joined the Madras Pioneers with whom he became Adjutant serving in the Black Mountain or First Hazara Expedition in 1888. He took command of the 1st Madras Pioneers in 1897, served in the Boxer Rebellion in 1900 where he was promoted to Lieutenant Colonel and Mentioned in Despatches. From 1907-09 he commanded the Secunderabad Brigade and from 1909-11 the Bangalore Brigade. He was promoted to Major General to command 26th Division who he led until

January 1917 first in France and then on the Salonika Front. He retired in 1919 when he was made a Knight Commander of the Order of the British Empire (KBE) having been awarded the Order of the Bath (CB) in June 1910.

Composition

Division	From	To
27th	18/09/1915	23/10/1915
26th	20/09/1915	22/09/1918
22nd	01/12/1915	30/09/1918
28th	28/12/1915	04/01/1916
60th	17/12/1916	10/06/1917
27th	01/07/1918	21/09/1918
28th	22/09/1918	30/09/1918

Battle Honours

Horseshoe Hill 10-18 August 1916 (22nd & 26th Divisions)

Machukovo 13-14 September 1916 (22nd Division)

Battle of Dojran 24-25 April and 8-9 May 1917 (22, 26th & 60th Divisions)

The Offensive

    Capture of the Roche Noire Salient 1-2 September 1918 (27th Division)

    Battle of Dojran 18-19 September 1918 (22nd & 26th Divisions, 83rd Brigade of 28th Division)

    Pursuit to the Strumica Valley 22-30 September 1918 (22nd & 28th Divisions)

Headquarters

5 September 1915	Doullens
24 September - 31 October 1915	Glisy
28 December 1915	Lembet Camp
30 July 1916	Kirec
10 October 1916	Janes
18 September 1918	Piton-Rocheux
19 September 1918	Janes
25 September 1918	Border Hill
27 September 1918	Cerniste

British Salonika Army

The British Salonika Army was formed on 15 October 1915 in Salonika to oppose Bulgarian advances in the Balkans on the Macedonian or Salonika Front. At first its commander was also commander of the Mediterranean Expeditionary Force (see VIII Corps). But Lieutenant General Bryan Mahon was put in charge in November 1915 as XII Corps arrived from France. He took all headquarters staff from XII Corps as his Army headquarters staff. In January 1916 Mahon was posted to Egypt to establish and run the newly formed Egyptian Expeditionary Force (see XX Corps). He was replaced in May 1916 by Lieutenant General George Milne. The Salonika Army had two Corps and became the Army of the Black Sea at the end of the war.

British Salonika Army

10th	01/11/1915	17/01/1916

XIII Corps

XIII Corps was formed in France on 15 November 1915 to be part of Third Army. It was first seriously engaged during the Battle of the Somme in 1916 when it was involved in every action serving with Fourth Army from 1 July until it was moved to the rear on 18 August. On the first day on the Somme the Corps held the southern flank of the British line next to the French. The Corps' objective was the village of Montauban, and it achieved one of the few successes of the day. After time in the rear to recover it moved to be part of Fifth Army and returned to the front line for the final action of the battle now serving on the northern part of the line at Serre and Hebuterne.

In 1917 it served in the Battle of Arras fighting near Vimy Ridge as part of First Army. Command of XIII Corps was offered to Lieutenant General Henry Hughes Wilson, who had been liaising with the French during the Nivelle Offensive having lost command of V Corps. However, he declined Haig's offer.

The Corps was also at Arras during the German advance in March 1918 still within First Army until it moved to Fifth Army on 1 July 1918. It played a role in the Advance to Victory as part of Fourth Army. On Armistice Day the Corps was at the La Capelle-Avesnes-Maubeuge road. It had halted its advance on 9 November except for a small mobile contingent called 'Bethells's Force'; named after the commanding officer of 66th Division, Major General Sir Hugh Keppel Bethell, KBE, CB, CMG, CVO, DSO, which continued to chase the German retreat until Armistice Day. Bethell's

Force had included 5th Cavalry Brigade, Cyclist battalions, two squadrons of the Royal Air Force, artillery, engineers, signal companies, 100th Battalion Machine Gun Corps, the South African Infantry Brigade, part of the 9th Gloucestershires and some Field Ambulances. It also had 199th Brigade from 10 November.

Commanding Officers

15 November 1915	Lieutenant General Sir Walter Norris Congreve, VC
10 August 1916	Lieutenant General Frederick Rudolph Lambart, the 10th Earl of Cavan (temp)
16 August 1916	Lieutenant General Sir Walter Norris Congreve, VC (wounded 12 June 1917)
17 June 1917	Lieutenant General Frederick William Nicholas McCracken
13 March 1918	Lieutenant General Henry de Beauvoir De Lisle
12 April 1918	Lieutenant General Sir Thomas Lethbridge Napier Morland

Lieutenant General Sir Walter Norris Congreve, VC – see X Corps

Lieutenant General Frederick Rudolph Lambart, the 10th Earl of Cavan – see XI Corps

Lieutenant General Sir Frederick William Nicholas McCracken, KCB, DSO, (18 August 1859 – 8 August 1949) was commissioned as a 2nd Lieutenant in the 49th Regiment of Foot, later the 1st Royal Berkshires, in 1879, promoted to Lieutenant in 1880, Captain in 1884, brevet Major in 1885, full Major in 1897, brevet Lieutenant Colonel in 1900, full Lieutenant Colonel in 1903 and brevet Colonel in 1905. He served in the Anglo-Egyptian War of 1882 and the Mahdist War of 1885 for which he was Mentioned in Despatches. He then was Deputy Assistant Adjutant-General in Barbados from 1892-97 before returning to the Berkshires. He served in the South African Wars taking command of the 2nd Royal Berkshires in 1901 receiving the Distinguished Service Order and being Mentioned in Despatches. After the war he went to serve with his battalion in Egypt commanding them until 1907 before taking staff roles in India until 1911. He was promoted to Brigadier General at Irish Command in 1911 before taking command of 7th Brigade in 1912 taking them to France in 1914 in 3rd Division. He was wounded at Le Cateau before he was promoted to Major General in October 1914 and appointed to be Inspector of Infantry. He was given command of 15th Division in December 1914 leading them until June 1917 being involved in the Battle of Loos, the Battle of the Somme, and the Battle of Arras. He was promoted to Lieutenant General to command XIII Corps remaining until just before the German attack in 1918. He was then demoted and sent home to lead Scottish Command until he retired in 1922. He was awarded the Order of the Bath (CB) in 1910 and made a Knight Commander of the Order of the Bath (KCB) in 1917

Lieutenant General Henry de Beauvoir De Lisle – see IX Corps

Lieutenant General Sir Thomas Lethbridge Napier Morland – see X Corps

Composition

Division	From	To
30th	18/11/1915	08/01/1916
36th	18/11/1915	19/01/1916
7th	06/12/1915	16/05/1916
51st	02/01/1916	29/02/1916
30th	05/02/1916	02/08/1916
18th	02/03/1916	21/07/1916
21st	30/03/1916	30/04/1916
9th	16/06/1916	23/07/1916
3rd	04/07/1916	16/08/1916
1st Cavalry	08/07/1916	14/07/1916
2nd Indian Cavalry/5th Cavalry/2nd Mounted	08/07/1916	14/07/1916
35th	12/07/1916	13/08/1916
2nd	21/07/1916	13/08/1916
55th	26/07/1916	14/08/1916
24th	01/08/1916	16/08/1916
33rd	02/09/1916	04/09/1916
2nd Canadian	05/09/1916	07/09/1916
25th	10/09/1916	25/09/1916
30th	18/09/1916	21/09/1916
48th	18/09/1916	30/09/1916
51st	30/09/1916	01/10/1916
51st	02/10/1916	25/11/1916

19th	06/10/1916	17/10/1916
31st	10/10/1916	22/02/1917
3rd	15/11/1916	22/11/1916
40th	15/11/1916	22/11/1916
7th	19/11/1916	23/11/1916
3rd	29/11/1916	31/01/1917
7th	29/11/1916	12/01/1917
2nd	09/01/1917	11/01/1917
63rd (RN)	15/01/1917	20/01/1917
11th	06/02/1917	23/02/1917
31st	25/03/1917	22/03/1918
2nd	26/03/1917	23/06/1917
63rd (RN)	26/03/1917	02/10/1917
5th	04/05/1917	24/09/1917
47th	19/09/1917	22/11/1917
59th	03/10/1917	08/10/1917
48th	09/11/1917	04/12/1917
2nd Canadian	13/11/1917	19/11/1917
21st	18/11/1917	01/12/1917
56th	05/12/1917	08/04/1918
62nd	06/12/1917	10/12/1917
62nd	18/12/1917	24/03/1918
3rd Canadian	28/03/1918	30/03/1918
40th	29/03/1918	30/03/1918
31st	02/04/1918	11/04/1918
16th	10/04/1918	04/05/1918
14th	11/04/1918	03/05/1918
3rd	23/04/1918	17/08/1918
4th	23/04/1918	25/08/1918
15th	25/04/1918	04/05/1918
46th	28/06/1918	10/09/1918

74th	30/06/1918	02/07/1918
19th	11/07/1918	25/09/1918
47th	10/09/1918	25/09/1918
50th	26/09/1918	28/09/1918
66th	26/09/1918	11/11/1918
74th	27/09/1918	30/09/1918
25th	28/09/1918	11/11/1918
50th	29/09/1918	11/11/1918
18th	01/10/1918	11/11/1918

Battle Honours

The Battles of the Somme 1916:

Battle of Albert 1-13 July 1916 (3rd, 9th, 18th, 30th & 35th Divisions in Fourth Army)

Capture of Montauban 1 July 1916 (30th Division in Fourth Army)

Capture of Bernafey Wood 3 July 1916 (9th Division in Fourth Army)

Fighting in Trones Wood 7-13 July 1916 (30th Division in Fourth Army)

Battle of Bazentin Ridge 14-17 July 1916 (3rd, 9th & 18th Divisions in Fourth Army)

Capture of Trones Wood 14 July 1916 (54th Brigade of 18th Division in Fourth Army)

Attack of Longueval 14-18 July 1916 (3rd & 9th Divisions in Fourth Army)

Battle of Delville Wood 15 July–16 August 1916 (2nd, 3rd, 9th, 18th & 24th Divisions in Fourth Army)

Capture and Consolidation of Delville Wood 27-28 July 1916 (2nd Division in Fourth Army)

Attack of Waterlot Farm-Guillemont 8-9 August 1916 (2nd Division in Fourth Army)

Battle of the Ancre 13-18 November 1916 (31st Division, 120th Brigade of 40th Division in Fifth Army)

Battles of Arras 1917

Battle of Vimy Ridge 9-14 April 1917 (2nd, 31st & 3rd Divisions in Reserve Army to 12 April 1917, then First Army)

Second Battle of the Scarpe 23-24 April 1917 (63rd Division in First Army)

Capture of Gavrelle 23 April 1917 (63rd Division in First Army)

Battle of Arleux 28-29 April 1917 (2nd & 63rd Divisions in First Army)

Third Battle of the Scarpe 3-4 May 1917 (2nd & 31st Divisions in First Army)

Capture of Oppy Wood 28 June 1917 (5th & 31st Divisions in First Army)

First Battles of the Somme 1918

First Battle of Arras 1918 28 March 1918 (56th & 3rd Canadian Divisions in First Army)

Battles of the Hindenburg Line

Battle of the St. Quentin Canal 1-2 October 1918 (18th & 50th Divisions in Fourth Army)

Battle of the Beaurevoir Line 3-5 October 1918 (25th & 50th Divisions in Fourth Army)

Capture of Beaurevoir 5 October 1918 (25th Division in Fourth Army)

Battle of Cambrai 8-9 October 1918 (25th, 50th & 66th Divisions in Fourth Army)

Pursuit to the Selle 9-12 October 1918 (25th, 50th & 66th Divisions in Fourth Army)

Final Advance in Picardy

Battle of the Selle 17-25 October 1918 (18th, 25th, 50th & 66th Divisions in Fourth Army)

Capture of Bousies 23 October 1918 (18th Division in Fourth Army)

Battle of the Sambre 4 November 1918 (18th, 25th & 50th Divisions in Fourth Army)

Passage of the Sambre-Oise Canal 4 November 1918 (25th Division in Fourth Army)

Final Operations 5-11 November 1918 (18th, 25th, 50th & 66th Divisions, Bethell's Force in Fourth Army)

Headquarters

15 November 1915	Doullens
30 November 1915	Domart-en-Ponthieu
30 December 1915	Vignacourt
5 February 1916	Heilly
29 April 1916	Corbie
27 June 1916	Chipilly
21 July 1916	Etinehem

15 August 1916	Domart-en-Ponthieu
4 October 1916	Couin
29 November 1916	Acheux
12 January 1917	Doullens
20 March 1917	La Beuvrière
12 April 1917	Ecoivres
28 March 1918	Acq
30 March 1918	Tinques
1 April 1918	Bryas
24 April 1918	Ferfay
26 September 1918	Villers-Bocage
1 October 1918	Bussu Wood near Aizecourt-le-Haut
13 October 1918	Elincourt
5 November 1918	Le Cateau
11 November 1918	Maroilles

XIV Corps

XIV Corps was formed in France on 3 January 1916 in Third Army. It first took part in the Battle of Mount Sorrel in the Ypres Salient, better known for being the first action in which the Canadian Corps took the lead role. XIV Corps later fought in the Battle of the Somme in 1916 in actions from August to October as part of Fourth Army having moved from Reserve Army.

In 1917 it saw action during the German Retreat to The Hindenburg Line and was then involved in almost every stage of Third Ypres. The Corps left from Ypres area on 2 November arriving at Pavia in Italy on 5 November 1917 and took over the Montello Sector of the Piave front on 4 December with three divisions.

On 24 February 1918, the other Corps in Italy, XI Corps, was ordered to return to France so XIV Corps remained with 7th, 23rd and 48th Divisions. On 9 March the Corps took over the Arcade Sector and at the end of the month moved to the Asiago Sector in the mountains. On 18 April, the headquarters staff became the GHQ British Force in Italy. So, the Corps ceased to exist temporarily, and the divisions were administered by the Italian Tenth Army. XIV Corps reformed between 9 and 16 October 1918, as part of the Italian Tenth Army under the Earl of Cavan, to take part in the final Italian offensive. On 4 November the armistice with Austria was agreed with the Corps located between Tagliamento, Udine and the coast, north-east of Venice.

Commanding Officers

11 January 1916	Lieutenant General Frederick Rudolph Lambart, the 10th Earl of Cavan
11 August 1916	Lieutenant General Edward Arthur Fanshawe (temp)
17 August 1916	Lieutenant General Sir Thomas Lethbridge Napier Morland (temp)
10 September 1916 – 10 March 1918	Lieutenant General Frederick Rudolph Lambart, the 10th Earl of Cavan
15 October 1918	Lieutenant General James Melville Babington

Lieutenant General Frederick Rudolph Lambart, the 10th Earl of Cavan – see XI Corps

Lieutenant General Edward Arthur Fanshawe – see V Corps

Lieutenant General Sir Thomas Lethbridge Napier Morland – see X Corps

Lieutenant General Sir James Melville Babington, KCB, KCMG, (31 July 1854 – 15 June 1936) was commissioned as a Lieutenant in the 16th Lancers in 1873, was a Captain in 1882, Major in 1892, and Colonel in 1902. He served as Adjutant from 1877-80, took part in the Bechuanaland Expedition of 1884, and took command of his regiment in 1892. He was Assistant Adjutant-General in India from 1896-99 and served in the South African Wars as commander of the 1st Cavalry Brigade. He was commander of the New Zealand Defence Force from 1902-07 and led the Lowland Mounted Brigade from 1908-13. When the war began, he was promoted to Major General to command 23rd Division who he led in France and Italy until October 1918. He was made a Lieutenant General to command XIV Corps and became Commander of the British Forces in Italy after the war. He was made a Knight of the Order of St Michael and St George (KCMG) in 1917 and Knight of the Order of the Bath (KCB) in 1919. His image was chosen by Paul McCartney and used by the Beatles as the fictional 'Sgt. Pepper' for the album Sgt. Pepper's Lonely Hearts Club Band in 1967. He had a reputation as being loved by his men as although he was 'elderly and fearless' he took care of them. For example, he acquired £17000 to spend on clothing for his division before they went overseas.

Composition

Division	From	To
55th	17/01/1916	31/01/1916
36th	19/01/1916	30/01/1916
46th	27/01/1916	31/01/1916
6th	01/02/1916	16/08/1916
14th	03/02/1916	22/02/1916
20th	04/02/1916	19/07/1916
Guards	17/02/1916	16/08/1916
36th	19/07/1916	22/07/1916
20th	21/07/1916	14/08/1916
4th	22/07/1916	30/07/1916
29th	28/07/1916	29/07/1916
25th	31/07/1916	11/08/1916
20th	15/08/1916	19/08/1916
35th	15/08/1916	30/08/1916
24th	16/08/1916	24/08/1916
3rd	16/08/1916	23/08/1916
6th	17/08/1916	29/08/1916
20th	20/08/1916	20/10/1916
5th	25/08/1916	28/09/1916
Guards	25/08/1916	01/10/1916
16th	28/08/1916	17/09/1916
56th	04/09/1916	11/10/1916
6th	07/09/1916	25/10/1916
4th	25/09/1916	07/11/1916
29th	08/10/1916	19/10/1916
8th	17/10/1916	20/11/1916
33rd	18/10/1916	10/11/1916
Guards	24/10/1916	31/10/1916
17th	31/10/1916	02/03/1917
29th	01/11/1916	30/03/1917

Guards	10/11/1916	18/10/1917
20th	16/11/1916	25/03/1917
1st	16/05/1917	12/06/1917
32nd	20/05/1917	12/06/1917
8th	27/05/1917	12/06/1917
51st	07/06/1917	12/06/1917
38th	12/06/1917	14/09/1917
29th	18/06/1917	16/10/1917
20th	20/07/1917	04/10/1917
4th	20/09/1917	17/10/1917
17th	04/10/1917	20/10/1917
34th	07/10/1917	29/10/1917
57th	11/10/1917	29/10/1917
35th	12/10/1917	29/10/1917
50th	19/10/1917	29/10/1917
23rd	05/11/1917	18/04/1918
7th	05/11/1917	22/02/1918
41st	11/11/1917	01/03/1918
48th	09/03/1918	18/04/1918
5th	09/03/1918	08/04/1918
7th	24/03/1918	18/04/1918
23rd	09/10/1918	11/11/1918
48th	09/10/1918	11/11/1918
7th	09/10/1918	11/11/1918

Italian Army

23rd	18/04/1918	09/10/1918
48th	18/04/1918	09/10/1918
7th	18/04/1918	09/10/1918

Battle Honours

The Battle of Mount Sorrel 2-13 June 1916 (20th Division in Second Army)
Battles of the Somme, 1916

> Battle of Delville Wood 17 August–3 September 1916 (20th & 24th Divisions in Fourth Army)
> Battle of Guillemont 3-6 September 1916 (5th, 16th & 20th Divisions in Fourth Army)
> Battle of Ginchy 9 September 1916 (16th & 56th Divisions in Fourth Army)
> Battle of Flers-Courcelette 15-22 September 1916 (Guards, 5th, 6th, 20th & 56th Divisions in Fourth Army)
> Battle of Morval 25-28 September 1916 (Guards, 5th, 6th, 20th & 56th Divisions in Fourth Army)
> Capture of Lesboeufs 25 September 1916 (Guards & 6th Divisions in Fourth Army)
> Capture of Combles 26 September 1916 (56th Division in Fourth Army)
> Battle of the Transloy Ridges 1-18 October 1916 (4th, 6th, 20th & 56th Divisions in Fourth Army)

German Retreat to the Hindenburg Line 14-25 March 1917 (Guards & 20th Divisions in Fourth Army)
Third Battles of Ypres

> Battle of Pilkem Ridge 31 July–2 August 1917 (Guards & 38th Divisions in Fifth Army)
> Battle of Langemarck 16–18 August 1917 (20th & 29th Divisions in Fifth Army)
> Fighting North of St Julien 27 August 1917 (38th Division in Fifth Army)
> Battle of the Menin Road 20-25 September 1917 (Guards, 20th & 29th Divisions in Fifth Army)
> Battle of Polygon Wood 26 September–3 October 1917 (4th, 20th & 29th Divisions in Fifth Army)
> Battle of Broodseinde 4 October 1917 (4th & 29th Divisions in Fifth Army)
> Battle of Poelcapelle 9 October 1917 (Guards, 4th & 29th Divisions in Fifth Army)
> First Battle of Passchendaele 12 October 1917 (Guards, 4th & 17th Divisions in Fifth Army)
> Fighting in the Houthulst Forest 22 October 1917 (34th & 35th Divisions in Fifth Army)

Second Battle of Passchendaele 26-29 October 1917 (35th, 50th & 57th Divisions in Fifth Army)

Battle of Vittorio Veneto

Capture of the Grave di Papadopoli 23-26 October 1918 (7th Division in Italian Tenth Army)

Passage of the Piave 26-28 October 1918 (7th & 23rd Divisions in Italian Tenth Army)

Passage of the Monticana 29 October 1918 (23rd Division in Italian Tenth Army)

Crossing of the Tagliamento 3 November 1918 (7th Division in Italian Tenth Army)

Headquarters

3 January 1916	Doullens
20 January 1916	Domart-en-Ponthieu
3 February 1916	Chateau Lovie near Poperinge
30 July 1916	Marieux
15 August 1916	Etinehem
20 August 1916	Méaulte
23 May 1917	Flêtre
19 June 1917	St. Sixte Convent near Poperinge
29 October 1917	Eperlecques
2 November 1917	Pavia
8 November 1917	Mantova
21 November 1917	Lonigo
28 November 1917	Fanzolo
18 March 1918	Noventa Padovana
29 March 1918 – 18 April 1918	Lonedo
9 October 1918	Lonedo
12 October 1918	Villa Marcello
15 October 1918	Dosson
22 October 1918	Villa Margherita
31 October 1918	Vazzola
3 November 1918	Pordenone
9 November 1918	Villa Margherita

XV Corps

XV Corps was formed in Egypt on 12 January 1916 with headquarters at Port Said. It was part of the Eastern Force protecting No. 3 Section of the Suez Canal defences. This was the northern section from Port Said to Ferdan. It comprised three divisions. At the end of February, it held the same area with two divisions. On 1 March 1916 it became part of the newly formed Egyptian Expeditionary Force but on 8 April 1916, the headquarters staff received orders to move to France leaving one division to man No. 3 Section of the Suez Canal. The handover took place on 12 April 1916 with the new headquarters formed in France on 22 April. The Corps' war diary for 12 April ends with the word 'finis'.

Once the Corps reformed in France with three members of the headquarters Staff that had been in Egypt, it took over part of the front from XIII Corps on 29 April 1916. It played a role in the Battles of the Somme in 1916 until mid-October as part of Fourth Army.

It had a relatively quiet 1917, still within Fourth Army, playing a part in a few small actions mainly defending the positions around Nieuwport on the Belgian coast for the second part of the year.

In 1918 it was involved in the Battle of the Lys, in First Army until 12 April and then in Second Army, and the Advance to Victory. During the Battles of the Lys, it put in the field a composite brigade of the 39th Division, which had been moved from the Somme having been decimated during the German advance. It also put in the field a 'Composite Force' of men from the division's schools, pioneers, entrenching battalions and reinforcement battalions.

During the advance it was on the right flank of Second Army but received orders to halt its advance on 10 November having crossed the River Schelde. It was withdrawn as X and XI Corps formed a link in front of its position. Hence, the Corps was in the rear on Armistice Day.

Commanding Officers

12 January – 12 April 1916 and from 22 April 1916	Lieutenant General Henry Sinclair Horne
29 September 1916	Lieutenant General Sir John Philip Du Cane
12 April 1918	Lieutenant General Sir Henry de Beauvoir de Lisle

General Henry Sinclair Horne, 1st Baron Horne, GCB, KCMG, (19 February 1861 – 14 August 1929) was commissioned as a Lieutenant into the Royal Artillery in May 1880, promoted to Captain in 1888, Major in 1898, brevet Lieutenant Colonel in 1900 and Lieutenant Colonel in 1905. He served in the South African Wars in the cavalry where he was Mentioned in Despatches. He returned to England after the war joining the Royal Horse Artillery and was promoted to Brigadier General to become Inspector of Artillery in 1912. When the war began, he was appointed to command the artillery in Haig's I Corps. His actions at Mons allowed Haig to retire and he developed his reputation in the actions of 1914. Consequently, he was promoted to Major General and given command of 2nd Division in January 1915 leading them at Festubert after which he suggested reorganisation of the artillery. He moved to the Middle East at the end of 1915, helping to organise the evacuation of the Gallipoli peninsula. Soon after he was given command of XV Corps in Egypt defending the Suez Canal. He took his Corps to France and led it in the Battles of the Somme suffering heavy casualties at Mametz and Fricourt on the first day. The Corps also suffered as the 38th (Welsh) Division got stuck in Mametz Wood in early July, for which Horne allowed the divisional commander to take the blame. He also successfully implemented the use of the creeping barrage. At the end of September, having been promoted to General, Horne was given command of First Army becoming only the first British artillery officer to command an Army in the war. He led them in the Battles of Arras but the Corps was side-lined for most of the remainder of 1917. It came back to action during the Battles of the Lys and, having stopped the German advance, the First Army played a role in the Advance to Victory in 1918. After the war he led Eastern Command from 1919 to his retirement in 1923. He was awarded the Order of the Bath (CB) in January 1915 and made a Knight Commander of the Order of the Bath (KCB) in September 1916. In 1919 he was created a Knight Commander of the Order of St Michael and St George (KCMG) and a Knight Grand Cross of the Order of the Bath (GCB). He was also made Baron of Stirkoke in the County of Caithness.

General Sir John Philip Du Cane, GCB, (5 May 1865 – 5 April 1947) was commissioned as a Lieutenant in the Royal Artillery in February 1884, promoted to Captain in 1893, Major in 1900 and brevet Lieutenant Colonel in 1902. He served in the South African Wars where he was Mentioned in Despatches. He was Brigade Major of the Royal Artillery from 1904-05, Deputy Assistant Adjutant General at the Staff College from 1905-07 and served on Staff from 1908-11. He was promoted to

Brigadier General to command 3rd Division's artillery from 1911-12 and returned to a Staff position from 1912-14. At the start of the war he remained on Staff, first at III Corps, then from 1915 as Major General, Royal Artillery and was attached to the Ministry of Munitions until 1916. It is considered that he laid the foundations for the reorganisation and expansion suggested by Horne after Festubert. Having never commanded a brigade or division he was appointed to lead XV Corps in September 1916. He was then appointed to be liaison officer between Haig and Foch in April 1918, a role he held until 1919. After the war he was Master-General of Ordnance from 1920-23, led Western Command from 1923-23, commanded the British Army on the Rhine from 1924-27 and was Governor and Commander-in-Chief of Malta from 1927 until he retired in 1931. He stood as a Unionist candidate for parliament in the constituency of Horncastle in 1923 but was defeated. He was awarded the Knight Grand Cross of the Order of the Bath (GCB) in 1919.

Lieutenant General Sir Henry de Beauvoir de Lisle – See IX Corps

Composition

Division	From	To
46th	19/12/1915	27/01/1916
31st	24/12/1915	29/02/1916
13th	22/01/1916	12/02/1916
52nd	27/01/1916	12/04/1916
11th	08/02/1916	20/06/1916
21st	30/04/1916	04/07/1916
7th	30/04/1916	21/07/1916
17th	12/06/1916	11/07/1916
38th	03/07/1916	12/07/1916
21st	10/07/1916	18/07/1916
33rd	12/07/1916	02/09/1916
2nd Indian Cavalry/5th Cavalry/2nd Mounted	14/07/1916	08/08/1916
5th	17/07/1916	06/08/1916
51st	21/07/1916	06/08/1916
17th	23/07/1916	21/08/1916
14th	07/08/1916	31/08/1916

5th	07/08/1916	25/08/1916
7th	07/08/1916	10/09/1916
24th	24/08/1916	04/09/1916
55th	30/08/1916	30/09/1916
41st	07/09/1916	16/10/1916
NZ Division	08/09/1916	06/10/1916
14th	12/09/1916	24/09/1916
21st	21/09/1916	02/10/1916
12th	30/09/1916	23/10/1916
30th	04/10/1916	26/10/1916
NZ Division	11/10/1916	10/10/1916
29th	19/10/1916	01/11/1916
5th Australian	19/10/1916	31/10/1916
1st Australian	23/10/1916	30/10/1916
2nd Australian	26/10/1916	31/10/1916
4th Australian	26/10/1916	01/11/1916
20th	31/10/1916	16/11/1916
Guards	31/10/1916	10/11/1916
60th	03/11/1916	30/11/1916
4th	07/11/1916	05/03/1917
33rd	10/11/1916	12/03/1917
8th	20/11/1916	27/05/1917
40th	22/11/1916	02/06/1917
20th	25/03/1917	23/05/1917
33rd	30/03/1917	03/04/1917
42nd	19/05/1917	02/06/1917
35th	23/05/1917	02/06/1917
59th	29/05/1917	02/06/1917
32nd	12/06/1917	26/10/1917
66th	24/06/1917	27/09/1917
1st	01/07/1917	25/10/1917

49th	12/07/1917	24/09/1917
33rd	31/07/1917	01/09/1917
42nd	22/09/1917	19/11/1917
41st	26/09/1917	11/11/1917
9th	26/10/1917	18/11/1917
38th	22/11/1917	01/04/1918
42nd	22/11/1917	20/12/1917
25th	23/11/1917	29/11/1917
12th	08/12/1917	24/03/1918
57th	04/01/1918	02/04/1918
34th	28/03/1918	12/04/1918
40th	30/03/1918	17/04/1918
50th	08/04/1918	12/04/1918
29th	09/04/1918	22/07/1918
31st	11/04/1918	26/06/1918
1st Australian	12/04/1918	06/08/1918
9th	07/05/1918	12/09/1918
40th	22/06/1918	11/11/1918
31st	02/07/1918	27/10/1918
61st	22/07/1918	01/08/1918
29th	01/08/1918	15/09/1918
14th	02/10/1918	11/11/1918
29th	27/10/1918	07/11/1918
36th	09/11/1918	11/11/1918

Battle Honours

Battles of the Somme, 1916

> Battle of Albert 1-13 July 1916 (7th, 17th, 21st, 33rd & 38th Divisions in Fourth Army)
>
> Capture of Mametz 1 July 1916 (7th Division in Fourth Army)
>
> Capture of Fricourt 2 July 1916 (17th Division in Fourth Army)
>
> Mametz Wood 7-11 July 1916 (38th Division in Fourth Army)

Battle of Bazentin Ridge 14-17 July 1916 (7th, 21st & 33rd Divisions in Fourth Army)

Attacks on High Wood 20-25 July 1916 (5th, 7th, 33rd & 51st Divisions in Fourth Army)

Capture of Longueval 29 July 1916 (5th Division in Fourth Army)

Battle of Delville Wood 31 August–3 September 1916 (5th, 7th, 14th & 24th Divisions in Fourth Army)

Battle of Guillemont 3-7 September 1916 (7th, 24th & 55th Divisions in Fourth Army)

Battle of Ginchy 9 September 1916 (55th Division in Fourth Army)

Battle of Flers-Courcelette 15-22 September 1916 (14th, 21st, 41st, 55th & New Zealand Divisions in Fourth Army)

Capture of Flers 15 September 1916 (41st & New Zealand Divisions in Fourth Army)

Battle of Morval 25-28 September 1916 (21st, 55th & New Zealand Divisions in Fourth Army)

Capture of Gird Trench 26 September 1916 (110th Brigade of 21st Division in Fourth Army)

Capture of Gueudecourt 26 September 1916 (110th Brigade of 21st Division in Fourth Army)

Battle of the Transloy Ridges 1-18 October 1916 (12th, 21st, 30th, 41st & New Zealand Divisions in Fourth Army)

Bouchavesnes 4 March 1917 (8th Division in Fourth Army)

German Retreat to the Hindenburg Line 14 March–5 April 1917 (8th, 20th & 40th Divisions in Fourth Army)

Capture of Fifteen Ravine, Villers Plouich, Beaucamp and La Vacquerie 21-25 April & 5 May 1917 (40th Division in Fourth Army)

Operations on the Flanders Coast 21 June–18 November 1917 (1st, 9th, 32nd, 33rd, 41st, 42nd, 49th & 66th Divisions in Fourth Army)

Defence of Nieuwpoort 10-11 July 1917 (1st & 32nd Divisions in Fourth Army)

Battles of the Lys

Battle of Estaires 9-11 April 1918 (29th, 31st, 34th, 40th & 50th Divisions, 74th Brigade of 25th Division, 147th Brigade of 49th Division in First Army)

Battle of Hazebrouck 12-15 April 1918 (29th 31st, 34th, 40th, 50th & 1st Australian Divisions, Composite Brigade of 39th Division, Composite Force in First Army to 12 April and then Second Army)

Defence of Nieppe Forest 12-15 April 1918 (29th, 31st & 1st Australian Divisions in Second Army)

Action of La Becque 28 June 1918 (31st Division in Second Army)

Capture of Méteren 19 July 1918 (9th Division in Second Army)

Advance to Victory

Advance in Flanders

Capture of Outtersteene Ridge 18 August 1918 (87th Brigade of 19th Division in Second Army)

Capture of Hoegenacker Ridge 18 August 1918 (9th Division in Second Army)

Capture of Ploegsteert and Hill 63 4 September 1918 (29th Division in Second Army)

Final Advance in Flanders:

Battle of Ypres, 1918 28 September-2 October 1918 (14th, 31st & 40th Divisions in Second Army)

Battle of Courtrai 14-19 October 1918 (14th Division in Second Army)

Headquarters

12 January 1916	Cairo
15 January 1916 to 12 April 1916	Port Said, Egypt
22 April 1916	Vignacourt
29 April 1916	Heilly
30 October 1916	Long
4 December 1916	Etinehem
29 March 1917	Poste de Commandement Chapeau de Gendarme North West of Curlu
17 April 1917	Camp on Haute Allaines – Moislains road
2 June 1917	Villers-Bretonneux
10 June 1917	Pernes
11 June 1917	Malo-les-Bains
29 June 1917	Bray-Dunes-Plage
2 September 1917	La Panne

19 September 1917	Bray-Dunes-Plage
19 November 1917	Lillers
22 November 1917	Hinges
30 January 1918	La Motte-au-Bois
11 April 1918	Wardreques
25 May 1918	Blaringhem
4 October 1918	St Jans Capel
21 October 1918	Mouvaux

XVI Corps

XVI Corps was formed in Salonika on 10 January 1916 as the War Office decided that the campaign in Macedonia needed two Corps and prepared to send several divisions to support XII corps already in the theatre. Formation was temporarily postponed from December as there were not enough divisions available to run a second Corps. But the commander of the Mediterranean Expeditionary Force insisted in January and a headquarters was formed. The two Corps formed the British Salonika Force or Army. However, the Force suffered as the senior staff at the War Office believed all 'sideshows' did not deserve the resources that were required in France and Flanders.

The campaign in 1916 and 1917 was a series of limited actions in terrain not designed for offensive warfare. Rather, it was well designed for defence across a series of hills and ravines which favoured the Bulgarians and Turks. The area was also very unhealthy with many casualties caused by malaria and other diseases rather than battle wounds. But casualties in battle were also high.

The Corps made limited progress until September 1918 at which time it broke the Bulgarian defences. The Corps then made progress through Bulgarian territory, with the Greek 14th Division crossing the Bulgarian border. The Bulgarians agreed an armistice on 30 September with the Corps located north of the Rover Strumica.

Commanding Officers

17 January 1916	Lieutenant General George Milne
17 May 1916	Lieutenant General Charles Briggs

Field Marshal George Francis Milne, 1st Baron Milne, GCB, GCMG, DSO, (5 November 1866 – 23 March 1948) was commissioned into the Royal Artillery in 1885, promoted to Captain in 1895, Major in 1900, brevet Lieutenant Colonel in 1902 and Colonel in 1905. He served in India from 1885-89 and was then posted to Aldershot, returning to India in 1891. He took part in the Suakin Expedition in 1896 and attended Staff College in 1897. He served in the Nile Expedition in 1898 and the South African Wars where he became Deputy Assistant Adjutant-General in February 1900 for which he was Mentioned in Despatches and awarded the Distinguished Service Order. He returned to England to become Deputy-Assistant Quartermaster-General in the intelligence division in 1903. He served on Staff at the North Midland Division from 1908-09, 6th Division from 1909-13 and as Brigadier General Royal Artillery for 4th Division from 1913 until January 1915. He then moved to III Corps and was promoted to Major General in February 1915 taking command of 27th Division in July 1915. He was given command of the newly formed XVI Corps in January 1916 to serve on the Macedonian Front. He was promoted to lead the British Salonika Army after a few months and almost simultaneously was made Commander-in-Chief of British Troops in Macedonia. His orders seem to have been to keep the French happy by being there but not to conduct any major offensive campaigns. Milne was promoted to full Lieutenant General on 1 January 1917. He was, however, undermined when his forces were placed under French control, with the French able to move British troops independently of his orders. In 1917 and 1918 he undertook a series of offensives to support the French and was successful in defeating the Bulgarians and Turks in Macedonia in September 1918. After the Macedonian Campaign he was put in charge of administration of the area including southern Russia, the Caucasus and Turkey as it formed out of the Ottoman Empire, Persia, Syria and Mesopotamia. He was promoted to General and appointed Lieutenant of the Tower of London in 1920. He led Eastern Command from 1923-26 when he became Chief of the Imperial General Staff where he served until he retired in 1933 during which time he was made a Baron and Field Marshal. He was awarded the Order of the Bath (CB) in 1912, made a Knight Commander of the Order of the Bath (KCB) in 1918, appointed a Knight Commander of the Order of St Michael and St George (KCMG) in January 1919, and Knight Grand Cross of the Order of St Michael and St George (GCMG) in June 1919. He was made Knight Grand Cross of the Order of the Bath (GCB) in 1927.

Lieutenant General Sir Charles James Briggs, KCB, KCMG, (22 October 1865 – 27 November 1941) was commissioned into the 1st (King's) Dragoon Guards in 1886, promoted to Captain in 1893, Major in 1902, Lieutenant Colonel in 1903 and Colonel in 1908. He served in Egypt from 1892-93, was Adjutant of his regiment from 1893-97 and Adjutant to 4th Cavalry Brigade from 1897-99. He served in the South African Wars as Adjutant to 3rd Cavalry Brigade. He returned to England in 1902 re-joining his regiment but was transferred in 1904 to the 6th (Inniskilling) Dragoons as second-in-command. He moved to southern Africa to command the Transvaal Volunteers in 1905, leading the campaign in the Bambatha Rebellion in 1906. Back in England he took command of the South Eastern Mounted Brigade in 1910. When the war began, he was given 1st Cavalry Brigade and was promoted to Major General to command 3rd Cavalry Division in May 1915. He moved to 28th Division in October 1915 and took command of XVI Corps in May 1916. After the war he was chief of the British Military Mission to South Russia from February to June 1919 before retiring in 1923. He was awarded the Order of the Bath (CB) in 1914, made a Knight Commander of the Order of the Bath (KCB) in 1917 and Knight Commander of the Order of St Michael and St George (KCMG) in 1918.

Composition

Divisions	From	To
28th	04/01/1916	10/06/1917
10th	17/01/1916	01/09/1917
27th	17/01/1916	01/07/1918
60th	08/12/1916	17/12/1916
28th	01/09/1917	22/09/1918
26th	22/09/1918	30/09/1918
27th	22/09/1918	30/09/1918

Battle Honours

Operations in the Struma Valley
>Capture of Karajakois 30 September–2 October 1916 (10th & 27th Divisions)
>Occupation of Mazirko 2 October 1916 (84th Brigade of 28th Division)
>Capture of Yenikoi 3-4 October 1916 (10th & 27th Divisions)
>Capture of Bairakli Jum'a 31 October 1916 (28th Division)
>Tumbitza Farm 17 November & 6-7 December 1916 (82nd Brigade of 27th Division)

Capture of Ferdie and Essex Trenches 15 May 1917 (28th Division)
Capture of Homondos 14 October 1917 (27th Division)
Capture of Bairakli and Kumli 16 October 1917 (28th Division)
The Offensive
>Battle of Dojran 18-19 September 1918 (28th Division, 228th Brigade, Greek Crete Division)
>Pursuit to the Strumica Valley 22-30 September 1918 (26th & 27th Divisions, Greek 14th Division)

Headquarters

17 January 1916	Kirechkoi
19 August 1916	Salonika-Seres Road
1 December 1916	Salonika
1 January 1917	Coles Kop
1 June 1917	Sivri
27 October 1917	Coles Kop
1 June 1918	Sivri
22 September 1918	Vergetor
24 September 1918	Stuiakuvo
29 September 1918	Dabilja

XVII Corps

XVII Corps was formed in France as XV Corps in December 1915 as the Indian Corps was disbanded and sent to Mesopotamia. Senior staff from the Indian Corps were transferred, by 21 December 1915, having been instructed to form the new Corps. It became XVII Corps on 9 January 1916, as another XV Corps was formed in Egypt, and moved into Third Army on 31 January 1916. As units began to join the Corps, the original Corps commander left. In March the Third Army moved to the Arras front so XVII Corps held this area for the rest of the war.

In April 1917, the Corps attacked to the east of Arras near the River Scarpe but became bogged down in rain and snow. This was its only significant action in 1917. In 1918 it faced some of the German advance and took part in the Advance to Victory breaking the Hindenburg Line in September 1918. It transferred from Third to First Army on 6 April 1918 returning to Third Army on 23 August. By Armistice Day the Corps was east of the Maubeuge to Mons road.

Commanding Officers

9 December 1915	Lieutenant General Sir Charles Alexander Anderson
12 February 1916	Major General the Honourable Edward James Montagu-Stuart-Wortley (acting)
27 February 1916	Lieutenant General the Honourable Sir Julian Hedworth George Byng
25 May 1916	Lieutenant General Sir Charles Fergusson, Bt

Lieutenant General Sir Charles Alexander Anderson – See I Corps

Major General The Honourable Edward James Montagu-Stuart-Wortley, CB, CMG, DSO, MVO, (31 July 1857 – 19 March 1934) was commissioned in the 60th Regiment of Foot, later the King's Royal Rifle Corps, in 1877, promoted to Lieutenant in 1880, Captain in 1885, Major in 1894, Lieutenant Colonel in 1901 and Colonel in 1907. He served during the Second Anglo–Afghan War from 1878–80, the Anglo-Egyptian War in 1882, the Nile Expedition in 1884-85 and the Mahdist War in 1885. He attended staff college in England from 1889-90 and was then a Brigade Major in Malta from 1893-96. He took part in another Nile Expedition in 1896 and commanded a battalion made up of King's Royal Rifle Corps and Rifle Brigade during the South African Wars. After the war he was Military Attaché to Paris for three years. He commanded 10th Brigade from 1908-12. He was promoted to Major

General in 1913 and took command of 46th (North Midland) Division on 1 June 1914 leading them to France in 1915. They attacked the Hohelzollern Redoubt during the Battle of Loos on the orders of the Corps commander, Haking, who overruled Wortley's concerns. The attack cost 180 officers and 3500 men. The division suffered high casualties again at Gommecourt, a diversionary attack on the first day of the Battle of the Somme. These two disasters damaged his reputation, with Haig and Haking politicking using Wortley as a tool in their plans after Loos. With the failure of the attack at Gommecourt in 1916 also being laid at Wortley's door, he was controversially relieved of command after the attack and moved to England to command the 65th Division on home service in Ireland. He retired in 1919. He was awarded the Order of St Michael and St George (CMG) in 1886 and the Distinguished Service Order in 1898. He was appointed a Member of the Royal Victorian Order (MVO) in 1903 and awarded the Order of the Bath (CB) in 1906. His nephew was the 1st Earl of Wharncliffe and his elder brother the 2nd Earl. His younger brother was a Lieutenant General who commanded divisions in the war.

Lieutenant General the Honourable Sir Julian Hedworth George Byng – See IX Corps

Lieutenant General Sir Charles Fergusson – See II Corps

Composition

Division	From	To
46th	31/01/1916	07/05/1916
55th	31/01/1916	09/02/1916
36th	07/02/1916	01/03/1916
51st	29/02/1916	15/07/1916
25th	10/03/1916	20/06/1916
38th	15/06/1916	28/06/1916
60th	25/06/1916	03/11/1916
1st Indian Cavalry/4th Cavalry/1st Mounted	19/07/1916	03/09/1916
39th	12/08/1916	24/08/1916
18th	25/08/1916	11/09/1916
24th	14/10/1916	21/10/1916
37th	14/10/1916	22/10/1916
3rd Canadian	22/10/1916	26/10/1916

9th	14/01/1917	31/07/1917
3rd	31/01/1917	08/02/1917
51st	08/02/1917	07/06/1917
34th	18/02/1917	01/05/1917
4th	22/03/1917	21/04/1917
37th	19/04/1917	30/04/1917
4th	28/04/1917	08/09/1917
17th	02/05/1917	31/05/1917
34th	28/05/1917	06/07/1917
17th	07/06/1917	25/09/1917
1st	17/06/1917	01/07/1917
12th	01/07/1917	01/11/1917
58th	31/07/1917	25/08/1917
21st	30/08/1917	15/09/1917
15th	08/09/1917	25/04/1918
61st	15/09/1917	30/11/1917
35th	04/10/1917	12/10/1917
4th	17/10/1917	13/04/1918
62nd	30/10/1917	14/11/1917
6th	01/11/1917	15/11/1917
51st	02/11/1917	17/11/1917
40th	16/11/1917	17/11/1917
59th	17/11/1917	19/11/1917
47th	22/11/1917	24/11/1917
36th	29/11/1917	04/12/1917
56th	03/12/1917	05/12/1917
62nd	04/12/1917	06/12/1917
Guards	05/12/1917	22/03/1918
55th	08/12/1917	14/12/1917
62nd	24/03/1918	25/03/1918
1st Canadian	28/03/1918	09/04/1918

33rd	06/04/1918	08/04/1918
56th	08/04/1918	21/08/1918
15th	04/05/1918	15/07/1918
51st	06/05/1918	14/07/1918
2nd Cavalry	14/07/1918	25/07/1918
59th	15/07/1918	26/07/1918
52nd	23/07/1918	21/08/1918
57th	29/07/1918	21/08/1918
1st Canadian	30/07/1918	06/08/1918
4th Canadian	01/08/1918	07/08/1918
51st	14/08/1918	23/08/1918
15th	18/08/1918	23/08/1918
2nd Canadian	20/08/1918	23/08/1918
3rd Canadian	23/08/1918	23/08/1918
52nd	25/08/1918	07/10/1918
56th	25/08/1918	06/09/1918
57th	25/08/1918	14/10/1918
33rd	27/08/1918	15/09/1918
63rd (RN)	31/08/1918	11/10/1918
50th	15/09/1918	26/09/1918
19th	04/10/1918	11/11/1918
24th	06/10/1918	11/11/1918
61st	06/10/1918	11/11/1918
20th	30/10/1918	11/11/1918

Battle Honours

German attack on Vimy Ridge 21 May 1916 (25th Division in Third Army)
Battles of Arras 1917

> First Battle of the Scarpe 9-14 April 1917 (4th, 9th, 34th & 51st Divisions in Third Army)
>
> Second Battle of the Scarpe 23-24 April 1917 (37th & 51st Divisions, 103rd Brigade of 34th Division in Third Army)
>
> Battle of Arleux 28-29 April 1917 (34th & 37th Divisions in Third Army)
>
> Third Battle of the Scarpe 3-4 May 1917 (4th & 9th Divisions in Third Army)

Capture and Defence of Roeux 13-14 May 1917 (17th & 51st Divisions in Third Army)
First Battles of the Somme 1918

> First Battle of Bapaume 24-25 March 1918 (15th Division in Third Army)
>
> First Battle of Arras 28 March 1918 (4th & 15th Divisions in Third Army)

The Advance to Victory
Second Battles of Arras 1918

> Battle of the Scarpe 26-30 August 1918 (52nd, 56th & 57th Divisions in Third Army)
>
> Battle of Drocourt-Quéant 2-3 September 1918 (52nd, 57th & 63rd Divisions in Third Army)

Battles of the Hindenburg Line

> Battle of the Canal du Nord 27 September–1 October 1918 (52nd, 57th & 63rd Divisions in Third Army)
>
> Battle of Cambrai 8-9 October 1918 (24th, 57th & 63rd Divisions in Third Army)
>
> Capture of Niergnies 8 October 1918 (63rd Division in Third Army)
>
> Capture of Cambrai 9 October 1918 (57th Division in Third Army)

Pursuit to the Selle 9-12 October 1918 (24th Division in Third Army)
Final Advance in Picardy

> Battle of the Selle 17-25 October 1918 (19th & 61st Divisions in Third Army)
>
> Battle of Valenciennes 1-2 November 1918 (61st Division in Third Army)
>
> Battle of the Sambre 4 November 1918 (19th & 24th Divisions in Third Army)
>
> Passage of the Grand Honelle 5-7 November 1918 (19th & 24th Divisions in Third Army)

Headquarters

9 January 1916	Norrent-Fontes
31 January 1916	Doullens
25 February 1916	Marieux
7 March 1916	Doullens
11 March 1916	Aubigny
28 October 1916	Aire
9 January 1917	Aubigny
20 April 1917	Etrun
9 November 1917	Duisans
15 July 1918	Bryas
30 July 1918	Duisans
24 August 1918	Fosseux
27 August 1918	Bretencourt
24 September 1918	Saint-Léger
29 September 1918	Louverval
10 October 1918	Nine Wood
15 October 1918	Cagnoncles
4 November 1918	Vendigies
9 November 1918	Genette

XVIII Corps

XVIII Corps was formed in France in January 1917 with two divisions in Third Army from 24 January taking over the front near Arras. For a period in March, and during the German Retreat to the Hindenburg Line, it had only one division in the Corps. It moved to Fifth Army in June 1917 and then took part in all of the actions of Third Ypres.

In 1918 it was involved in facing the German advance in March and April. However, on 27-28 March, all of its divisions were handed to other units and it ceased to be a fighting formation as Corps headquarters withdrew to Pont Remy. It moved to St Pol in April when it took two divisions under its control. With these it took over the line near Lens as part of First Army in May 1918. On 2 July Corps headquarters merged with VIII Corps headquarters under the commander and Staff of VIII Corps. The Corps ceased to exist at this point in July 1918.

Commanding Officers

15 January 1917	Lieutenant General Sir Frederick Ivor Maxse
22 June – 2 July 1918	Lieutenant General Sir Aylmer Gould Hunter-Weston

General Sir Frederick Ivor Maxse, KCB, CVO, DSO, (22 December 1862 – 28 January 1958) was commissioned as a Lieutenant into the 7th Royal Fusiliers in 1882, promoted to Captain in 1889, Major in 1897, brevet Lieutenant Colonel in 1900, Lieutenant Colonel in 1903 and brevet Colonel in 1905. He transferred to the Coldstream Guards in 1891, served in the Egyptian Army during the Nile Expedition in 1897-98 and the Mahdist War in 1899. He served in the South African Wars and then commanded 1st Coldstream Guards from 1903-07. In 1910 he took command of the 1st Guards Brigade who he took to France in August 1914. He was promoted to Major General in August 1914 and commanded 18th Division from October 1914 to January 1917 when he took command of XVIII Corps. His division took all of its objectives on the first day of the Battle of the Somme. He led the Corps during Third Ypres but, following Gough's orders in March 1918, led a retreat on the Somme that forced other Corps on his flank to retreat though this was against Gough's wishes. By the time Gough got revised orders to Maxse the Corps could only hold its position with the help of 'Harman's Detachment', one of several ad hoc formations that helped face the Germans during their rapid advance. Maxse's Corps did manage to hold their line by 26 March. Nonetheless, as Gough was removed, Maxse left soon after in April 1918 and became Inspector-General of Training in France. This was a role in which he was well placed having been an innovative trainer of his men throughout the war. After the war he took command of IX Corps as part of the Army on the Rhine. He led Northern Command from 1919-23 and retired in 1926. His father was an Admiral and his great grandfather the Earl of Berkeley. He was awarded the Distinguished Service Order in 1898, the Order of the Bath (CB) in 1900, became a Commander of the Royal Victorian Order (CVO) in 1907 and was made a Knight of the Order of the Bath (KCB) in 1917.

Lieutenant General Sir Aylmer Gould Hunter-Weston – See VIII Corps

Composition

Division	From	To
46th	24/01/1917	20/02/1917
49th	24/01/1917	04/03/1917
58th	31/01/1917	19/03/1917
46th	01/03/1917	07/03/1917
33rd	12/03/1917	30/03/1917
17th	15/03/1917	17/03/1917
50th	26/03/1917	02/04/1917
29th	30/03/1917	12/04/1917
33rd	03/04/1917	12/04/1917
17th	04/04/1917	12/04/1917
50th	07/04/1917	11/04/1917
14th	12/04/1917	24/04/1917
30th	12/04/1917	19/04/1917
37th	12/04/1917	19/04/1917
12th	14/04/1917	23/04/1917
56th	19/04/1917	26/04/1917
4th	21/04/1917	28/04/1917
17th	26/04/1917	02/05/1917
29th	26/04/1917	03/05/1917
50th	26/04/1917	02/05/1917
37th	30/04/1917	19/05/1917

34th	01/05/1917	08/05/1917
50th	04/05/1917	19/05/1917
15th	06/05/1917	23/05/1917
3rd	19/05/1917	31/05/1917
50th	23/05/1917	26/05/1917
12th	24/05/1917	07/06/1917
17th	31/05/1917	07/06/1917
37th	03/06/1917	07/06/1917
51st	12/06/1917	29/09/1917
39th	13/06/1917	07/08/1917
11th	22/06/1917	11/10/1917
48th	23/07/1917	16/09/1917
58th	25/08/1917	29/09/1917
18th	24/09/1917	29/10/1917
9th	01/10/1917	26/10/1917
63rd (RN)	02/10/1917	02/11/1917
48th	03/10/1917	12/10/1917
2nd	15/10/1917	08/11/1917
58th	21/10/1917	01/11/1917
1st	25/10/1917	02/11/1917
32nd	26/10/1917	11/11/1917
Guards	02/11/1917	11/11/1917
17th	03/11/1917	08/11/1917
57th	08/11/1917	08/12/1917
50th	11/11/1917	01/12/1917
63rd (RN)	11/11/1917	01/12/1917
58th	27/11/1917	01/12/1917
61st	23/12/1917	28/03/1918
36th	26/12/1917	28/03/1918
14th	03/01/1918	07/01/1918
30th	07/01/1918	27/01/1918

30th	10/02/1918	28/03/1918
20th	24/02/1918	28/03/1918
14th	28/03/1918	01/04/1918
50th	01/04/1918	04/04/1918
39th	02/04/1918	10/04/1918
16th	03/04/1918	10/04/1918
61st	03/04/1918	07/04/1918
66th	05/04/1918	16/04/1918
24th	07/04/1918	01/07/1918
14th	10/04/1918	11/04/1918
20th	11/04/1918	01/07/1918
52nd	06/05/1918	01/07/1918

Battle Honours

German Retreat to the Hindenburg Line 14-19 March 1917 (58th Division in Third Army)

Third Battles of Ypres

> Battle of Pilkem Ridge 31 July–2 August 1917 (39th & 51st Divisions in Fifth Army)
>
> The Battle of Langemarck 16–18 August 1917 (11th & 48th Divisions in Fifth Army)
>
> The Cockcroft 19 August 1917 (11th & 48th Divisions in Fifth Army)
>
> Fighting in Defence of St Julien 22 August 1917 (11th & 48th Divisions in Fifth Army)
>
> Fighting North of St Julien 27 August 1917 (11th & 48th Divisions in Fifth Army)
>
> Battle of the Menin Road 20-25 September 1917 (51st & 58th Divisions in Fifth Army)
>
> Battle of Polygon Wood 26 September–3 October 1917 (11th, 48th & 55th Divisions in Fifth Army)
>
> Battle of Broodseinde 4 October 1917 (11th & 48th Divisions in Fifth Army)
>
> Battle of Poelcapelle October 1917 (11th & 48th Divisions, 189th Brigade of 63rd Division in Fifth Army)
>
> First Battle of Passchendaele 12 October 1917 (9th & 18th Divisions in Fifth Army)

Fighting East of Poelcapelle in Houthulst Forest 22 October 1918 (18th Division in Fifth Army)

Second Battle of Passchendaele 26 October–2 November 1917 (58th & 63rd Divisions in Fifth Army)

First Battles of the Somme 1918

Battle of St. Quentin 21-23 March 1918 (20th, 30th, 36th & 61st Divisions in Fifth Army)

Actions at the Somme Crossings 24-25 March 1918 (20th, 30th, 36th & 61st Divisions in Fifth Army)

Battle of Rosières 26-27 March 1918 (20th, 30th & 36th Divisions in Fifth Army)

Headquarters

24 January 1917	Pas-en-Artois
2 April 1917	Hauteville
20 April 1917	Fosseux
13 June 1917	Vogeltje Convent near Poperinge
2 November 1917	Esquelbecq
3 December 1917	Villers-Bretonneux
12 December 1917	Querrieu
14 January 1918	Ham
22 March 1918	Nesle
23 March 1918	Roye
25 March 1918	Moreuil
28 March 1918	Saint-Sauflieu
1 April 1918	Pont-Remy
16 April 1918	Roellecourt
25 April 1918	Bryas
2 May 1918	Chateau de la Haie
7 May 1918	Camblain-l'Abbé

XIX Corps

XIX Corps was formed in France on 4 February 1917 at Flers near St Pol. It went into the line for the first time on 12 June 1917 north of Ypres serving in Fifth Army. In 1917 it fought in Third Ypres, from the first day of the battle to the last, though primarily in August and the final assault on the village of Passendale. In 1918, during the German Spring advance, it was driven back 20 miles in five days and found itself in disarray. Notably, on 27 March, the war diary records that 50th and 39th Divisions had broken while 66th Division was trying to hold their line. The Corps had been given responsibility for destroying the bridges over the Somme and some key ammunition dumps such was the haste of the retreat.

On 27 March, the Corps was given responsibility for 'Carey's Force', an ad hoc formation created by Gough on 24-25 March 1918, who ordered the disused Amiens Defence Line, east of Villers-Bretonneux, to be brought in to use and manned by all available troops. A task force of about 3000 men was put together mainly of British engineers, though it also included 500 American railway troops, 400 officers and men of the 2nd Battalion Canadian Railway Troops, and a ten-gun battery made from newly arrived reinforcements for the 1st Canadian Motor Machine Gun Brigade. It was named after Brigadier General George Glas Sandeman Carey, CB, who went on to command 20th Division in April. Other forces improvised by Gough include 'Hunt's Force' and 'Harman's Detachment'. From 27 March 'Carey's Force' also took in the remains of 66th Division so that XIX Corps comprised their battered divisions and 'Carey's Force'. They held off several German attacks and even counter attacked on at least one occasion. By 30 March, the force had been so depleted that it was effectively being commanded by Lieutenant Colonel Sir Francis Henry Douglas Charlton Whitmore, 10th Hussars, and became known as 'Whitmore's Composite Force' such that 'Carey's Force' cease to exist on 3 April. The force continued to hold the sector from the Roman road to the Somme until 5 April, when its troops were sent back to their own formations.

By November 1918 the Corps, as an element of Second Army on the left of the line, was one of the most northerly British military formations on the Western Front. It crossed the Schelde on 9 November 1918 and was located at the River Dendre at the armistice.

Commanding Officers

4 February 1917	Lieutenant General Sir Herbert Edward Watts

Lieutenant General Sir Herbert Edward Watts, KCB, KCMG, (14 February 1858 – 15 October 1934) was commissioned as a 2nd Lieutenant into the 14th Regiment of Foot, later the West Yorkshires, in April 1880, was promoted to Lieutenant in 1881, Captain in 1889 and Major in 1899. He served in the South African Wars during which he was five times Mentioned in Despatches and promoted to Lieutenant Colonel. He was promoted to Colonel in 1908 and finished his army career as the commander of No. 9 District in Eastern Command from 1910-14 when he retired. When the war began, he was brought back from retirement, promoted to Brigadier General and given command of 21st Brigade. He led them until the Battle of Loos when the divisional commander was killed, and he was promoted to Major General to command 7th Division. He took command of 38th Division briefly in 1916 during the Battle of Mametz Wood but remained at 7th Division until promoted to lead the newly formed XIX Corps in February 1917. He stayed there until the end of the war. He received the Order of the Bath (CB) in 1912, Order of St Michael and St George (CMG) in 1915, became a Knight of the Order of the Bath (KCB) in 1918 and Knight of the Order of St Michael and St George (KCMG) 1919.

Composition

Division	From	To
17th	17/03/1917	23/03/1917
58th	01/04/1917	06/04/1917
30th	30/04/1917	17/05/1917
34th	08/05/1917	28/05/1917
61st	21/05/1917	24/05/1917
15th	23/05/1917	08/09/1917
29th	04/06/1917	18/06/1917
55th	12/06/1917	15/09/1917
16th	20/06/1917	28/08/1917
36th	07/07/1917	25/08/1917
61st	15/08/1917	07/09/1917
42nd	23/08/1917	07/09/1917

59th	01/09/1917	07/09/1917
18th	07/09/1917	24/09/1917
48th	16/09/1917	03/10/1917
5th	24/09/1917	28/09/1917
58th	29/09/1917	21/10/1917
11th	11/10/1917	16/10/1917
Guards	18/10/1917	02/11/1917
17th	20/10/1917	03/11/1917
18th	29/10/1917	04/02/1918
34th	29/10/1917	02/11/1917
35th	29/10/1917	14/11/1917
50th	29/10/1917	11/11/1917
57th	29/10/1917	08/11/1917
17th	08/11/1917	12/12/1917
58th	15/11/1917	27/11/1917
1st	27/11/1917	30/01/1918
57th	08/12/1917	04/01/1918
29th	04/01/1918	04/01/1918
66th	18/02/1918	05/04/1918
24th	09/03/1918	07/04/1918
3rd Cavalry	09/03/1918	21/03/1918
1st Cavalry	13/03/1918	24/03/1918
50th	21/03/1918	01/04/1918
8th	22/03/1918	12/04/1918
16th	25/03/1918	03/04/1918
39th	25/03/1918	02/04/1918
20th	28/03/1918	11/04/1918
2nd Cavalry	28/03/1918	03/04/1918
61st	28/03/1918	03/04/1918
3rd Cavalry	31/03/1918	06/04/1918
14th	01/04/1918	05/04/1918

58th	03/04/1918	05/04/1918
18th	04/04/1918	06/04/1918
5th Australian	05/04/1918	05/04/1918
61st	07/04/1918	10/04/1918
66th	16/04/1918	21/04/1918
66th	02/05/1918	22/06/1918
30th	24/05/1918	27/06/1918
21st	22/06/1918	01/07/1918
8th	23/06/1918	26/06/1918
41st	30/06/1918	11/11/1918
6th	01/07/1918	02/09/1918
35th	02/07/1918	14/07/1918
34th	28/08/1918	23/09/1918
35th	15/09/1918	11/11/1918
14th	20/09/1918	02/10/1918
31st	05/11/1918	11/11/1918

Battles Honours

The Third Battles of Ypres

Battle of Pilkem Ridge 31 July–2 August 1917 (15th, 16th & 55th Divisions in Fifth Army)

Battle of Langemark 16–18 August 1917 (15th, 16th, 36th & 61st Divisions in Fifth Army)

Fighting south of Fortuin 22 August 1917 (15th & 61st Divisions in Fifth Army)

Fighting north-west of Zonnebeke 27 August 1917 (61st Division in Fifth Army)

Second Battle of Passchendaele 26 October–10 November 1917 (17th, 18th, 35th, 50th & 57th Divisions in Fifth Army)

First Battles of the Somme 1918:

Battle of St. Quentin 21-23 March 1918 (8th, 24th, 50th & 66th Divisions in Fifth Army)

Actions at the Somme crossings 24-25 March 1918 (8th, 24th, 39th, 50th & 66th Divisions in Fifth Army)

Battle of Rosières 26-27 March 1918 (8th, 16th, 24th, 39th, 50th & 66th Divisions in Fifth Army)

The Battle of the Avre 4 April 1918 (14th, 18th & 24th Divisions; 5th Australian Brigade of 2nd Australian Division; 9th Australian Brigade of 3rd Australian Division; 8th & 15th Australian Brigades of 5th Australian Division; 3rd Cavalry Division in Fifth Army)

Advance in Flanders 18 August–6 September 1918 (6th, 34th & 41st Divisions with 27th American Division in Second Army)

The Final Advance in Flanders

Battle of Ypres, 1918 28 September-2 October 1918 (14th, 35th & 41st Divisions in Second Army)

Battle of Courtrai 14-19 October 1918 (35th & 41st Divisions in Second Army)

Ooteghem 25 October (41st Division in Second Army)

Tieghem 31 October (35th Division in Second Army)

Headquarters

4 February 1917	Flers (near Frévent, Pas-de-Calais)
2 May 1917	St. Pol-sur-Ternoise
12 June 1917	Ten Elms Camp near Poperinge
8 September 1917	Eperlecques
29 October 1917	St. Sixte convent near Poperinge
2 February 1918	Moreuil
23 February 1918	Villers-Carbonnel
9 March 1918	Le Catelet
22 March 1918	Villers-Carbonnel
23 March 1918	Foucaucourt
24 March 1918	Harbonnières
25 March 1918	Villers-Bretonneux
28 March 1918	St. Fuscien
5 April 1918	Molliens-Vidame
13 April 1918	Belloy St. Leonard
17 April 1918	Pont-Rèmy
2 May 1918	Bernaville
28 May 1918	Pont-Rèmy
27 June 1918	Herzeele
29 June 1918	Winnezeele
29 September 1918	Orwell Farm south of Poperinge

13 October 1918	St. Dunstan's Camp west of Ypres
17 October 1918	Clapham Junction east of Ypres on the Menin Road
19 October 1918	Moorsele
25 October 1918	Pottelberg

XX Corps

XX Corps was formed in Palestine on 2 August 1917 and was created as the new commander of the Egyptian Expeditionary Force, Allenby, wanted to reform the force following the British failure in the Second Battle of Gaza. The infantry component of the force was divided into two Corps with each Corps initially comprised of two infantry divisions but two more were added within months. XX Corps was responsible for the right section of line, from Sheik Abbas towards Beersheba.

The Corps first saw action in the Beersheba phase of the Third Battle of Gaza on 31 October 1917. The 60th and 74th Divisions captured Turkish outposts west of the town but were not involved in the final assault. Following Beersheba, on 6 November, the Corps made a frontal assault against the Turkish fortifications at Sheria.

In 1918 the Corps took control of the inland areas driving from there into the coastal zone captured by XXI Corps. They spent the last weeks of the campaign in support, the Turks having been beaten, as XXI Corps mopped up the coastal ports.

Commanding Officers

2 August 1917	Lieutenant General Sir Philip Walhouse Chetwode, Bt
20 August 1917	Major General John Stuart Mackenzie Shea (acting)
31 August 1917	Lieutenant General Sir Philip Walhouse Chetwode, Bt

Field Marshal Philip Walhouse Chetwode, 1st Baron Chetwode, 7th Baronet of Oakley, GCB, OM, GCSI, KCMG, DSO, (21 September 1869 – 6 July 1950) was commissioned into the 3rd Oxfordshire and Buckinghamshire Light Infantry in 1888 before moving to the 19th Hussars in 1889. He was promoted to Lieutenant in 1890, Captain in 1897, Major in 1901 and Lieutenant Colonel in 1908. He served in the Chin Hills Expedition in Burma in 1892-93 and the South African Wars where he was twice Mentioned in Despatches and awarded the Distinguished Service Order. He became assistant military secretary to Sir John French in 1906 and took command of the 19th Hussars in 1908. He was promoted to Colonel in 1912 to lead the London Mounted Brigade and became Brigadier General in May 1914 to command the 5th Cavalry Brigade from August 1914. He was promoted to Major General to take charge of 2nd Cavalry Division in July 1915. He moved to the Middle East to command the Desert Mounted Column as a Lieutenant General in November 1916. When Allenby took command of the Egyptian Expeditionary Force in June 1917, Chetwode was given command of XX Corps. He was eight times Mentioned in Despatches during the Palestine Campaign. He was made a Knight Commander of the Order of St Michael and St George (KCMG) in the Birthday Honours List in June 1917, Knight Grand Cross of the Order of the Bath (GCB) in the Birthday Honours List in 1929 having been made a Knight of the Order of the Bath (KCB) in January 1918 and awarded the Order of the Bath (CB) in February 1915. He was made a Knight Grand Commander of the Order of the Star of India (GCSI) in June 1934 and awarded the Order of Merit (OM) in January 1936. After the war he took several senior Staff positions before moving to India in 1928 as Chief of the General Staff in India and Commander-in-Chief, India in November 1930. He was promoted to Field Marshal in February 1933 and created Baron Chetwode of Chetwode in 1945. His son was killed on active service in 1940 and his daughter married John Betjeman, the poet laurate.

General Sir John Stuart Mackenzie Shea, GCB, KCMG, DSO, (17 January 1869 – 1 May 1966) was commissioned into the Royal Irish Regiment as a 2nd Lieutenant in February 1888, was promoted to Lieutenant on 11 February 1890, Captain in 1899 and Major in 1902. He moved to the Indian Army in 1889 to serve with the 15th Bengal Lancers taking part in the Chitral Expedition in 1895. He served in the South African Wars for which he was awarded the Distinguished Service Order. He became an Instructor at the Staff College in Quetta in 1906. He started the war as a General Staff Officer first with the British Expeditionary Force and then with 6th Division. He was promoted to Brigadier General to command 151st Brigade in 1915 and Major General to command 30th Division in 1916. He went to Egypt with Allenby to command 60th Division. He led 'Shea's Force' at the Battle of Amman in March 1918 consisting of his infantry division, the Anzac Mounted Division, and the Imperial Camel Brigade. The force, with 'Chaytor's Force' were to raid Amman, which they did for four days, and then withdraw to the River Jordan. The force was successful but did not fulfill all its objectives as rain had slowed their advance so the Turks had reinforced the city. After the war he commanded 3rd (Lahore) Indian Division in 1919 and was General Officer Commanding Central Provinces District in India in 1921. He went on to be Adjutant-General, India in 1924 and General Officer Commanding-in-Chief, Eastern Command, India in 1928 before retiring in 1932. He was awarded the Order of the Bath (CB) in 1915, made a Knight Commander of the Order of the Bath (KCB) in 1923, a Knight Grand Cross of the Order of the Bath (GCB) in 1929, awarded the Order of St Michael and St George (CMG) in 1918 and made a Knight of the Order of St Michael and St George (KCMG) in 1919.

Composition

Division	From	To
53rd	02/08/1917	12/08/1917
60th	02/08/1917	01/11/1917
74th	02/08/1917	03/05/1918
53rd	28/08/1917	30/10/1918
10th	26/09/1917	30/10/1918
60th	10/11/1917	01/04/1918
52nd	28/11/1917	02/12/1917
54th	28/11/1917	02/12/1917
75th	28/11/1917	02/12/1917
Yeomanry Mounted	28/11/1917	01/04/1918
ANZAC Mounted	06/01/1918	05/04/1918
60th	14/05/1918	06/09/1918
3rd (Lahore) Indian	22/10/1918	30/10/1918

Battle Honours

Invasion of Palestine

> Third Battle of Gaza 31 October–6 November 1917 (10th, 53rd, 60th & 74th Divisions)
>
> Capture of Beersheba 31 October 1917 (53rd, 60th & 74th Divisions, Imperial Camel Brigade)
>
> Capture of Tell Khuweilfe 3–7 November 1917 (53rd Division)
>
> Capture of Sheria Position 6 November 1917 (10th, 60th & 74th Divisions)

Jerusalem Operations

Turkish Counter-Attacks in Defence of Jerusalem 28 November–3 December 1917 (52nd, 60th, 74th & Yeomanry Mounted Divisions)

Capture of Jerusalem 7–9 December 1917 (10th, 60th & 74th Divisions; Mott's Detachment)

Defence of Jerusalem 26–30 December 1917 (10th, 53rd, 60th & 74th Divisions)

Operations in the Jordan Valley

Capture of Jericho 19–21 February 1918 (60th Division)

Tell 'Asur 8–12 March 1918 (10th, 53rd & 74th Divisions; 181st Brigade of 60th Division; Auckland Mounted Brigade of Australian & New Zealand Mounted Division)

The Final Offensive

Battles of Megiddo

Battle of Nablus 19–21 September 1918 (10th & 53rd Divisions; Watson's Force)

Headquarters

2 August 1917	Deir el Balah
18 August 1917	Wadi es Selka
1 September 1917	Deir el Belah
3 September 1917	El Fuqari
30 October 1917	El Baqqar
2 November 1917	Beersheeba
18 November 1917	Red House, North Bank of Wadi el Ghazze
23 November 1917	Junction Station
28 November 1917	Latron
4 January 1918	Mount of Olives, Jerusalem
19 September 1918	Ramallah
22 September 1918	Huwara
24 September 1918	Nablus
30 October 1918	Haifa

Egyptian Expeditionary Force

When the war began the British Force in Egypt was made up of the 10th and 11th Indian Divisions, the Imperial Service Cavalry Brigade, the Bikaner Camel Corps, three batteries of Indian mountain artillery and one Egyptian artillery battery with volunteers of the Egyptian Army. Its main task was to protect the Suez Canal to the east of Egypt. The British evacuated the Sinai and set defences along the canal. The Turks attacked in 1915 initiating the Senussi Campaign on the western border of Egypt with Libya that lasted to 1917. In response the British created the Western Frontier Force, utilising the camel corps, two composite brigades, though not of brigade strength, and several other units. Defending the Suez was the Eastern Frontier Force which faced Turkish attacks in late 1914 and 1915.

As the Gallipoli campaign came to an end, while some troops went to Salonika and some to France, others were sent to Egypt to expand the forces in the area, support the defence of the Suez Canal and fulfil a desire to move on to the offensive against the Turks. The need for a properly coordinated 'army' in the area, separate from the Mediterranean Expeditionary Force who had responsibility for all forces in the east, led to the formation of the Egyptian Expeditionary Force on 1 March 1916.

While the Western Force continued the Senussi campaign, the Eastern Force defended the canal with headquarters at Port Said. It was comprised of three sectors:

- No. 1 (Southern) Sector covered Suez to Kabrit with headquarters at Suez. It was controlled by IX Corps, but they moved to France in June 1916.
- No. 2 (Central) Sector covered Kabrit to Ferdan with headquarters at Ismailia. It was controlled by I ANZAC Corps, formerly the Australian and New Zealand Army Corps, who moved to France in February 1916.
- No. 3 (Northern) Sector covered Ferdan to Port Said. It was controlled by XV Corps who moved to France in April 1916.

The Western Force beat the attacking Turks at the Battle of Romani in August 1916 and then followed the Turks into Sinai and Palestine. By 1917 it had several divisions, the Desert Column, later Corps, and a number of ad hoc formations. The Eastern Force had achieved several victories and were well established in Ottoman territory. At this time, the new commander of the Egyptian Expeditionary Force, Allenby, reorganised the force with the creation of the two new Corps and the Desert Mounted Corps. These moved north in Palestine, defeating the Turks, and captured Jerusalem by the end of 1917. Serious losses on the Western Front in March 1918 during the German Spring Offensive, forced the British to take reinforcements for France from the Egyptian Expeditionary Force. This slowed the advance, but Allenby got them moving again in April achieving a series of victories leading to the Ottoman Empire agreeing an armistice at the end of October 1918.

Egyptian Expeditionary Force

Division	From	To
11th Indian	24/12/1914	31/05/1915
63rd (RN)	10/01/1916	29/04/1916
53rd	01/04/1916	20/05/1916
52nd	12/04/1916	01/10/1916
42nd	22/04/1916	22/02/1917
ANZAC Mounted	01/06/1916	01/12/1916
53rd	03/06/1916	01/03/1917
52nd	01/10/1916	22/12/1916
52nd	01/03/1917	12/08/1917
74th	04/03/1917	02/08/1917
53rd	01/04/1917	02/08/1917
54th	01/06/1917	12/08/1917
60th	12/06/1917	02/08/1917
2nd Indian Cavalry/5th Cavalry/2nd Mounted	10/05/1918	02/07/1918
ANZAC Mounted	13/08/1918	11/11/1918

Indian Expeditionary Forces E & F

Indian Expeditionary Forces E & F fought from 1914 to 1918 in Egypt, Sinai and Palestine. They began with divisions, brigades and units sent from India, both cavalry and infantry as well as specialist formations. Several infantry divisions were formed in the theatre or sent from India and 36 battalions were sent to reinforce the units in the area. Some units remained from Indian Expeditionary Force G that had served at Gallipoli. Two Indian cavalry divisions were sent from England in 1918. They defended the Suez Canal from 1914 and then took part in the push into Palestine in 1917-18. Some units left the area to join Indian Expeditionary Force D in Mesopotamia.

XXI Corps

XXI Corps was formed in Egypt in August 1917 with the headquarters coming together from 12 August. It formed part of the Egyptian Expeditionary Force that served in the Sinai and Palestine Campaign and was created as the new commander of the Egyptian Expeditionary Force, Allenby, wanted to reform the force. The Corps took over 52nd, 54th and 75th Divisions. It was responsible for the left section of the line from the Jordan Valley at Sheik Abbas to the sea at Gaza and was joined on its right by XX Corps, with the Desert Mounted Corps held in reserve to the south east. After the success at Sharon the Turkish Army collapsed and the Corps concentrated at Haifa. Its task in the last weeks of the war was to secure the coastal area, especially the ports such as Beirut and Tripoli.

Commanding Officers

18 August 1917	Lieutenant General Edward Stanislaus Bulfin
13 June 1918	Major General Sir Vere Bonamy Fane (acting)
14 August 1918	Major General Arthur Reginald Hoskins (acting)
19 August 1918	Lieutenant General Sir Edward Stanislaus Bulfin

General Sir Edward Stanislaus Bulfin, KCB, CVO, (6 November 1862 – 20 August 1939) was commissioned into the Yorkshires in 1884, promoted to Captain in 1895, Brigade Major to the 9th Brigade in 1899 and brevet Major in November 1900. He went to India in 1890, was Garrison Adjutant at Dover in 1898 and fought in the South African Wars. After the war he became a brevet Lieutenant Colonel when he returned to England to be Deputy Assistant Adjutant-General with I Corps from 1902-04 followed by time as second in command of the Royal Welsh Fusiliers. From 1906-10 he was Assistant Adjutant and Quartermaster-General for the Cape Colony. When he returned to England, he was given command of 2nd Brigade in 1913 as a Brigadier General, having never commanded a battalion, and took them to war in 1914. He led six battalions at Ypres in late 1914 known as 'Bulfin's Force' which played a part in holding the German attacks. In December 1914, he was promoted to Major General to command the newly formed 28th Division leading them through Second Ypres and the Battle of Loos. He became ill and could not return to command until June 1916 when he was given 60th Division and took them to the Salonika Front in December 1916. He was promoted to Lieutenant General to command the newly formed XXI Corps in Palestine in June 1917. After the war he held several Staff positions until retiring in 1926. He was made Commander of the Royal Victorian Order (CVO) in 1910 and a Knight Commander of the Order of the Bath (KCB) in 1918.

Major General Sir Vere Bonamy Fane, KCB, KCIE, (16 June 1863 – 23 May 1924) was commissioned as a Lieutenant in the Manchesters in 1884 and transferred to the Bengal Staff Corps in India in 1888. He was promoted to Captain in 1895 and was appointed Deputy Assistant Adjutant-General with the Punjab Command in 1900. Soon after he went to China to serve during the Boxer Rebellion on the Staff of the Indian Cavalry Brigade and from October 1900, he was Provost Marshal to the British Forces in China. Returning to India in 1902 he was promoted to Major, brevet Lieutenant Colonel in 1903 and brevet Colonel in 1909 to command 21st Punjabis, taking part in the Mohmand Expedition of 1908. When the war began, he was promoted to Brigadier General to lead the Jhelum Brigade. He commanded the Bannu Brigade on the North West Frontier in 1915 and was awarded the Order of the Indian Empire (CIE). Fane was promoted to Major General in 1916 to serve in Palestine and Mesopotamia commanding the 7th (Meerut) Indian Division for which he was made a Knight Commander of the Order of the Indian Empire (KCIE) and twice Mentioned in Despatches as well as receiving the Croix de Guerre and the Order of the Nile (2nd class). After the war he continued to serve with the Indian Army, being a district commander in Burma and was made a Knight Commander of the Order of the Bath (KCB) having been awarded the Order of the Bath (CB) in 1914.

Major General Sir Arthur Reginald Hoskins, KCB, CMG, DSO, (30 May 1871 – 7 February 1942) was commissioned into the North Staffordshires in 1891, promoted to Lieutenant in 1895, Captain in 1900 and brevet Major the same year. He served with the Egyptian Army from 1896-1900, fought in the Mahdist War between 1897-99 where he was Mentioned in Dispatches and received the Order of the Medjidie (4th Class). He served in the South African Wars where he was awarded the Distinguished Service Order. He fought in the Somaliland Campaign in 1903 and was again Mentioned in Despatches before moving to England to attend the Staff College. From 1905 he served as a Staff Officer in Egypt and at the Staff College and moved to East Africa as Inspector of the Kings African Rifles in 1913. At the start of the war he was appointed as Assistant Adjutant and Quartermaster General of the 8th Division and soon became Chief of Staff to Major General Sir Thompson Capper at 7th Division. In March 1915 Hoskins was promoted to Brigadier General and given command of the 8th Brigade. In early 1916 he was promoted to Major General and transferred to the East African Campaign as commander of the 1st East African Division for which he was awarded the Order of St Michael and St George (CMG). Hoskins became Commander-in-Chief of British forces in East Africa in January 1917 but was replaced in April. He was given command of the 3rd (Lahore) Indian Division in Mesopotamia and Palestine until the end of the war at which time he was made a Knight Commander of the Order of the Bath (KCB). He commanded 46th Division after the war until he retired in 1923.

Composition

Division	From	To
52nd	12/08/1917	28/11/1917
53rd	12/08/1917	28/08/1917
54th	12/08/1917	20/11/1917
75th	12/08/1917	28/11/1917
52nd	02/12/1917	04/04/1918
54th	02/12/1917	30/10/1918
75th	02/12/1917	03/10/1918
Yeomanry Mounted	11/12/1917	28/11/1917
ANZAC Mounted	24/12/1917	29/12/1917
7th (Meerut) Indian	10/01/1918	30/10/1918
Imperial Mounted/Australian Mounted	04/04/1918	23/04/1918
3rd (Lahore) Indian	22/06/1918	22/10/1918
60th	06/09/1918	24/09/1918

Battle Honours

Invasion of Palestine
Third Battle of Gaza
> Attack on Gaza Defences —3 November 1917 (54th Division and 156th Brigade of 52nd Division)
> Capture of the Wadi el Hesi Defences 8 November (52nd Division)
> Burqa 12 November 1917 (156th Brigade of 52nd Division)
> El Maghar 13 November 1917 (52nd & 75th Divisions)

Occupation of Junction Station 14 November 1917 (52nd & 75th Divisions)
Jerusalem Operations
Battle of Nabi Samweil 17–24 November 1917 (52nd & 75th Divisions)
Turkish Counter-Attacks in Defence of Jerusalem 27–28 November 1917 (52nd, 54th & 75th Divisions)
Battle of Jaffa 11, 15 & 20–22 December 1917 (52nd, 54th & 75th Divisions)
Passage of the Nahr el Auja 21 December 1917 (52nd Division)
Tell 'Asur 8–12 March 1918 (54th & 75th Divisions)
Fight at Ras el 'Ain 12 March 1918 (162nd Brigade of 54th Division)
Berukin 9–10 April 1918 (7th (Meerut) Indian, 54th, & 75th Divisions; Australian Mounted Division of the Desert Mounted Corps)
Final Offensive
Battles of Megiddo
Battle of Sharon 19–21 September 1918 (3rd (Lahore) Indian, 7th (Meerut) Indian, 54th, 60th & 75th Divisions)

Headquarters

12 August 1917	Deir el Balah
11 November 1917	Deir Sneid
13 November 1917	South of Es Suafir el Gharbiye
14 November 1917	Jewish Colony
19 November 1917	El Qubab, North-East of Junction Station
28 November 1917	Bir Salem near Er Ramle
4 January 1918	Jaffa
1 April 1918	Jerishe on the Nahr el Auja
19 September 1918	Bulfin Hill West of Mulebbis
24 September 1918	Tul Karm
28 September 1918	Karmelheim
8 October 1918	Beirut

XXII Corps

XXII Corps was formed in France on 31 December 1917, from what was left of II ANZAC Corps, once the Australian divisions had left to form the Australian Corps. When II ANZAC Corps was disbanded its New Zealand units moved to XXII Corps. The New Zealand Division was attached to VII Corps from March 1918, but the other New Zealand units remained part of XXII Corps. It took over a front from IX Corps on 30 January 1918. In June 1918, after the German offensives, it became a reserve Corps utilised for training and reconstruction of divisions ready to head to the front line. It was given four British divisions, the 15th (Scottish), the 34th, the 51st (Highland) and the 62nd (West Riding). It then returned to front line action in July 1918 aiding the French with the 51st and 62nd Divisions in the Second Battle of the Marne and at Soissons. XXII Corps was returned to Haig in August 1918 for the Advance to Victory. On 9 November 1918, the Corps crossed the Maubeuge-Mons road and at the time of the armistice, the Corps was located to the south-east and east of Mons.

Commanding Officers

31 December 1917	Lieutenant General Alexander John Godley
27 August 1918	Lieutenant General Sir Walter Pipon Braithwaite (temp)
12 September 1918	Lieutenant General Sir Alexander John Godley

General Sir Alexander John Godley – See III Corps
General Sir Walter Pipon Braithwaite, GCB – See IX Corps

Composition

Division	From	To
49th	31/12/1917	10/04/1918
66th	31/12/1917	18/02/1918
NZ Division	31/12/1917	24/03/1918
20th	30/01/1918	24/02/1918
37th	30/01/1918	25/03/1918
6th	27/03/1918	12/05/1918
21st	06/04/1918	14/05/1918
39th	06/04/1918	05/06/1918

39th	10/04/1918	17/04/1918
9th	11/04/1918	07/05/1918
30th	18/04/1918	27/04/1918
49th	20/04/1918	12/05/1918
25th	25/04/1918	08/05/1918
19th	26/04/1918	09/05/1918
33rd	01/05/1918	12/05/1918
59th	06/05/1918	08/05/1918
30th	12/05/1918	24/05/1918
34th	12/05/1918	05/06/1918
37th	05/06/1918	14/06/1918
12th	06/06/1918	16/06/1918
58th	06/06/1918	15/06/1918
47th	15/06/1918	20/06/1918
63rd (RN)	15/06/1918	19/06/1918
8th	26/06/1918	14/07/1918
50th	03/07/1918	14/07/1918
12th	14/07/1918	16/07/1918
51st	14/07/1918	02/08/1918
62nd	14/07/1918	06/08/1918
15th	15/07/1918	18/08/1918
34th	15/07/1918	06/08/1918
16th	09/08/1918	22/08/1918
39th	16/08/1918	11/11/1918
4th	25/08/1918	28/08/1918
51st	29/08/1918	10/10/1918
11th	30/08/1918	25/09/1918
1st	04/09/1918	10/09/1918
56th	06/09/1918	10/10/1918
4th	17/09/1918	11/11/1918
1st Canadian	07/10/1918	10/10/1918

2nd Canadian	11/10/1918	11/10/1918
49th	11/10/1918	04/11/1918
51st	11/10/1918	11/11/1918
11th	12/10/1918	11/11/1918
56th	31/10/1918	11/11/1918
63rd (RN)	05/11/1918	11/11/1918

Battles Honours

Battles of the Lys 1918

Battle of Bailleul 13-15 April 1918 (9th Division and 62nd Brigade of 62nd Division in Second Army)

First Battle of Kemmel 17-19 April 1918 (9th & 21st Divisions, 39th Division Composite Brigade, 146th Brigade of 49th Division in Second Army)

Second Battle of Kemmel 25-26 April 1918 (6th, 9th, 21st, 25th, 30th and 49th Divisions in Second Army)

Battle of the Scherpenberg 29 April 1918 (6th, 21st, 25th, 30th & 49th Divisions, 39th Division Composite Brigade, South African Brigade of 9th Division in Second Army)

The Advance to Victory

Battle of Tardenois 20-31 July 1918 (51st & 62nd Divisions in French Fifth Army)

Second Battles of Arras 1918

Battle of the Scarpe 1918 26-30 August 1918 (51st & 11th Divisions in First Army)

Battle of Drocourt-Quéant 2-3 September 1918 (11th & 51st Divisions in First Army)

Battles of the Hindenburg Line

Battle of the Canal du Nord 27 September–1 October 1918 (4th & 56th Divisions in First Army)

Battle of Cambrai 1918 8-9 October 1918 (56th & 1st Canadian Divisions in First Army)

Pursuit to the Selle 9-12 October 1918 (49th, 51st, 56th, 1st & 2nd Canadian Divisions in First Army)

Final Advance in Picardy

Battle of the Selle 17-25 October 1918 (4th, 49th & 51st Divisions in First Army)

Battle of Valenciennes 1-2 November 1918 (4th & 49th Divisions in First Army)

Battle of the Sambre 4 November 1918 (11th & 56th Divisions in First Army)

Passage of the Grand Honelle 5-7 November 1918 (11th, 56th & 63rd Divisions in First Army)

Headquarters

31 December 1917	Abeele
4 March 1918	Mont Noir
11 April 1918	Steenvoorde
20 April 1918	Zuytpeene
15 May 1918	Bollezeele
5 June 1918	Molliens-Vidame
14 July 1918	Vitry-le-Francois
15 July 1918	Romilly-sur-Seine
17 July 1918	Vertus
20 July 1917	Haut Villers
22 July 1918	Mareuil-sur-Ay
6 August 1918	Bryas
29 August 1918	Ecoivres
11 October 1918	Quarry Wood
16 October 1918	Escaudoeuvres
5 November 1918	Verchain
9 November 1918	Sebourg

XXIII Corps

XXIII Corps was formed in the United Kingdom on 16 February 1918 as a Home Forces formation to reinforce units in France. It only functioned in the United Kingdom and acted as a holding Corps for divisions on home service and a few divisions from France who returned from the Western Front in 1918 for restructuring and training new men. The Corps saw no action.

Commanding officers

16 February 1918	Lieutenant General Sir William Pulteney Pulteney
7 May 1918	Lieutenant General Sir Thomas D'Oyly Snow
5 August 1918	Lieutenant General Sir William Pulteney Pulteney

Lieutenant General Sir William Pulteney Pulteney – See III Corps
Lieutenant General Sir Thomas D'Oyly Snow - See VII Corps

Composition

Division	From	To
67th Division	16/02/1918	11/11/1918
68th Division	16/02/1918	11/11/1918
69th Division	16/02/1918	11/11/1918
64th Division	01/04/1918	11/11/1918
16th Division	18/06/1918	27/07/1918
25th Division	30/06/1918	28/09/1918

Headquarters

| 16 February 1916 | Brentwood |
| 5 August 1918 | Bury St Edmunds |

Home Forces
While dealing with the Home Forces Corps, I feel it is important to look briefly at the other 'Home Forces' commands. Preparation for a potential war had seen plans to use the Territorial forces, some parts of the 'Regular' army, about 42000 men mostly from the Royal Garrison Artillery and the Royal Engineers, and the police, to protect ports, railways and other vital installations in the United Kingdom from invasion and sabotage. Additional coastal security was to be provided by seven Territorial divisions of about 73000 men, and 101 battalions of the Special and Extra Reserves.

The remaining seven Territorial divisions, about 195000 men, were allocated to the Central Force, who were to move to engage the enemy once the location of any potential invasion became known. On mobilisation, these divisions were to concentrate mainly north of London in locations with good transport links which could be used to place them on the enemy's approach to the capital. This force was organised into four commands: the Mounted Division, comprising four yeomanry brigades and two cyclist battalions, headquartered at Bury St. Edmunds, Suffolk; First Army, of one infantry division and one mounted brigade, headquartered at Bedford; Second Army, of two infantry divisions, two yeomanry brigades and three cyclist battalions, headquartered at Aldershot; and Third Army, of four infantry divisions, two yeomanry brigades and one cyclist battalion, headquartered at Luton.

This plan was enacted in August 1914 but, as the war progressed, the plan had to react to circumstances. Kitchener began to recruit for the long war he expected, losses in 1914 were high and the Territorials were mobilised to go overseas to fight or to relieve battalions of Regulars moving to the front line from places like Malta and India. The war was more widespread than expected with the need for forces to be active in the Middle East and Africa. Hence, the plan had to evolve and react to circumstances.

In 1915, it was decided that two New Army divisions would be made available to the home army should it be required. Hence, the home forces gained men who had been recruited to the New Armies. Further developments came in 1916 as Field Marshal French returned from France to take command of the home forces. He was not impressed by what he found and felt that a focus on potential invasion from the east coast need to be the primary focus. He also recognised the role of home forces as first, defending the country and second, training troops to go overseas. Hence, he found that as divisions were brought up to strength and provided with equipment, they were posted overseas. As such, he disbanded the forces that existed at that time and replaced them with new commands.

The Central Force armies were replaced by the Northern Army, headquartered at Mundford in Suffolk with a cyclist division, two Territorial divisions, 13 Provisional Battalions in three brigades and a Territorial infantry division for training; and the Southern Army, headquartered at Brentwood in Essex with a cyclist division, three Territorial divisions, 24 Provisional Battalions in six brigades and a mounted division for training. Two more Territorial divisions were emergency reserves. A 'Local

Force' remained, of two Territorial divisions, two cyclist brigades, twelve cyclist battalions, three mounted brigades and 30 battalions of the Special, Extra and Local Reserve. Additional Home Army forces were Special Reserve brigades defending seven ports, fifteen Second Reserve and eleven Local Reserve brigades located near the coast or at inland training centres, third-line Territorial units located across the country, and cavalry and guards reserve battalions in London. In November 1916, he gained the 71st, 72nd and 73rd Divisions only created for home service, to add to the eleven Territorial divisions under his command. He went on to undertake further reforms such as the creation of the Royal Defence Force, the Volunteer Force and the Training Reserve.

At the end of 1917, the huge losses suffered during Third Ypres, the implications of the October Revolution in Russia, the Austro-German success on the Italian Front and the anticipated German Spring offensive generated a surge in demand for manpower. As a result, in January 1918 the home army was again searched for drafts to be sent overseas, losing around 50000 of its 400000 troops. The 65th (Lowland) Division and the 71st, 72nd and 73rd Divisions were disbanded. In May 1918 French was replaced by General Sir William Robert Robertson and became Lord Lieutenant of Ireland.

Composition

Division	From	To
1st Mounted	31/08/1914	01/11/1916
2nd Mounted	31/08/1914	10/04/1915
63rd	31/08/1914	21/07/1916
64th	31/08/1914	01/04/1918
65th	31/08/1914	18/03/1918
67th	31/08/1914	16/02/1918
68th	31/08/1914	16/02/1918
69th	31/08/1914	16/02/1918
2nd/2nd Mounted/3rd Mounted/1st Mounted/1st Cyclist	06/03/1915	11/11/1918
4th Mounted/2nd Cyclist	20/03/1916	16/11/1916
72nd	01/11/1917	08/04/1918

| 71st | 11/11/1917 | 08/04/1918 |
| 73rd | 11/11/1917 | 08/04/1918 |

Central Force

Central Force, based in London, was formed on 5 August 1914 under Sir Ian Hamilton, who had the title of Commander-in-Chief Home Army though this did not give him command of all troops on home service. Under this were the three Armies below and attached to Central Force were the 1st and 2nd Mounted Divisions, the West Riding Division, and the Northumbrian Division. Central Force was disbanded and redesignated as Home Forces in December 1915 when Sir John French was appointed Commander-in-Chief, Home Forces.

Commanding officers

| 5 August 1914 | General Sir Ian Standish Monteith Hamilton |
| 13 March 1915 – 12 March 1916 | General Sir Henry Macleod Leslie Rundle |

Sir Ian Standish Monteith Hamilton, GCB, GCMG, DSO, (16 January 1853 – 12 October 1947) was commissioned into the Suffolks in 1871, but soon transferred to the 2nd Gordon Highlanders in India where he took part in the Afghan Campaign. He served in the First Boer War from 1880-81 where he was severely wounded and suffered from the wound to his hand for the rest of his life. He was promoted to Captain in 1882, Major in 1885 and Lieutenant Colonel in 1887. From 1895–98 he held the post of Deputy Quarter Master General in India. He served in the Nile Expedition of 1884-85, the Chitral Expedition of 1895 for which he was awarded the Order of the Bath (CB), the Tirah Campaign of 1897-98 where he commanded the 3rd Brigade and was again wounded. He was awarded the Distinguished Service Order in 1891. He returned to England in April 1898 to be Commandant of the School of Musketry. He was sent to South Africa in 1899 as Chief Staff Officer (Assistant Adjutant General) to Lieutenant General White so served in the South African Wars commanding several formations and for which he was frequently Mentioned in Despatches. He was promoted to Major General and made a Knight Commander of the Order of the Bath (KCB) in 1900, as well as being recommended twice for the Victoria Cross but on the first occasion was considered too young, and on the second too senior. He returned to London to the War Office but was sent back to South Africa as Chief of Staff to Lord Kitchener and was promoted to Lieutenant General. After the war he served in the United Kingdom as Military

Secretary at the War Office and Quartermaster-General to the Forces from 1903-04. From 1904-05, Hamilton was the military attaché of the British Indian Army serving with the Japanese army in Manchuria during the Russo-Japanese War where he saw prolonged trench warfare for the first time and began to realise that cavalry tactics had become redundant. Hamilton went on to serve as General Officer Commanding Southern Command from 1905-09, Adjutant-General to the Forces from 1909-10 for which he was made a Knight Grand Cross of the Order of the Bath (GCB), Inspector-General of Overseas Forces from 1911-13 and General Officer Commanding-in-Chief Mediterranean Command from 1913-14 returning to England in July 1914. Hamilton was a very highly regarded soldier before the war. Too senior to be appointed to a Corps position under French, he was appointed Commander-in-Chief, Home Army and commander of the Central Force at the start of the war. He was appointed to the post of commander of the Mediterranean Expeditionary Force, with orders to gain control of the Dardanelles straits from the Ottoman Empire and to capture Constantinople. With the failure of the Gallipoli campaign, he was recalled to London in October 1915 and his career ended. He spoke German, French and Hindi. He was made a Knight Commander of the Order of St Michael and St George (KCMG) in 1919.

General Sir Henry Macleod Leslie Rundle, GCB, GCMG, GCVO, DSO, (6 January 1856 – 19 November 1934) was commissioned into the Royal Artillery in 1876. He fought in the Zulu War in 1879, the First Boer War of 1881, the Anglo-Egyptian War of 1882, the Nile Expedition 1884-85 and the Khartoum Expedition in 1898 having joined the Egyptian Army in 1893, remaining for fifteen years. He was awarded the Distinguished Service Order in 1887 and the Order of Osmanieh (third class). In 1889 he was Mentioned in Despatches, one of ten 'Mentions' before 1902, and awarded the 2nd Class Order of Medijidieh, as well as being promoted to Lieutenant Colonel. He was promoted to Major General in November 1896 and was awarded the Order of St Michael and St George (CMG). He was made a Knight of the Order of the Bath (KCB) in 1898 and returned to England to become General Officer Commanding South-Eastern District. At the start of the South African Wars he was Deputy Adjutant General at the War Office but was soon given command of the 8th Division of the South African Field Force being promoted to Lieutenant General. He led them throughout the war for which he was made a Knight Commander of the Order of St Michael and St George (KCMG). Returning to England he was given command of South-Eastern District and 5th Division from

1902-03 and Northern Command from 1903-06 before temporary retirement. He was promoted to Knight Grand Cross of the Order of the Bath (GCB) in 1911, Knight Grand Cross of the Royal Victorian Order (GCO) in 1912, and Knight Grand Cross of the Order of St Michael and St George (GCMG) in 1914. In 1909, now promoted to General, he became Governor General of Malta until his return to England in 1915 to take command of Central Force. When it was disbanded, he did not receive another post retiring in 1919.

First Army

First Army was formed on 5 August 1914 under the command of Central Force. It was based at Bedford with Sir Bruce Hamilton as commander. Units attached to the Army were the Highland Division and the Highland Mounted Brigade. First Army kept its name even after the establishment of a First Army in the British Expeditionary Force in December 1914. It was disbanded on 12 March 1916 and reformed as Northern Army.

Commanding Officers

5 August 1914	General Sir Bruce Meade Hamilton
22 June 1915	General Sir Horace Lockwood Smith Dorrien
11 December 1915- 12 March 1916	Lieutenant General Sir Alfred Edward Codrington

Northern Army

Northern Army was responsible for the defence of East Anglia. It was formed on 11 April 1916 under the command of Sir Bruce Hamilton, with headquarters at Mundford. The Army was composed of 1st Cyclist Division, 62nd (2nd West Riding) Division, 64th (2nd Highland) Division and four provisional brigades (3rd, 4th, 5th and 6th), with 68th (2nd Welsh) Division attached for training purposes. The Army was disbanded on 16 February 1918

Commanding Officers

11 April 1916 – 16 February 1918	General Sir Bruce Meade Hamilton

Second Army

Second Army was formed on 5 August 1914 under the command of Central Force. It was based at Aldershot with Sir Frederick Stopford as commander. Units attached to the Army were the 1st London Division, the Home Counties Division, and the South Eastern Mounted Brigade. By November 1914 headquarters had moved to

Tunbridge Wells. Second Army kept its name even after the establishment of a Second Army in the British Expeditionary Force in December 1914. It was disbanded on 12 March 1916 and reformed as Southern Army.

Commanding Officers

5 August 1914	Lieutenant General Sir Frederick William Stopford
7 June 1915 – 12 March 1916	Lieutenant General Charles Louis Woollcombe

Southern Army

Southern Army was responsible for the defence of South-East England, including both sides of the Thames Estuary. It was formed on 11 April 1916 under the command of Sir Arthur Paget, with headquarters at Brentwood, Essex. The Army was composed of the 2nd Cyclist Division, 65th (2nd Lowland) Division, 66th (2nd East Lancashire) Division until February 1917, 67th (2nd Home Counties) Division, 71st Division from March 1917 and six provisional brigades (1st, 2nd, 7th, 8th, 9th and 10th), with the 1st Mounted Division attached for training purposes. Southern Army was disbanded on 16 February 1918

Commanding Officers

11 April 1916 – 16 February 1918	General Right Honourable Sir Arthur Henry Fitzroy Paget

Third Army

Third Army, based at Luton, was formed on 6 September 1914 under the command of Central Force. Sir Alfred Codrington was appointed commander on 30 October after the death of Sir William Franklyn. Units attached to the Army were the East Anglian Division, the North Midland Division, the South Midland Division, the 2nd London Division, the North Midland Mounted Brigade, and the 2nd South Western Mounted Brigade. Third Army kept its name even after the establishment of a Third Army in the British Expeditionary Force in July 1915. It was disbanded on 11 December 1915 following the appointment of Sir John French as Commander-in-Chief, Home Forces.

Commanding Officers

6 September 1914	Lieutenant General Sir William Edmund Franklyn
30 October 1914 – 11 December 1915	Lieutenant General Sir Alfred Edward Codrington

Aldershot Command

In 1901 the army planned for six Army Corps based on six regional commands. I Corps based on Aldershot, II Corps on Southern Command, III Corps on Irish Command, IV Corps on Eastern Command, V Corps on Northern Command and VI Corps on Scottish Command. In August 1914, Aldershot Command became I Corps under Haig. Then Central Force took over with Second Army headquartered at Aldershot. For the first two years of the war, command at Aldershot was divided between the Major General, Administration, held by Major General Alexander Hamilton-Gordon, and the commander of Aldershot Training Centre, held by General Sir Archibald Hunter. Aldershot Command was reinstated in 1916 under Hunter.

Commanding Officers

5 August 1914	Major General Alexander Hamilton-Gordon
8 May 1916	General Sir Archibald Hunter
1 October 1917	Lieutenant General Sir Archibald James Murray

Eastern Command

When Kitchener started recruiting the New Armies in 1914, each division was to be under the administration of one of the Home Commands, and Eastern Command, also the core of IV Corps, formed what became the 12th (Eastern) Division followed by 18th (Eastern) Division in September 1914. During the war, headquarters of Eastern Command was in London, initially at Horse Guards, and from February 1916 at 50 Pall Mall, London. In 1919 it moved to 41 Queen's Gardens, Bayswater.

Commanding Officers

5 August 1914	Lieutenant General Charles Louis Woollcombe
7 June 1915	General Sir Henry McLeod Leslie Rundle
5 May 1916	Lieutenant General Sir James Wolfe Murray
1 September 1917	Lieutenant General Sir Henry Hughes Wilson
19 February 1918	General Sir William Robert Robertson
29 June 1918	Lieutenant General Sir Charles Louis Woollcombe

Irish Command

Irish Command, also the core of III Corps, formed what became the 10th (Irish) Division followed by 16th (Irish) Division in September 1914. Its headquarters was in Dublin.

Commanding Officers

5 August 1914	Major General Right Honourable Lovick Bransby Friend
27 April 1916	General Right Honourable Sir John Grenfell Maxwell
15 November 1916	Lieutenant General Right Honourable Sir Bryan Thomas Mahon
13 May 1918	Lieutenant General Right Honourable Sir Frederick Charles Shaw

London District

London District (LONDIST) was established in 1870 as Home District. It was re-formed in 1905 as London District to be an independent district within the larger command structure of the army and has remained so ever since. In 1906, when the Chief of the General Staff moved to the Old War Office Building, headquarters of London District moved to Horseguards.

Commanding Officers

5 August 1914	Major General Sir Francis Lloyd (Lieutenant General from 1 January 1917)
1 October 1918	Major General Geoffrey Percy Thynne Feilding

Northern Command

Northern Command, also the core of V Corps, formed the 11th (Northern) Division followed by the 17th (Northern) Division in September 1914. At the end of 1914, Lieutenant General Sir Herbert Plumer, left Northern Command to form V Corps in France, and Major General Henry Lawson was placed in temporary command, followed by Lieutenant General Sir John Maxwell after he had suppressed the Easter Rising in Ireland. Its headquarters was at York.

Commanding Officers

5 August 1914	Lieutenant General Sir Herbert Charles Onslow Plumer
1 January 1915	Major General Henry Merrick Lawson
16 November 1916	Lieutenant General Right Honourable Sir John Grenfell Maxwell

Scottish Command

Scottish Command, also the core of VI Corps, formed what became the 9th (Scottish) Division followed by 15th (Scottish) Division in September 1914. The 64th

(2nd Highland) Division was established in the Command by 1915 after the departure of 51st (Highland) Division for France. Scottish Command was established in 1905 at Edinburgh Castle.

Commanding Officers

| 5 August 1914 | Lieutenant General Sir John Spencer Ewart |
| 5 May 1918 | Lieutenant General Sir Frederick William Nicholas McCracken |

Southern Command

Southern Command was the home of II Corps. Southern Command was initially based at Tidworth Camp but moved to Salisbury. At the end of 1914, Lieutenant General Sir Horace Smith-Dorrien left Southern Command to form II Corps in France, and Lieutenant General William Campbell was placed in command.

Commanding Officers

5 August 1914	General Sir Horace Lockwood Smith Dorrien
21 August 1914	Lieutenant General William Pitcairn Campbell
8 March 1916	Lieutenant General Sir Henry Chrichton Sclater

Western Command

Western Command was established in 1905 and was originally called the Welsh & Midland Command before changing its name in 1906. In 1907 Western Command relocated to Chester. Western Command formed the 13th (Western) Division followed by 19th (Western) Division in September 1914.

Commanding Officers

5 August 1914	General Sir William Henry Mackinnon
8 March 1916	Lieutenant General Sir William Pitcairn Campbell
5 August 1918	Lieutenant General Sir Thomas D'Oyly Snow

XXIV Corps

It was felt in early 1918 that the Egyptian Expeditionary Force needed an extra Corps to command the two Indian divisions about to reinforce the force. On 15 March 1918, the creation of XXIV Corps was authorised. A Corps commander, Lieutenant General Sir George de Symons Barrow, GCB, KCMG, was in place from 20 March. However, the German advance in March to April 1918 highlighted the need for troops on the Western Front that the restructuring of the army in France, and the arrival in France of young conscripts from the United Kingdom, had failed to fulfil. Hence, two divisions left Palestine for the Western Front. The new Corps became redundant and after ten days it ceased to exist, having consisted of little more than a few senior officers at headquarters in Cairo. Lieutenant General Barrow returned to his post in command of the Yeomanry Mounted Division while his replacement at the Yeomanry Mounted Division, Major General Sir Henry John Milnes MacAndrew, had his promotion cancelled.

Reserve Corps

Reserve Corps began to form at Wailly on 4 April 1916 and existed for just over six weeks. Headquarters moved to Regniere Ecluse on 12 May 1916. To create the new Reserve Corps, Haig disbanded the Cavalry Corps in March 1916 and distributed the divisions to the armies and the Reserve Corps. It became Reserve Army on 22 May 1916 in preparation for the Battles of the Somme. Reserve Army subsequently became Fifth Army in October 1916. Its commanding officer was Lieutenant General Hubert de la Poer Gough (see I Corps) who had been moved from command of I Corps on 1 April 1916.

ANZAC Corps (1915)

The Australian and New Zealand Army Corps was part of the Mediterranean Expeditionary Force. It was formed in Egypt in November 1914, arrived in Egypt in December 1914, and operated during the Gallipoli Campaign. It was originally intended to name the Corps the Australasian Army Corps but complaints from New Zealand recruits led to adoption of the name Australian and New Zealand Army Corps.

It consisted mostly of troops from the Australian Imperial Force and New Zealand Expeditionary Force in two divisions, the Australian Division and the New Zealand and Australian Division. There were also British and Indian units attached at times throughout the campaign including the 7th Indian Mountain Artillery Brigade, the Ceylon Planters Rifle Corps, the Zion Mule Corps, and men of the Royal Naval Division.

The First Australian Imperial Force was formed on 15 August 1914, initially with a strength of one division and one light horse brigade. The division fought at Gallipoli, being reinforced by a second division and three light horse brigades. After being evacuated to Egypt the Australian Imperial Force was expanded to five divisions, who fought in France and Belgium on the Western Front.

The New Zealand Expeditionary Force was formed upon the outbreak of war when New Zealand offered two brigades, one infantry and one mounted, with 8500 men to fight for the Empire. The forces in New Zealand were 'territorial' so, as with the men of territorial units in the United Kingdom, and with the Australian forces, the men going overseas had to volunteer for service. The first troops in the New Zealand Expeditionary Force left New Zealand in October 1914 and arrived in Egypt with the first men of the Australian Imperial Force in November 1914. Used with the Australians at Gallipoli, there were not enough New Zealanders to form a Division, so they formed the New Zealand and Australian Division in 1915. The division was disbanded in early 1916 following a reorganisation of the Australian and New Zealand forces after the evacuation from Gallipoli.

The British Secretary of State for War, Kitchener, appointed General William Birdwood, an officer of the British Indian Army, to command the Corps and he furnished most of the Corps Staff from the Indian Army as well. Birdwood arrived in Cairo on 21 December 1914 to assume command.

The Corps disbanded on 15 February 1916, following the Allied evacuation of the Gallipoli peninsula. The troops from the Corps formed I ANZAC Corps under Birdwood and II ANZAC Corps commanded by Lieutenant General Alexander Godley. These were also helped with the expansion of the Australian Imperial Force and the creation of the New Zealand Division. These two Corps went to France and Belgium leaving behind in Egypt, to fight in the Sinai and Palestine, were men who then formed the ANZAC Mounted Division and the Imperial Mounted Division. A sixth division was partially raised in 1917 in the United Kingdom but was broken up and used as reinforcements following heavy casualties.

Commanding Officers

21 December 1914 to 27 January 1916	General William Riddell Birdwood

Field Marshal William Riddell Birdwood, 1st Baron Birdwood, GCB, GCSI, GCMG, GCVO, CIE, DSO, (13 September 1865 – 17 May 1951) was commissioned into the 4th (Militia) Royal Scots Fusiliers in 1883, and transferred as a Lieutenant into the 12th (Prince of Wales's) Royal Lancers in 1885. He was promoted to Captain in 1896, brevet Major in November 1901 and local Lieutenant Colonel in October 1901, full Major in 1903, Lieutenant Colonel in 1904 and Colonel in 1905. He went to India in 1885 before joining the Bengal Staff Corps at the end of 1886 and then the 11th Bengal Lancers in 1887. He served on the North West Frontier in 1891 on the Isazai Campaign and the Tirah campaign in 1897. He served in the South African Wars initially as Brigade-Major with a mounted brigade from January 1900 and then as Deputy-Assistant Adjutant-General from October 1900 being Mentioned in Despatches. He followed Lord Kitchener to India in 1902 as his assistant military secretary and interpreter. He took command of the Kohat Brigade on the North West Frontier in 1908 being promoted to Brigadier General in 1909. He took part in the Mohmand Field Force actions in 1908 for which he was awarded the Distinguished Service Order. He was promoted to Major General in 1911 to become Quartermaster General in India, a member of the Viceroy's Legislative Council in 1912 and Secretary of the Indian Army Department in 1913. In November 1914 he was tasked with forming a Corps of Australian and New Zealand troops for which he was promoted to Lieutenant General. This Corps was to attack Gallipoli at Gaba Tepe, now ANZAC Cove, in April 1915, now celebrated as ANZAC Day. Birdwood became commander of the Australian Imperial Force shortly after the landings. The campaign went very badly with the last offensive in August 1915. From then preparations were underway for a withdrawal, one of the few successes of the campaign, in December 1915. In October 1915, Birdwood was given command of the Dardanelles Army. In February 1916, the ANZAC Corps was disbanded in Egypt with the troops forming I and II ANZAC Corps made up of two Australian divisions in each Corps with Birdwood commanding II ANZAC Corps. When I ANZAC Corps became the first to depart for France, Birdwood, as senior Corps commander, took over. He was made a General in October 1917 commanding the newly formed Australian Corps as I ANZAC and II ANZAC were merged. Birdwood was given command of Fifth Army in May 1918 leading it until the end of the war. After the war he was made a baronet and promoted to Field Marshal. He was commanding the Northern Army in India from 1920-25 and became Commander in Chief in India in 1925 until he retired in 1930. He was made Baron Birdwood of Anzac and of Totnes in 1938. He was awarded the Order of the Bath (CB) in 1911, made a Knight of the Order of the Bath (KCB) in 1917 and Knight Grand Cross of the Order of the Bath (GCB) in 1923. He was made a Knight of the Order of St Michael and St George (KCMG) in 1915 and Knight Grand Cross of the Order of St Michael and St George (GCMG) in 1919. He was made a Knight Grand Cross of the Royal Victorian Order (GCVO) in 1937. He became a Knight Grand Commander of the Order of the Star of India (GCSI) in 1930 and Companion of the Order of the Indian Empire (CIE) in 1908.

Composition

Division	From	To
1st Australian	01/12/1914	15/02/1916
NZ & Australian Division	21/12/1914	15/02/1916
2nd Australian	01/07/1915	15/02/1916
13th	16/07/1915	28/08/1915

Battle Honours

Landing at Anzac Cove 25 April-5 May 1915 (1st Australian & ANZAC Divisions)
    Attack on Baby 700 2 May 1915 (ANZAC Division)
    Gaba Tepe 4–5 May 1915 (1st Australian & ANZAC Divisions)
Second Battle of Krithia 6–9 May 1915 (1st Australian & ANZAC Divisions)
Defence of Anzac-Turkish Attack 19 May 1915 (1st Australian & ANZAC Divisions)
Quinn's Post 2, 9, 13 and 29 May 1915 (1st Australian & ANZAC Divisions)
Turkish attack at The Nek 29 June 1915 (ANZAC Division)

Battle of Sari Bair 6 August 1915 (ANZAC Division)

  Lone Pine 6–10 August 1915 (1st Australian Division)

  The Nek 7 August 1915 (ANZAC Division)

Hill 60 21, 22, and 27 August 1915 (2nd Australian & ANZAC Divisions)

Evacuation of Anzac 19–21 December 1915 (1st & 2nd Australian & ANZAC Divisions)

Headquarters

23 December 1914	Cairo
25 April 1915	ANZAC Cove or Gaba Tepe
21 December 1915	Cairo
4 January to 15 February 1916	Ismailia

The Dardanelles Army

The Dardanelles Army was formed in late 1915 made up of three Corps at Gallipoli, VIII Corps, IX Corps and Australian and New Zealand Army Corps as well as the 1st Newfoundland Regiment. It was created because of the reorganisation when the Salonika Front began. The Dardanelles Army was created to manage operations at Gallipoli while the Salonika Army was responsible for operations at Salonika. Both armies came under the direction of the Mediterranean Expeditionary Force. The Dardanelles Army was short-lived as, by the time of its creation, offensive operations at Gallipoli had ceased and plans for the evacuation were being made. For most of its existence, the Army was commanded by Lieutenant General William Birdwood who was also in charge of all Australian forces and the ANZAC Corps at Gallipoli. It was disbanded in the restructuring of early 1916.

I ANZAC Corps

I ANZAC Corps was formed at Ismailia in Egypt on 15 February 1916 as part of the reorganisation and expansion of the Australian Imperial Force and the New Zealand Expeditionary Force to accommodate five Australian and one New Zealand divisions following the evacuation of Gallipoli in December 1915. The Australian and New Zealand Army Corps was disbanded and reformed as two Corps who spent a short time in Egypt protecting the Suez Canal before being moved to France in March 1916. I ANZAC was formed with three divisions, two Australian and the newly formed New Zealand Division. On 28 March its headquarters staff was exchanged with that of II ANZAC as I ANZAC Corps moved to France arriving at Marseilles from Alexandria on 4 April 1916.

In France, the Corps began in a quiet sector of northern France near the Belgian border, within Second Army, known as the 'nursery' as it replaced a Corps on the way to the Somme. But it soon moved south to the Somme in July 1916 where it played a major role as part of Fifth Army from July to August at Pozieres. At this point the New Zealand Division moved to II ANZAC Corps and was replaced by an Australian division. The Corps captured the village of Pozieres and rotated its three divisions over the next six weeks to hold German counter-attacks and shelling. After the heavy casualties suffered in this battle the Corps was withdrawn to recover for the rest of the year. The battle at Pozieres was so significant in the history of the country that Australians will tell you that if you dig six inches into the soil at Pozieres you will still find Australian blood.

In 1917 the Corps was involved in the German retreat, but more well-known is its contribution to the Battles of Bullecourt in April and May. It then helped to capture Messines in June and took part in Third Ypres, notably at Polygon Wood and on the Broodseinde Ridge, near what is now the largest Commonwealth War Graves Commission military cemetery in the world at Tyne Cot, a couple of kilometres from Passendale. The atrocious weather and heavy casualties meant that, by early November, I ANZAC Corps was withdrawn from the line around Ypres.

In November 1917, the five Australian infantry divisions in France were grouped together to become the Australian Corps and on 31 December 1917 I and II ANZAC Corps ceased to exist, though I ANZAC had effectively become the Australian Corps on 15 November 1917.

Commanding Officers

15 February 1916	Lieutenant General Sir Alexander John Godley
23 March 1916 – 15 November 1917	Lieutenant General Sir William Riddell Birdwood

Lieutenant General Sir Alexander John Godley – See III Corps

Lieutenant General Sir William Riddell Birdwood – See ANZAC Corps 1915

Composition

Division	From	To
1st Australian	15/02/1916	08/04/1916
2nd Australian	15/02/1916	08/04/1916
NZ Division	15/02/1916	21/06/1916
ANZAC Mounted	01/03/1916	01/06/1916
1st Australian	13/04/1916	28/08/1916
2nd Australian	13/04/1916	17/06/1917
4th Australian	12/07/1916	03/09/1916
1st Australian	03/09/1916	20/10/1916
4th Australian	05/09/1916	26/10/1916
23rd	15/10/1916	24/10/1916
47th	16/10/1916	24/10/1916
41st	20/10/1916	24/10/1916
1st Australian	30/10/1916	01/11/1917
2nd Australian	31/10/1916	17/06/1917
5th Australian	31/10/1916	26/05/1917
4th Australian	01/11/1916	17/05/1917
15th	03/02/1917	18/02/1917
11th	19/04/1917	19/05/1917
48th	12/05/1917	25/05/1917
20th	23/05/1917	26/05/1917
5th Australian	17/06/1917	01/11/1917
2nd Australian	28/07/1917	01/11/1917
4th Australian	02/09/1917	01/11/1917

| 25th | 05/09/1917 | 10/09/1917 |
| 47th | 10/09/1917 | 19/09/1917 |

Battle Honours

The Battles of the Somme, 1916:

The Battle of Pozières 15 July–3 September 1916 (1st, 2nd & 4th Australian Divisions)

Fighting for Mouquet Farm (1st, 2nd & 4th Australian Divisions)

Operations on the Ancre 11 January–13 March 1917 (1st, 2nd & 4th Australian Divisions)

Capture of the Thilloys 25 February–2 March (1st, 2nd & 5th Australian Divisions)

Capture of Irles 10 March (2nd Australian Division)

German Retreat to the Hindenburg Line 14 March–5 April 1917 (4th & 5th Australian Divisions)

Capture of Bapaume 17 March (2nd Australian Division)

Battles of Arras 1917

First Battle of Bullecourt 11 April 1917 (4th & 5th Australian Divisions)

German Attack on Lagnicourt 15 April 1917 (1st & 2nd Australian Divisions)

Second Battle of Bullecourt 3-17 May 1917 (1st & 2nd Australian Divisions)

Actions on the Hindenburg Line 20 May–16 June 1917 (5th Australian Division)

Third Battles of Ypres

Battle of the Menin Road 20-25 September 1917 (1st, 2nd & 4th Australian Divisions)

Battle of Polygon Wood 26 September–3 October 1917 (1st, 2nd, 4th & 5th Australian Divisions)

Battle of Broodseinde 4 October 1917 (1st & 2nd Australian Divisions)

Battle of Poelcapelle 9 October 1917 (1st & 2nd Australian Divisions)

First Battle of Passchendaele 12 October 1917 (4th & 5th Australian Divisions)

Second Battle of Passchendaele 26 October–10 November 1917 (1st, 2nd & 5th Australian Divisions)

Headquarters

15 February 1916	Ismailia
28 March 1916	Alexandria
4 April 1916	Marseilles
8 April 1916	Chateau La Motte-aux-Bois
3 July 1916	Bailleul
10 July 1916	Vignacourt
19 July 1916	Contay
3 September 1916	Abeele
26 October 1916	Villers-Bocage
30 October 1916	Heilly
28 January 1917	Hénencourt
11 April 1917	Grévillers
26 May 1917	Querrieu
26 July 1917	Hazebrouck
5 September 1917	Hoograaf

II ANZAC Corps

II ANZAC Corps was formed at Ismailia in Egypt on 15 February 1916 as part of the reorganisation and expansion of the Australian Imperial Force and the New Zealand Expeditionary Force to accommodate five Australian and one New Zealand divisions following the evacuation of Gallipoli in December 1915. The Australian and New Zealand Army Corps was disbanded and reformed as two Corps who spent a short time in Egypt protecting the Suez Canal before being moved to France in March 1916. II ANZAC was formed with two divisions newly created by the expansion of the Australian Imperial Force. On 28 March its headquarters staff was exchanged with that of I ANZAC and it set sail for France, shortly after I ANZAC Corps, under Lieutenant General Godley who had moved from his brief command of I ANZAC Corps. It departed from Alexandria for Marseilles on 7 June 1916.

In July 1916, following the arrival of II ANZAC in France, the Australian 4th Division was swapped for the New Zealand Division from I ANZAC, and II ANZAC took over a quiet sector of front-line near Armentières known as 'the nursery' relieving I ANZAC Corps who moved to the Somme. In mid-July, they lent the 5th Australian

Division to XI Corps for a diversionary operation that became known as the Battle of Fromelles. However, the Corps saw little action in 1916. The Corps was often made up of an Australian division, the New Zealand Division and a couple of British divisions. The 3rd Australian Division did not arrive in France until November 1916. In June 1917, the Corps took part in the capture of Messines south of Ypres with the New Zealand Division, 3rd and 4th Australian Divisions and British 25th Division and was then also involved in Third Ypres. The casualties sustained made it difficult to maintain the strength of the Australian divisions so a partially formed 6th Australian Division was disbanded to provide reinforcements.

Hence, in November 1917, the five Australian infantry divisions in France were grouped together to form the Australian Corps so that on 31 December 1917 I and II ANZAC Corps ceased to exist, though I ANZAC had effectively become the Australian Corps on 15 November with the transfer of 3rd Australian Division from II ANZAC Corps. The New Zealand Division and the British divisions moved to XXII Corps, newly formed at the end of December.

Commanding Officers

15 February 1916	Lieutenant General Sir William Riddell Birdwood
28 March 1916	Lieutenant General Sir Alexander John Godley

Lieutenant General Sir William Riddell Birdwood – See ANZAC Corps
Lieutenant General Sir Alexander John Godley – See III Corps

Composition

Division	From	To
4th Australian	15/02/1916	12/07/1916
5th Australian	15/02/1916	16/07/1916
53rd	20/05/1916	03/06/1916
NZ Division	21/06/1916	20/08/1916
5th Australian	21/07/1916	18/10/1916
18th	26/07/1916	25/08/1916
51st	11/08/1916	30/09/1916
34th	20/08/1916	18/02/1917
NZ Division	10/10/1916	17/10/1917
3rd Australian	26/11/1916	17/10/1917

57th	15/02/1917	20/05/1917
25th	21/03/1917	25/06/1917
4th Australian	17/05/1917	02/09/1917
8th	19/08/1917	02/09/1917
14th	29/08/1917	02/09/1917
7th	03/09/1917	25/09/1917
49th	24/09/1917	31/12/1917
66th	27/09/1917	31/12/1917
3rd	28/09/1917	02/10/1917
59th	28/09/1917	03/10/1917
3rd Canadian	17/10/1917	22/10/1917
4th Canadian	17/10/1917	22/10/1917
3rd Australian	22/10/1917	15/11/1917
NZ Division	22/10/1917	31/12/1917

Battle Honours

Battle of Messines 7-14 June 1917 (25th, 3rd & 4th Australian, New Zealand Divisions)

Third Battles of Ypres

Battle of Polygon Wood 26 September–3 October 1917 (3rd & 59th, 3rd Australian & New Zealand Divisions)

Battle of Broodseinde 4 October 1917 (3rd Australian & New Zealand Divisions

Battle of Poelcapelle 9 October 1917 (49th & 66th Divisions)

First Battle of Passchendaele 12 October 1917 (3rd Australian & New Zealand Divisions)

Headquarters

15 February 1916	Ismailia
12 June 1916	Marseilles
16 June 1916	Hazebrouck
20 June 1916	Bailleul
4 July 1916	Chateau de la La Motte-aux-Bois
19 July 1916	Advanced HQ established at Fort Rompu
12 September 1916	Bailleul

14 July 1917	Flêtre
2 September 1917	Lumbres
28 September 1917	Ten Elms Camp near Poperinge
18 October 1917	Hazebrouck
15 November 1917	Abeele

Australian Corps 1918

The Australian Corps was formed on 15 November 1917 with the disbanding and merging of I ANZAC and II ANZAC Corps. The five Australian divisions had suffered heavily on the Western Front in 1916 and 1917. The country did not introduce conscription so, by the end of 1917, many battalions were beginning to struggle for manpower. The British solution was to merge and disband battalions but the Australian troops rebelled at this idea when it was tried with the disbandment of the 4th Division. Hence, the emerging 6th Division was abandoned, and the men sent to reinforce the other divisions. As such, the Australian Corps spent its winter months in 1917-18 in a 'quiet' zone at Messines, with the intention of bringing units up to strength and allowing for the sick and wounded to return to their units.

Birdwood, commander of the Australian Imperial Force and I ANZAC Corps at the time, suggested the creation of the Australian Corps. It became the largest Corps on the Western Front with over 100000 men. As a purely Australian Corps, with Australian artillery and Australian Flying Corps units attached, it was felt politically sensitive to appoint Australian officers to all senior command positions. However, Birdwood remained in command of the Corps.

When Birdwood took command of the Fifth Army, the way was open for an Australian to command the Corps. General John Monash, commander of the 3rd Australian Division, who was the senior Australian candidate, had experience commanding troops in battle and was preferred by Haig and Birdwood, got the post in May 1918 and was promoted to Lieutenant General.

The Corps saw actions throughout 1918 from March, with all five divisions involved. During the German advance in April 1918, part of the Corps made a stand and counter-attack at Villers Bretonneux on the third anniversary of the first ANZAC Day, which in some ways began to turn the tide of the war in 1918. It was also involved in what is possibly the first 'modern' battle, at Le Hamel in July 1918, when an 'all arms' assault took place. During the Advance to Victory parts of the Corps had notable successes such as at Mont St Quentin near Peronne. The Corps was effectively withdrawn in early October and spent the rest of the war in redevelopment.

Commanding Officers

15 November 1917	Lieutenant General Sir William Riddell Birdwood
31 May 1918	Lieutenant General John Monash

Lieutenant General Sir William Riddell Birdwood – See ANZAC Corps

General Sir John Monash, GCMG, KCB, VD, (27 June 1865 – 8 October 1931) was a German speaker, genuinely multi-lingual and graduated with post-graduate degrees in Engineering. He joined the militia when he was at university in 1884, became a Lieutenant in 1887, Captain in 1895, Major in 1897 and Lieutenant Colonel in the Intelligence Corps in 1908. He became a Colonel in 1913 having taken command of the 13th Australian Brigade in 1912. When the war began, he was given a desk job but was moved to command the 4th Australian Brigade in September 1914. He took them overseas in December 1914 and landed at Gallipoli with the brigade on 26 April 1915. He was promoted to Brigadier General at Gallipoli having demonstrated leadership and organisational skills. He left the peninsula in August returning in November to cover the withdrawal. In Egypt, the brigade was restructured and defended the Suez Canal before they moved to France. He was promoted to Major General in July 1916 to command the 3rd Australian Division leading them in 1917 at Messines and Third Ypres and in 1918 at Villers Bretonneux. He was promoted to Lieutenant General on 1 July 1918 having taken command of the Australian Corps in May. He led it through the Battle of Le Hamel and then in the Advance to Victory. He was made Director-General of Repatriation and Demobilisation in Australia at the end of the war. He was awarded the Order of the Bath (CB) in September 1915 and made a Knight Commander of the Order of the Bath (KCB) on the battlefield in 1918, the first such award in 200 years. He was made a Knight Grand Cross of the Order of St Michael and St George (GCMG) on 1 January 1919 and was promoted to General in 1929.

Composition

Division	From	To
1st Australian	01/11/1917	03/04/1918
2nd Australian	01/11/1917	03/04/1918
4th Australian	01/11/1917	09/01/1918
5th Australian	01/11/1917	27/03/1918
3rd Australian	15/11/1917	24/03/1918
4th Australian	12/01/1918	27/03/1918
19th	29/03/1918	08/04/1918
25th	30/03/1918	03/04/1918
21st	01/04/1918	03/04/1918
9th	01/04/1918	04/04/1918
1st Australian	06/04/1918	12/04/1918
2nd Australian	06/04/1918	11/11/1918
35th	06/04/1918	06/04/1918
3rd Australian	06/04/1918	11/11/1918
4th Australian	06/04/1918	11/11/1918
8th	12/04/1918	18/04/1918
5th Australian	21/04/1918	24/04/1918
5th Australian	27/04/1918	11/11/1918
47th	29/04/1918	05/05/1918
18th	05/05/1918	25/05/1918
12th	28/07/1918	31/07/1918
1st Australian	06/08/1918	11/11/1918
2nd Cavalry	11/08/1918	14/08/1918
17th	13/08/1918	18/08/1918
32nd	30/08/1918	11/09/1918
1st	10/09/1918	11/09/1918

Battle Honours

Actions of Villers-Bretonneux 24-25 April 1918 (4th & 5th Australian Divisions)
Capture of Hamel 4 July 1918 (2nd, 3rd & 4th Australian Divisions)
Battle of Amiens 8-11 August 1918 (1st, 4th & 5th Australian Divisions)
Second Battles of the Somme 1918

Battle of Albert 21-23 August 1918 (1st, 3rd, 4th & 5th Australian Divisions, 32nd Division)
Second Battle of Bapaume 31 August–3 September 1918 (2nd, 3rd & 5th Australian Divisions, 32nd Division)
Capture of Mont St Quentin 31 August–3 September 1918 (2nd Australian Division)

Battles of the Hindenburg Line

Battle of Epehy 18 September 1918 (1st & 4th Australian Divisions)
Battle of the St. Quentin Canal 29 September–2 October 1918 (2nd, 3rd & 5th Australian Divisions)
Battle of Beaurevoir 3-5 October 1918 (2nd Australian Division)
Capture of Montbrehain 3-5 October 12918 (2nd Australian Division)

Headquarters

1 November 1917	Hoograf
17 November 1917	Flêtre
3 April 1918	Bernaville
5 April 1918	Villers-Bocage
6 May 1918	Bertangles
12 August 1918	Glisy
31 August 1918	Méricourt
11 September 1918	Belloy Wood
10 October 1918	Eu
11 November 1918	Le Cateau

Canadian Corps

The Canadian Corps was formed from the Canadian Expeditionary Force, which was the 1st Canadian Division, in September 1915 after the arrival of the 2nd Canadian Division in France. The 1st Canadian Division had fought well during Second Ypres, facing the gas attack at the start of the German attack, and holding the line to allow the British to move reinforcements to the front. Pressure was for a united Canadian force once the 2nd Canadian Division arrived and a Canadian Corps was inevitable, notably as the Minister of Militia and Defence insisted that Canadian troops remain under national command and as one entity.

On 13 September 1915 Alderson opened his Headquarters at Bailleul. He was not Canadian, and it was not until 1917 that the Corps gained a Canadian commander. Canada's shortage of officers trained for Staff roles meant that the principal Staff appointments in the Corps were given to British officers though this was to change a little during the course of the war.

The Corps was expanded by the addition of the 3rd Canadian Division in December 1915 and the 4th Canadian Division in August 1916. The organization of the 5th Canadian Division began in February 1917, but it was still not fully formed when it was broken up in February 1918 and its men used to reinforce the other four divisions. The Corps grew from an initial two divisions with approximately 35000 troops to a force of four divisions with 100000 troops by early 1917.

Although the Corps was within, and under the command of, the British Expeditionary Force, there was considerable political pressure in Canada, especially following the Battle of the Somme in 1916, to have the Corps fight as a single unit rather than have the divisions dispersed through the army. It was a mainly volunteer force, and although Canada introduced conscription, this was to have a minimal contribution.

The Corps were at Ypres during the start of the Battle of the Somme facing the Germans at Mount Sorrell, sometimes called Hill 62, in June 1916. They were then moved to the Somme to relieve the Australians and played a significant role in the later fighting on the Somme.

The Corps continued to be heavily involved in 1917, attacking and capturing Vimy Ridge, now the site of the national monument to the missing in France. Currie called it 'the grandest day the Corps ever had.' It was the first time all four Canadian divisions fought together bringing Anglophone and Francophone battalions together in the field at the same time. They continued at Third Ypres capturing the objective of Passendale in the final months of the campaign as part of Second Army. In 1918 the Corps was involved in a small way in the German advance at the start of the year but played a large role in the Advance to Victory at the end of the war. On Armistice Day the Corps were east of Mons and at the vanguard of the Allied line. The last official British and Empire casualty of the war was a Canadian.

Commanding Officers

13 September 1915	Lieutenant General Sir Edwin Alfred Hervey Alderson
29 May 1916	Lieutenant General the Honourable Sir Julian Hedworth George Byng
9 June 1917	Lieutenant General Sir Arthur William Currie

Lieutenant General Sir Edwin Alfred Hervey Alderson, KCB, (8 April 1859 – 14 December 1927) was commissioned into the Norfolk Artillery Militia, transferred to the 1st Regiment of Foot (later the Royal Scots) in 1878 as a 2nd Lieutenant and transferred again ten days later, to his father's regiment, the 97th Regiment of Foot (later the Queen's Own Royal West Kents) which was serving in Canada. He moved to Malta and then South Africa where he served with the Mounted Infantry, a post for developing the skills of young officers regarded as having the potential for promotion and success. He was promoted to Captain in 1884, brevet Lieutenant Colonel in 1896 and brevet Colonel in 1900. He served in the First Boer War in 1881, the Anglo-Egyptian War in 1882, the Nile Expedition of 1884 and then moved to Aldershot at the European Mounted Infantry Depot. For rescuing a soldier from the Nile in 1885 he won a medal from the Royal Humane Society. He served on Staff attending Staff College before being sent to Mashonaland as commander of a regiment of local troops during the Second Matabele War. He then returned to Aldershot as Deputy Assistant Adjutant-General and wrote books on military tactics and methods. He served in the South African Wars commanding the Mounted Infantry which included Canadian troops who grew to like and respect Alderson. He was promoted to Brigadier General in 1900 as a result of his successful leadership in the war and given command of 2nd Brigade in 1903. He was promoted to Major General in 1906 and posted to India in 1908 to command the 6th (Poona) Indian Division. He returned to England in 1912 in semi-retirement. When the war began, he was given command of the 1st Mounted Division but was soon promoted to lead the Canadian Expeditionary Force, then just one division, because of his experience with the Canadians in South Africa. He took the division to France in February 1915 where it gained experience of trench life in northern France before some battalions found themselves in the face of the German gas attack at the start of Second Ypres. The Canadian battalions held the Germans for two days to allow the British to get reinforcements forward suffering nearly 50% casualties. In addition, Alderson felt out of touch, found the rifles did not work and some of his Staff officers were not up to the task. The division went on to do poorly at Festubert and Givenchy in 1915. Even so, Alderson was given command of the Corps when the 2nd Division arrived in September 1915. Despite further failures at the St Eloi Craters in March to April 1916, politicians in Canada refused the changes in Staff officers required to improve the situation. They wanted Alderson gone to which Haig offered a compromise. Alderson was made Inspector-General of Canadian Forces. He was moved from any association with the Canadians in September 1916 when he was made Inspector of Infantry in the British Army a post in which he remained until he retired in 1920. He was awarded the Order of the Bath (CB) in 1901 and made a Knight Commander of the Order of the Bath (KCB) in 1916.

Lieutenant General the Honourable Sir Julian Hedworth George Byng – See IX Corps

General Sir Arthur William Currie, GCMG, KCB, (5 December 1875 – 30 November 1933) joined the Militia as a gunner in 1897 as a part time soldier while working as a teacher. He was a Corporal when he was commissioned in 1900, promoted to Captain in 1901, Major in 1906 and Lieutenant Colonel in 1909. From 1909, by now having left teaching and being involved in business, he commanded the 5th Regiment and in 1913, he took command of the newly created 50th Regiment Gordon Highlanders of Canada. At the start of the war he was promoted to Brigadier General to command the 2nd Canadian Brigade, having turned down the position of commander of Military District No. 11, taking the brigade to France as part of 1st Canadian Division. The brigade was in the front line on the first day of Second Ypres facing the German gas attack. He was promoted to Major General in May 1915 to command 1st Canadian Division when Alderson became Corps commander. He led the division at the Battle of Mount Sorrel and on the Somme in 1916 where he was gradually developing a good reputation as leader. In 1917 he led the division at the Battle of Vimy Ridge where they took all their objectives in April snow. Currie had been tasked with planning the offensive by looking at the failures and successes in Allied offensives in the past few years. He identified careful Staff work, thorough artillery preparation and support, the element of surprise, a high state of training in the infantry units detailed for the assault, and restructuring of the platoon units as the key to success. Therefore, Currie was promoted to Lieutenant General to command the Canadian Corps. He planned an attack on Lens in 1917 to stop the Germans from reinforcing their troops at Ypres. The Corps was then moved to be involved in the final push of Third Ypres. Currie predicted that the attack would cost him a division, about 16000 casualties, which proved to be remarkably accurate. He fought against integration with the American forces arriving in 1918 so the Canadians played a significant role under Currie in the advance of 1918. After the war Currie was appointed Inspector-General of the Armed Forces in 1919 and promoted to General, retiring in 1920. He became principal and vice-chancellor of McGill University in May 1920. In 1927 he took a newspaper to court for libel when they accused him of ordering unnecessary attacks on the last day of the war and won his case. He was awarded the Order of the Bath (CB) in June 1915 and made a Knight Commander of the Order of the Bath (KCB) in 1918. Currie was knighted and appointed Knight Commander of the Order of St Michael and St George (KCMG) in June 1917 and made a Knight Grand Cross of the Order of St Michael and St George (GCMG) in 1919.

Composition

Division	From	To
1st Canadian	13/09/1915	03/04/1916
2nd Canadian	13/09/1915	03/04/1916
3rd Canadian	24/12/1915	22/03/1916
24th	22/03/1916	03/04/1916
50th	03/04/1916	04/04/1916
1st Canadian	04/04/1916	12/10/1917
2nd Canadian	04/04/1916	05/09/1916
3rd Canadian	04/04/1916	22/10/1916
4th Canadian	15/08/1916	28/08/1916
4th	25/08/1916	03/09/1916
1st Australian	28/08/1916	03/09/1916
4th Australian	03/09/1916	05/09/1916
2nd Canadian	07/09/1916	12/10/1916
4th Canadian	05/10/1916	17/10/1916

24th	21/10/1916	28/10/1916
2nd Canadian	21/10/1916	12/10/1917
3rd Canadian	26/10/1916	17/10/1917
4th Canadian	03/12/1916	17/10/1917
5th	27/03/1917	04/05/1917
3rd Australian	17/10/1917	22/10/1917
NZ Division	17/10/1917	22/10/1917
2nd Canadian	18/10/1917	13/11/1917
1st Canadian	21/10/1917	26/03/1918
3rd Canadian	22/10/1917	28/03/1918
4th Canadian	22/10/1917	01/08/1918
2nd Canadian	19/11/1917	14/03/1918
3rd Canadian	30/03/1918	26/06/1918
1st Canadian	09/04/1918	30/07/1918
74th	23/05/1918	26/06/1918
2nd Canadian	01/07/1918	29/07/1918
59th	03/07/1918	15/07/1918
3rd Canadian	25/07/1918	20/08/1918
2nd Canadian	01/08/1918	20/08/1918
1st Canadian	06/08/1918	20/08/1918
32nd	07/08/1918	30/08/1918
4th Canadian	07/08/1918	11/11/1918
15th	23/08/1918	26/08/1918
2nd Canadian	23/08/1918	11/10/1918
3rd Canadian	23/08/1918	11/11/1918
51st	23/08/1918	29/08/1918
1st Canadian	25/08/1918	07/10/1918
4th	28/08/1918	03/09/1918
11th	29/08/1918	30/08/1918
1st	31/08/1918	04/09/1918
11th	25/09/1918	12/10/1918

49th	07/10/1918	11/10/1918
1st Canadian	10/10/1918	11/11/1918
51st	10/10/1918	11/10/1918
56th	10/10/1918	31/10/1918
2nd Canadian	11/10/1918	11/11/1918

Battle Honours

Actions of St. Eloi Craters 27 March–16 April 1916 (2nd Canadian Division)

Battle of Mount Sorrel 2-13 June 1916 (1st & 3rd Canadian Divisions)

Battles of the Somme, 1916

> Battle of Flers-Courcelette 15-22 September 1916 (1st, 2nd & 3rd Canadian Divisions)
>
> Battle of Thiepval 26-28 September 1916 (1st, 2nd & 3rd Canadian Divisions)
>
> Battle of Le Transloy 1-18 October 1916 (1st, 2nd, 3rd & 4th Canadian Divisions)
>
> Battle of the Ancre Heights 1 October–11 November 1916 (1st, 2nd & 3rd Canadian Divisions)

Battles of Arras, 1917

> Battle of Vimy 9-14 April 1917 (5th British, 1st, 2nd, 3rd & 4th Canadian Divisions)
>
> Attack on La Coulotte 23 April 1917 (5th, 2nd & 3rd Canadian Divisions)
>
> Battle of Arleux 28-29 April 1917 (1st & 2nd Canadian Divisions)
>
> Third Battle of the Scarpe 3-4 May 1917 (5th British, 1st, 2nd & 3rd Canadian Divisions)

Flanking Operations towards Lens 3 June–26 August 1917 (1st, 2nd, 3rd & 4th Canadian Divisions)

> Affairs South of the Souchez River 3-25 June 1917 (3rd & 4th Canadian Divisions)
>
> Capture of Avion 26-29 June 1917 (3rd & 4th Canadian Divisions)
>
> Battle of Hill 70 15-25 August 1917 (2nd, 3rd & 4th Canadian Divisions)

Third Battles of Ypres

> Second Battle of Passchendaele 26 October–10 November 1917 (1st, 2nd, 3rd & 4th Canadian Divisions)

Advance to Victory

Battle of Amiens 8-11 August 1918 (32nd British, 1st, 2nd, 3rd & 4th Canadian Divisions)

Actions around Damery 15-17 August 1917 (1st, 2nd, 3rd & 4th Canadian Divisions)

Second Battles of Arras, 1918

Battle of the Scarpe, 1918 26-30 August 1918 (4th & 51st British, 1st, 2nd & 3rd Canadian Divisions)

Battle of Drocourt-Quéant 2-3 September 1918 (1st & 4th British, 1st & 4th Canadian Divisions)

Battles of the Hindenburg Line

Battle of the Canal du Nord 27 September–1 October 1918 (11th British, 1st, 3rd & 4th Canadian Divisions)

Battle of Cambrai, 1918 8-9 October 1918 (11th British, 1st, 2nd & 3rd Canadian Divisions)

Pursuit to the Selle 9-12 October 1918 (11th, 49th & 51st British Divisions, 2nd Canadian Division)

Final Advance in Picardy

Battle of Valenciennes 1-2 November 1918 (3rd & 4th Canadian Divisions)

Battle of the Sambre 4 November 1918 (4th Canadian Division)

Passage of the Grand Honelle 5-7 November 1918 (2nd & 4th Canadian Divisions)

Capture of Mons 11 November 1918 (3rd Canadian Division)

Headquarters

13 September 1915	Bailleul
4 April 1916	Abeele
3 September 1916	Contay
17 October 1916	Ranchicourt
24 March 1917	Camblain-l'Abbé
25 July 1917	Hersin Coupigny
5 October 1917	Camblain-l'Abbé
12 October 1917	Lillers
15 October 1917	Poperinge
18 October 1917	Ten Elms Camp North of Poperinge
18 November 1917	Camblain-l'Abbé
7 May 1918	Pernes
26 May 1918	Bryas
15 July 1918	Duisans
30 July 1918	Molliens-Vidame
7 August 1918	Dury
8 August 1918	Gentelles
10 August 1918	Demuin
19 August 1918	Dury
22 August 1918	Hautecloque
24 August 1918	Noyelle Vion
3 September 1918	Neuville Vitasse
28 September 1918	Queant
14 October 1918	Chateau Lewarde
4 November 1918	Denain
10 November 1918	Valenciennes

Indian Corps

The Indian Army Corps was formed and mobilised in India in August 1914. The Indian Army, over 160000 strong, seemed an obvious source of trained men, and the Lahore and Meerut infantry divisions were selected for service in Europe. However, its training emphasised combat in open terrain against a mobile enemy not equipped with artillery. It was not meant to take part in a European war. However, following the Retreat from Mons, when the British Expeditionary Force found itself seriously undermanned, it was decided to call on the Indian Army.

The Corps moved to France as part of Indian Expeditionary Force A with the first arrivals at the end of September. 3rd (Lahore) Indian Division began landing at Marseilles on 26 September 1914 and headquarters staff arrived at Marseilles on 30 September 1914 with both Indian divisions concentrated in northern France by 29 October 1914. The force was made up of the Indian Corps of two Indian divisions and the Indian Cavalry Corps. In France, the divisions were known as 'Lahore' and 'Meerut' Divisions, to distinguish them from the 3rd and 7th British divisions.

The Corps went into battle in October and November 1914 suffering heavy casualties. The Indian Corps was ordered to hold a line seventeen kilometres long, i.e. one-third of the line held by the British First Army and faced severe German attacks without proper artillery cover. Most battalions were down to 50% of their strength, from when they landed in France, by the end of First Ypres after which the Corps was were taken out of the line to rest and recover.

In 1915 the Corps was involved in some of the heaviest fighting providing a significant force at the Battle of Neuve Chapelle in March where it took some positions from the Germans despite fierce resistance, but had to withdraw due to insufficient artillery preparation. The Lahore Division was pushed into Second Ypres in April leading a counter-attack and it was also involved at Aubers Ridge and Festubert. The Indians again took heavy losses at the Battle of Loos in September. These losses affected morale despite reinforcements arriving from India and it was thought unwise to expose them to another winter on the Western Front. It also made strategic sense to concentrate the Indian Army in the Middle East, where it was easier to send reinforcements and supplies from India. Hence, on 22 November 1915 the Indian Corps was the subject of a Special Order of the Day from Field Marshal Sir John French, ordering the Indian Corps to leave France and move to

Mesopotamia. Indian Corps in France ceased to exist on 9 December 1915 and the Corps headquarters was notified that it would form a headquarters for XV Corps.

Commanding Officers

29 October 1914	Lieutenant General Sir James Willcocks
7 September 1915 – 9 December 1915	Lieutenant General Sir Charles Alexander Anderson

General Sir James Willcocks, GCB, GCMG, KCSI, DSO, (1 April 1857 – 18 December 1926) was commissioned into the 100th Regiment of Foot (later the Leinsters) in the Punjab in 1878, was promoted to Lieutenant in 1879, Captain in 1884, Major in 1893, brevet Lieutenant Colonel in 1898, Lieutenant Colonel in 1899, brevet Colonel in 1900 and Colonel in 1902. He served as a Transport Officer in the Second Anglo-Afghan War in 1879, as a Transport Officer in the Mahsud Waziri Expedition in 1881 and served with the Army Transport Department in Burma in 1884. He served in the Suakin Expedition in Sudan in 1885–86 before returning to Burma in 1886 for which he was awarded the Distinguished Service Order in 1887. At the end of the year he was offered a position in the Commissariat and Transport Department but chose to become Adjutant in the 1st Leinsters. He was intelligence officer in the Chin-Lushai Expedition in 1889 and the Manipur Expedition in 1891. He was Deputy Assistant Adjutant General in Bombay from 1894-97 before moving to Africa at the end of the year to become second-in-command of the newly formed West African Frontier Force commanding it from 1900 serving in the Ashanti War in 1900. He moved to South Africa in 1902 on Staff during the South African Wars. He returned to India in late 1902 as a Brigadier General to command the Nowshera Brigade. He was promoted to Major General in 1906 to command the Peshawar Division from 1908. He commanded the Zakka Khel Expedition and the Mohmand Expedition in 1908 after which he was promoted to Lieutenant General. In October 1910 he was appointed to command the Northern Army. In 1914 Willcocks was given command of the Indian Corps in France and promoted to General in May 1915. He resigned in September 1915 after friction with Sir Douglas Haig and was made Governor of Bermuda. He was appointed Companion of the Order of St Michael and St George (CMG) in 1899, Knight Commander of the Order of St Michael and St George (KCMG) a year later and made a Knight Grand Cross of the Order of St Michael and St George (GCMG) in 1915. He was awarded the Order of the Bath (CB) in 1907, made a Knight Commander of the Order of the Bath (KCB) in

1914 and a Knight Grand Cross of the Order of the Bath (GCB) in 1921. He was appointed Knight Commander of the Order of the Star of India (KCSI) in 1913.
Lieutenant General Sir Charles Alexander Anderson – See I Corps

Composition

Division	From	To
7th (Meerut) Indian	14/10/1914	22/12/1914
3rd (Lahore) Indian	17/10/1914	23/10/1914
3rd (Lahore) Indian	30/10/1914	24/04/1915
1st Indian Cavalry/4th Cavalry/1st Mounted	07/11/1914	18/12/1914
8th	14/11/1914	14/11/1914
7th (Meerut) Indian	27/12/1914	30/11/1915
51st	02/05/1915	14/05/1915
3rd (Lahore) Indian	03/05/1915	09/12/1915
1st Canadian	14/05/1915	17/05/1915
51st	18/05/1915	31/05/1915
49th	31/05/1915	28/06/1915
8th	31/05/1915	29/06/1915
51st	26/06/1915	21/07/1915
19th	24/07/1915	03/11/1915

Battle Honours

Battle of La Bassée 1914 10 October–2 November 1914 (3rd (Lahore) & 7th (Meerut) Indian Divisions)

Defence of Festubert 23-24 November 1914 (7th (Meerut) Indian Division)

Defence of Givenchy 20-21 December 1914 (3rd (Lahore) & 7th (Meerut) Indian Divisions)

Battle of Neuve Chapelle 10-13 March 1915 (3rd (Lahore) & 7th (Meerut) Indian Divisions)

Battle of Aubers 9 May 1915 (3rd (Lahore) & 7th (Meerut) Indian Divisions)

Battle of Festubert 15-25 May 1915 (3rd (Lahore) & 7th (Meerut) Indian Divisions)

Battle of Loos 25 September–8 October 1915(19th British & 7th (Meerut) Indian Divisions)

Headquarters

12 September 1914	Bombay
30 September 1914	Marseilles
11 October 1914	Orléans
29 October 1914	Merville
31 October 1914	Hinges
23 December 1914	Lillers
2 February 1915	Saint-Venant
9 March 1915	Cix Marmuse Farm near Lestrem
16 March 1915	Lestrem
23 July 1915	Merville
24 September 1915	Fosse Chateau
9 November 1915	Norrent-Fontes

Several Divisions were sent to India to release the forces of the Indian Army and British units stationed in India.

43rd	09/11/1914	11/11/1918
44th	03/12/1914	11/11/1918
45th	08/01/1915	11/11/1918

Indian Cavalry Corps

The Indian Cavalry Corps was formed in France on 18 December 1914 made up of two divisions of cavalry that moved from India in November and December of 1914. These included a mix of Indian and British regiments. Together with the Indian Corps the two divisions of the Indian Cavalry Corps formed Indian Expeditionary Force A.

Indian divisions and brigades were named after the area from which they originated, or their home stations, eg. 'Lucknow' and 'Meerut'. It should also be remembered that each Indian brigade contained one British regiment, as well as British artillery and supporting units. The high number of officer casualties, mostly British men, influenced its performance. British officers that understood the language, customs, and psychology of their men could not be easily replaced when they became casualties.

Following, and possibly reflecting the lack of mounted action by the cavalry at Loos, on 12 March 1916 both the British and the Indian Cavalry Corps were broken up and the divisions were attached to individual Armies, though the Indian divisions had effectively moved on 3 March. Hence, by 1916 the Indian cavalry divisions were the only Indian divisions remaining in France and were thus referred to simply as 1st and 2nd 'Indian Cavalry Divisions'. Later these were to become the 4th and 5th Cavalry Divisions.

Commanding Officers

14 December 1914 to 3 March 1916	Lieutenant General Michael Rimington

Lieutenant General Sir Michael Frederic Rimington, KCB, CVO, (23 May 1858 – 19 December 1928) was commissioned in 1881 as a Lieutenant in the 6th (Inniskilling) Dragoons, was promoted to Captain in 1887, Major in 1897, Lieutenant Colonel in 1900 and brevet Colonel in 1902. He served in the Warren Expedition in 1884 to suppress the Boers in part of South Africa, the campaign against Dinizulu, last leader of the Zulu nation, in 1888 and returned to England in 1890. He went to South Africa again in 1899 and raised an ad hoc unit known as 'Rimington's Guides' or 'Rimington's Tigers' to serve during the South African Wars. He was promoted to Brigadier General to command the 3rd Cavalry Brigade in 1903 and moved to India to command the Secunderabad Cavalry Brigade in 1907. In 1911 he became Inspector-General of cavalry units in India. When the war began, he was promoted to Major General to command the 1st Indian Cavalry Division taking them to France. When the Indian Cavalry Corps was formed in December 1914, he was promoted to Lieutenant General to command the Corps. Following the disbandment of the Corps, Rimington was given command of a reserve centre in the United Kingdom from April 1916 to January 1918, and retired from the Army in 1919. He was five times Mentioned in Despatches in South Africa, was awarded the Order of the Bath (CB) in 1901 and made a Knight of the Order of the Bath (KCB) in 1921. He was appointed a Commander of the Royal Victorian Order (CVO) in 1911. He was knighted in 1919. His son was killed in action in North Africa on 10 April 1941 serving with the Royal Tank Regiment as a Brigadier commanding an armoured brigade.

Composition

1st Indian Cavalry/4th Cavalry/1st Mounted	18/12/1914	23/05/1915
2nd Indian Cavalry/5th Cavalry/2nd Mounted	18/12/1914	03/03/1916
1st Indian Cavalry/4th Cavalry/1st Mounted	14/06/1915	03/03/1916

Battle Honours

None

Headquarters

18 December 1914	Lozinghem
23 December 1914	Chateau St Andre, Aire-sur-la-Lys
25 April 1915	Oxelaere
5 May 1915	Chateau St Andre, Aire-sur-la-Lys
17 May 1915	Lillers
19 May 1915	Chateau St Andre, Aire-sur-la-Lys
2 August 1915	Flixecourt
23 September 1915	Doullens
22 October 1915	Hallencourt
17 December 1915	Gamaches

Desert Mounted Corps

The Desert Column was formed in December 1916 as part of the Eastern Force in the Egyptian Expeditionary Force. The commander was Lieutenant General Philip Chetwode (See XX Corps) who handed over to Chauvel when Chetwode was promoted to command Eastern Force. Under Chetwode the Column comprised the 42nd (East Lancashire) Division, the 52nd (Lowland) Division, the ANZAC Mounted Division with the Imperial Camel Brigade but was later made up of the ANZAC Mounted Division, Australian Mounted Division and the Yeomanry Mounted Division. It was involved in several battles in early 1917 but was halted at Gaza.

As the campaigns in the Middle East were not progressing well with the failure at Gallipoli, the stalemate in Sinai and the loss of the 6th (Poona) Indian Division at Kut Al Amara, the new commander of the Egyptian Expeditionary Force, Allenby, wanted to make positive progress and felt the mounted troops would be important in any advance. As such he wanted to restructure his command so Eastern Force was abolished and two Corps were formed, XX Corps under Chetwode and XXI Corps under Bulfin with the Desert Mounted Corps as mounted troops. It had been intended to use the title II Cavalry Corps, but the name was chosen in recognition of its predecessor the Desert Column. The Corps was formed on 12 August 1917 from the Desert Column with three divisions, two extra brigades, and units including artillery and a machine gun section.

The first battle in which the Desert Mounted Corps was involved was the Battle of Beersheba at the end of October. They pressed the advantage of the victory leading to the capture of Jerusalem in December. In 1918, the Corps was involved in the capture of Jericho, the attack on Amman and capture of the Jordan Valley. However, the reorganisation of the army on the Western Front led to changes in Palestine. The yeomanry was sent to France to be replaced by the 4th and 5th Calvary Divisions from France, formerly the 1st and 2nd Indian Cavalry Divisions. The Corps now had four divisions in which to attack the Turks in September 1918. One of the divisions, the ANZAC Mounted Division, formed part of an ad hoc formation known as 'Chaytor's Force', which existed from August 1918 to attack the Jordan Valley. Operating under the Egyptian Expeditionary Force, it captured Amman and the valley before the armistice. The success at Megiddo and capture of Damascus led to the armistice on 30 October 1918. The Desert Mounted Corps was disbanded in June 1919.

Commanding Officers

12 August 1917	Lieutenant General Henry 'Harry' George Chauvel

General Sir Henry George Chauvel, GCMG, KCB, (16 April 1865 – 4 March 1945) was commissioned as a 2nd Lieutenant in the Upper Clarence Light Horse, a unit organised by his father, in 1886 and transferred to the Queensland Mounted Infantry in 1890. He became a 'Regular' officer in 1896, was promoted to Lieutenant in 1890, Captain in 1896, Major in 1899, brevet Lieutenant Colonel in 1902 and Colonel in 1913. He served in the South African Wars and returned to Australia to command the 7th Australian Commonwealth Horse. In 1911 he became Adjutant General and second member of the Military Board and in 1914 he was sent to London to be Australian representative on the Imperial General Staff. He served at the War Office until he went to Egypt in December 1914 to meet the Australian Imperial Force which he had been instrumental in arranging to be diverted on its way to France. He was promoted to Brigadier General to command the 1st Light Horse Brigade at Gallipoli. He was promoted to Major General in November 1915 to command the 1st Australian Division. Chauvel was acting commander of the New Zealand and Australian Division for short periods in September and October 1915. In March 1916 he took command of the ANZAC Mounted Division. He was then given command of the Desert Column in April 1917 before taking command of the newly formed Desert Mounted Corps in August 1917, becoming the first Australian to command a Corps in the war and the first to reach the rank of Lieutenant General. After the war he was appointed Inspector General of the Australian Army and was also Chief of the General Staff from 1923 until his retirement in 1930 having in 1929 become the first Australian to be promoted to General. During the Second World War, he was recalled to duty as Inspector in Chief of the Volunteer Defence Corps. For his services in South Africa, he was awarded the Order of St Michael and St George (CMG), Mentioned in Despatches and made a brevet Lieutenant Colonel. He was awarded the Order of the Bath (CB) in January 1916 for his role at Gallipoli and a made a Knight Commander of the Order of the Bath (KCB) in the 1918 New Year Honours List. In January 1917 he was appointed a Knight Commander of the Order of St Michael and St George (KCMG) and Knight Grand Cross of the Order of St Michael and St George (GCMG) in June 1919.

Composition – Desert Mounted Corps

Division	From	To
ANZAC Mounted	12/08/1917	24/12/1917
Imperial Mounted/Australian Mounted	12/08/1917	04/04/1918
Yeomanry Mounted	12/08/1917	11/12/1917
60th	01/11/1917	10/11/1917
54th	20/11/1917	28/11/1917
ANZAC Mounted	29/12/1917	06/01/1918
60th	01/04/1918	14/05/1918
Yeomanry Mounted	01/04/1918	25/04/1918
ANZAC Mounted	05/04/1918	13/08/1918
Imperial Mounted/Australian Mounted	23/04/1918	11/11/1918
1st Indian Cavalry/4th Cavalry/1st Mounted	24/04/1918	11/11/1918
2nd Indian Cavalry/5th Cavalry/2nd Mounted	24/04/1918	10/05/1918
2nd Indian Cavalry/5th Cavalry/2nd Mounted	02/07/1918	11/11/1918

Composition – Desert Column

Division	From	To
ANZAC Mounted	01/12/1916	12/08/1917
52nd	22/12/1916	01/03/1917
Imperial Mounted/Australian Mounted	01/01/1917	12/08/1917
53rd	01/03/1917	01/04/1917
Yeomanry Mounted	20/06/1917	12/08/1917

Battle Honours

Third Battle of Gaza

> Capture of Beersheba 31 October 1917 (Australian Mounted & Yeomanry Mounted Divisions)
>
> Capture of Sheira Position 6 November 1917 (Yeomanry Mounted Division)
>
> El Maghar 13-14 November 1917 (Australian Mounted Division & Yeomanry Mounted Divisions)

Battle of Nabi Samweil 17-24 November 1917 (Yeomanry Mounted Division)

Defence Against Counter-Attacks before Jerusalem 27 November–2 December 1917 (Australian Mounted Division)

Second Trans-Jordan Raid 30 April–4 May 1918 (ANZAC Mounted, Australian Mounted, 1st Mounted (4th Cavalry), 2nd Mounted (5th Cavalry) & 60th Divisions)

Affair of Abu Tulul 14 July 1918 (ANZAC Mounted & 2nd Mounted (5th Cavalry) Divisions)

The Final Offensive

> Battle of Meggido 19-25 September 1918 (4th Cavalry (1st Mounted) & 5th Cavalry (2nd Mounted) Divisions)
>
> Capture of Haifa 23 September 1918 (5th Cavalry (2nd Mounted) Division)
>
> Capture of Samakh 25 September 1918 (Australian Mounted Division)
>
> Capture of Damascus 1 October 1918 (Australian Mounted, 4th Cavalry (1st Mounted) & 5th Cavalry (2nd Mounted) Divisions)
>
> Affair of Haritan 26 October 1918 (5th Cavalry (2nd Mounted) Division)
>
> Occupation of Aleppo 26 October 1918 (5th Cavalry (2nd Mounted) Division)

Headquarters

12 August 1917	Beni Sela
26 October 1917	Abasan
28 October 1917	Esani
30 October 1917	Asluj
30 October 1917	Source of Wadi Imshash near Beersheeba
7 November 1917	Sharia Station
8 November 1917	Muntar
9 November 1917	Huj
10 November 1917	Julis
19 November 1917	Deiran
25 April 1918	Talat ed Dumm
16 September 1918	Jerisheh
20 September 1918	El Lejjun
27 September 1918	Tiberias
28 September 1918	Nr Roshpina
29 September 1918	Kuneitra
30 September 1918	Khan esh Shina
1 October 1918	Nr Daraya Station
2 October 1918	Salahiye
3 October 1918	Damascus

Tigris Corps

Indian Expeditionary Force D

The largest Indian Army force to serve abroad was the Indian Expeditionary Force D in Mesopotamia, under the command of Lieutenant General Sir John Nixon. The first unit sent in November 1914, was the 6th (Poona) Indian Division and they were tasked with guarding British oil installations in and around Basra. In March 1915, the force was doubled in size, renamed the Indian Expeditionary Force D, and ordered to push on to Baghdad. They started with an offensive that saw early victories until the Battle of Ctesiphon in November 1915. Following this, the Poona

Division withdrew to Kut, where they came under siege by the Turks. In early 1916 the British tried to break the siege at heavy cost, but the spread of disease and lack of food led the force at Kut to surrender and the 6th (Poona) Indian Division ceased to exist. This was one of the factors that led to the call for the Indian troops on the Western Front to be moved to Mesopotamia.

Tigris Corps

The Indian infantry divisions were withdrawn from France and arrived at Basra in early 1916, though the 3rd (Lahore) Indian Division did not complete its move until April 1916. On arrival they, with other British divisions in Mesopotamia, formed the Tigris Corps out of Indian Expeditionary Force D in December 1915. The Corps spent most of 1916 in a rebuilding program after the fall of Kut as the Indian Expeditionary Force D became the Mesopotamian Expeditionary Force. The divisions were involved in a series of engagements. On 15 November 1916, the Tigris Corps was split to form I Indian and III Indian Corps and ceased to exist. The Tigris Corps was often called III Indian Corps in 1916 but its staff and commander, Cobbe, went on to command I Indian Corps.

Commanding Officers

Indian Expeditionary Force D to August 1916, then Mesopotamian Expeditionary Force	
9 April 1915	General Sir John Eccles Nixon
18 January 1916	Lieutenant General Sir Percy Henry Noel Lake
28 August 1916	Lieutenant General Sir Frederick Stanley Maude
18 November 1917 to 30 October 1918	Lieutenant General Sir William Raine Marshall

General Sir John Eccles Nixon, GCMG, KCB, (16 August 1857 – 15 December 1921) was commissioned into the 75th Regiment of Foot, later the 1st Gordon Highlanders, in 1875, was promoted to Captain in 1886, Major in 1895, Lieutenant Colonel in 1896 and Colonel in 1899. He transferred to the Bengal Staff Corps in 1878, was posted to the 18th Bengal Lancers and then served in the Second Anglo-Afghan War where he was Mentioned in Despatches. He served in the Mahsud Waziri Expedition in 1881, the Chitral Relief Force in 1895, the Tochi Field Force in 1897 and then became Assistant Quartermaster General in charge of intelligence at Indian Headquarters. He served in the South African Wars as a cavalry brigade commander for which he was Mentioned in Despatches. He returned to India to be Assistant Quartermaster General (Intelligence). He was promoted to Brigadier General to command the Bangalore Brigade from 1903-06, became Inspector General of Cavalry in India from 1906-08 and was promoted to Major General in 1904 to command the 7th (Meerut) Division from 1908-10, the 1st (Peshawar) Division from 1910-12 when he took command of the Southern Army in India having been made a Lieutenant General in 1909 and General in 1914. In 1915 he was given command of the Northern Army in India. In April 1915 he took command of the Indian Expeditionary Force in Mesopotamia as its first official commander when it expanded beyond one division. He planned an advance on Bagdad with no reference to London as this was the way the Indian Army had always operated ie with reference to Delhi not London. However, although the advance was initially successful, it led to the loss of the 6th (Poona) Indian Division at Kut having been ordered by Nixon to remain there after an unsuccessful attempt by Nixon to relieve them. A second relief attempt also failed before the force at Kut surrendered. Nixon was replaced and retired to India in January 1916. He was awarded the Order of the Bath (CB) in 1902, made a Knight of the Order of the Bath (KCB) in 1911, and Knight Grand Cross of the Order of St Michael and St George (CGMG) in 1919.

Lieutenant General Sir Percy Henry Noel Lake, KCB, KCMG, (29 June 1855 – 17 November 1940) was commissioned as a Sub-Lieutenant in the 59th Regiment of Foot, later the East Lancashires, in 1873 and was promoted to Lieutenant in the same year. He served in the Second Anglo-Afghan War in 1878 and in Sudan in 1885. He became Deputy Assistant Adjutant General and Quartermaster General in Egypt in 1885, Staff Captain at Army Headquarters in 1887 and Deputy Assistant Adjutant General (Intelligence) at Army Headquarters in 1888-92, Deputy Assistant Adjutant General at Dublin District in Ireland in 1892-93, Quartermaster General for the Canadian Militia in 1893-99, Assistant Quartermaster General at Army Headquarters in 1899-1904, Chief Staff Officer for II Corps 1904-05, Chief of the Canadian General Staff 1905-08 as a Major General and Inspector General of the Canadian Militia in 1908-11 as a Lieutenant General from 1911. He commanded 7th (Meerut) Indian Division 1911-12 and then became Chief of the General Staff in India from 1912. He took command of the Indian Expeditionary Force in Mesopotamia in January 1916 but following the fall of Kut he was recalled to London in August 1916 and attached to the Ministry of Munitions in 1917 retiring in 1919. He was awarded the Order of the Bath (CB) in 1902 and made a Knight

Commander of the Order of the Bath (KCB) on 1 January 1916. He was awarded the Order of St Michael and St George (CMG) in 1905 and made a Knight Commander of St Michael and St George (KCMG) in 1908.

Lieutenant General Sir Frederick Stanley Maude, KCB, CMG, DSO, (24 June 1864 – 18 November 1917) was commissioned into the Coldstream Guards in February 1884, was promoted to Captain in 1891, Major in 1899, Lieutenant Colonel in 1907 and Colonel in 1911. He served in Egypt in 1885 and the South African Wars where he was Mentioned in Despatches and awarded the Distinguished Service Order. He became Military Secretary to the Earl of Minto, Governor General of Canada from 1901-04 and then served on Staff in London. He started the war on Staff with III Corps and was promoted to Brigadier General in October 1914 to command 14th Brigade. After a period at home to recover from a wound from April to May 1915 he was promoted to Major General to command the 33rd Division. He was moved to 13th Division serving at Gallipoli, being the last man evacuated from Suvla Bay, and then at Mesopotamia from March 1916 being promoted to Lieutenant General soon after his arrival. He replaced General Gorringe as commander of the Tigris Corps in July 1916 and became commander of all Allied forces in Mesopotamia in late July 1916, replacing Lake. He led an advance in 1917 capturing Bagdad in March 1917 before moving further up the river systems towards Turkey. In November 1917 Maude contracted cholera from which he died in the same house as German Field Marshal von der Goltz nineteen months earlier. He is buried in Baghdad (North Gate) War Cemetery. He was awarded the Order of St Michael and St George (CMG) in 1901, the Order of the Bath (CB) in 1915 and was made a Knight Commander of the Order of the Bath (KCB) in June 1916. His father was Sir Frederick Francis Maude, a General who had been awarded the Victoria Cross during the Crimean War.

Lieutenant General Sir William Raine Marshall, GCMG, KCB, KCSI, (29 October 1865 – 29 May 1939) was commissioned into the Sherwood Foresters in 1886, was promoted to Captain in 1893, Major in 1900, brevet Lieutenant Colonel in 1902 and full Lieutenant Colonel in 1912. He served on the Malakand Expedition 1897-98, on the North West Frontier and on the Tirah Expedition in 1897-98 before serving in the South African Wars. He was Assistant Commandant, School of Instruction for Mounted Infantry in 1911. He started the war as commander of the 1st Sherwood Foresters taking them to France, was promoted to Brigadier General in 1915 to command the 87th Brigade at Gallipoli in 1915 and was promoted to Major General in 1915 to command in turn the 42nd, 29th and 53rd Divisions. He was promoted to Lieutenant General in 1916 to command III Indian Corps in Mesopotamia when it was created in November 1916. When Maude died in November 1917, he was promoted to command all forces in Mesopotamia. He held this post until the Turkish surrender in October 1918. After the war he returned to India to command the Southern Army from 1919-23 retiring in 1924. Marshall was awarded the Order of the Bath (CB) in 1916, made a Knight Commander of the Order of the Bath (KCB) in 1917, awarded Knight Commander of the Order of the Star of India (KCSI) in 1918 and Knight Grand Cross of the Order of St Michael and St George (GCMG) in 1919.

Tigris Corps	
9 December 1915	Lieutenant General Sir Fenton John Aylmer
12 March 1916	Lieutenant General Sir George Frederick Gorringe
11 July 1916	Lieutenant General Sir Frederick Stanley Maude
23 August 1916 to 15 November 1916	Lieutenant General Sir Alexander Stanhope Cobbe

Lieutenant General Sir Fenton John Aylmer, 13th Baronet, VC, KCB, (5 April 1862 – 3 September 1935) was promoted Lieutenant in the Royal Engineers in 1880, Major in 1893, Brevet Major in 1892, brevet Lieutenant Colonel in 1895 and Colonel in 1901. He served in the Burma Expedition from 1886-87 and the Hunza–Nagar Campaign in 1891 when he won the Victoria Cross as a Captain. The citation reads 'On 2 December 1891 during the assault on Nilt Fort, British India, Captain Aylmer, with the storming party, forced open the inner gate with gun-cotton which he had placed and ignited, and although severely wounded, fired 19 shots with his revolver, killing several of the enemy, and remained fighting until, fainting from loss of blood, he was carried out of action'. He served in the Isazai Expedition in 1892 and the Chitral Expedition in 1895. He was appointed Assistant Quartermaster General in India in 1901 and Adjutant-General, India as a Major General from 1912-15. He was promoted to Lieutenant General in 1914. He was sent to command the newly formed Tigris Corps in December 1915 with orders to relieve the force trapped at Kut. The two Indian divisions had a little success, but, although joined by the 3rd (Lahore) Indian Division from England, could not reach Kut. A fourth division, the British 13th Division, arrived but could still not relieve Kut and Aylmer was replaced in March 1916. He did not command in battle again, though he commanded the 5th (Mhow) Indian Division from May 1916 to June 1917, retiring from the British Army in 1919. He was awarded the Order of the Bath (CB) in 1907 and made a Knight Commander of the Order of the Bath (KCB) in 1916. He was made a baronet in 1928.

Lieutenant General Sir George Frederick Gorringe, KCB, KCMG, DSO, (10 February 1868 – 24 October 1945) was commissioned into the Royal Engineers in 1888, was promoted to Lieutenant in 1891, Captain in February 1899 and brevet Major the following day, Lieutenant Colonel in 1900, brevet Colonel in 1904 and Colonel in 1906. He was attached to the Egyptian Army from 1892-99 serving with the Dongola Expedition of 1896 and the Nile Expeditions of 1897-1899. In the Sudan in 1899 when he commanded a battalion of Sudanese troops during the operations leading to the defeat of the Khalifa for which he was Mentioned in Despatches. He served in the South African Wars before returning to the Egyptian Army in the Sudan from 1902-04. He was promoted to Brigadier General to command the 18th Brigade in 1909 and Major General in 1911 to command the Bombay Brigade in India until 1915. He commanded the 12th Indian Division in Mesopotamia from March 1915 to 31 March 1916 when the division was disbanded but he was promoted to Lieutenant General. He was made commander of the Tigris Corps in March 1916 holding the post until July. In October 1916 he was given command of 47th (2nd London) Division until the end of the war. After the war, he commanded the 10th Division in Egypt from 1919-21, was promoted to Lieutenant General in 1921 and retired in 1924. He was awarded the Order of St Michael and St George (CMG) in 1900, made a Knight Commander of the Order of St Michael and St George (KCMG) in 1918, a Knight Commander of the Order of the Bath (KCB) in March 1916 and was knighted in 1915.

Lieutenant General Sir Frederick Stanley Maude – See Above

General Sir Alexander Stanhope Cobbe, VC, GCB, KCSI, DSO, (6 June 1870 – 29 June 1931) was commissioned a 2nd Lieutenant in the South Wales Borderers in 1889, was promoted to Lieutenant in 1892, Captain in 1900, Major in 1907, brevet Lieutenant Colonel in 1907 and Colonel in 1911. He moved to the Indian Army in 1892 and from the South Wales Borderers to the Indian Army Staff Corps a couple of years later. He was on the Chitral Campaign in 1895 and then served in Africa for a few years where he became second in command of the 1st Central African Rifles in 1899. He took command in 1900 and was involved in the final Ashanti Wars known as the War of the Golden Stool for which he was Mentioned in Despatches and awarded the Distinguished Service Order. He was involved in the Somaliland

Campaign in 1902-04 during which he was awarded the Victoria Cross. The citation reads 'During the action at Erego, on 6 October 1902, when some of the Companies had retired, Lieutenant Colonel Cobbe was left by himself in front of the line, with a Maxim gun. Without assistance he brought in the Maxim, and worked it at a most critical time. He then went out under an extremely hot fire from the enemy about 20 yards in front of him, and from his own men (who had retired) about the same distance behind, and succeeded in carrying in a wounded Orderly.' After this campaign he returned to Staff with the Indian Army until 1914. He went to France in 1914 where he was appointed Deputy Adjutant and Quartermaster General in February 1915 as a Brigadier General. In March 1916 he was posted back to India as Director of Staff Duties and Military Training in Army Headquarters. He was promoted to Major General in June 1916 and Lieutenant General in August 1916 to take command of the Tigris Corps in Mesopotamia. He became commander of I Indian Corps when it was created in November 1916 and stayed until the end of the war leading the Corps to victory over the Turks. After the war he was appointed Military Secretary to the India Office in 1920. He was promoted to General in 1926 to command India's Northern Command returning to his post as Military Secretary to the India Office in 1930. He was awarded the Order of the Bath (CB) in June 1915, made a Knight Commander of the Order of the Bath (KCB) in March 1917 and Knight Grand Cross of the Order of the Bath (GCB) in 1928. In March 1919 he was appointed Knight Commander of the Order of the Star of India (KCSI). His father was Lieutenant General Sir Alexander Hugh Cobbe. His son, Flying Officer William 'Bill' Cobbe was killed on 8 September 1940 during the Battle of Britain.

Composition

Division	From	To
12th Indian	09/12/1915	10/03/1916
6th (Poona) Indian	09/12/1915	29/04/1916
7th (Meerut) Indian	03/01/1916	15/11/1916
3rd (Lahore) Indian	17/01/1916	15/11/1916
13th	27/02/1916	15/11/1916
14th Indian	12/05/1916	15/11/1916

Battle Honours

Seige of Kut 9 December 1915–29 April 1916 (6th (Poona) Indian Division)

Action of Sheikh Saad 6-8 January 1916 (7th (Meerut) Indian)

Action of the Wadi River 13 January 1916 (7th (Meerut) Indian)

Affair of Butaniya 14 January 1916 (12th Indian Division)

First Attack on Hanna 21 January 1916 (3rd (Lahore) Indian & 7th (Meerut) Indian Divisions)

Attack on the Dujaila Redoubt 8 March 1916 (3rd (Lahore) Indian & 7th (Meerut) Indian Divisions)

Capture of Hanna and Fallahiya 5 April 1916 (British 13th Division)

First Attack on the Sannaiyat 6 April 1916 (7th (Meerut) Indian)

Second Attack on Sanniyat 9 April 1916 (British 13th & 7th (Meerut) Indian Divisions)

Bait 'Isa 17-18 April 1916 (British 13th & 3rd (Lahore) Indian Divisions)

Third Attack on Sanniyat 22 April 1916 (British 13th & 7th (Meerut) Indians)

Headquarters

9 December 1915	Basra
12 December 1915	Amara
2 January 1916	Ali Al Gharbh
7 January 1916	Musandaq Reach
9 January 1916	Sheikh Saad
14 January 1916 – 15 November 1916	Wadi River at Falahiyeh

Mesopotamia I Indian Corps

While the decision to remove the Indian Corps from France seemed to originate around the time of the Battle of Loos and due to the issues surrounding the Corps involvement in the battles of 1915, in fact before then, in August 1915, the commander of Indian Expeditionary Force D in Mesopotamia, had already requested that one of the Indian infantry divisions in France be sent to Mesopotamia as reinforcements for his advance on Baghdad. At the same time, the Secretary of State for India had stated that he was keen that the Indian infantry were withdrawn from France before they had to endure another winter. Indian battalions were becoming very weak after the heavy casualties they had suffered and it was felt that it was becoming too difficult to get reinforcements to France whereas it was significantly easier to get Indian troops to the Middle East, especially Mesopotamia on India's doorstep.

The Indian infantry divisions were withdrawn from France and arrived at Basra in early 1916, though the 3rd (Lahore) Indian Division did not complete its move until April 1916. On arrival they, with other British divisions in Mesopotamia, formed the Tigris Corps. In November 1916, the Tigris Corps was split to form I Indian and III Indian Corps. At the same time, headquarters staff was substantially reorganised with many senior officers being sent from the Western Front. While the Tigris Corps had also been called the III Indian Corps at the time, the Staff and headquarters went with the new I Indian Corps in November 1916 so there is the potential for confusion.

In 1917, I and III Indian Corps again went on the offensive under a new Indian Expeditionary Force D commander, Frederick Stanley Maude, and advanced towards Baghdad which was captured in March. The offensive and advance continued in 1918 until October when an armistice was signed with the Turks. The Mesopotamian Campaign was largely an Indian Army campaign as the only British formations involved were the 13th (Western) Division and British battalions assigned to Indian brigades. However, more than just the two Indian divisions sent from France were involved in the campaign. The two Corps were often referred to as 'Cobbe's Column or Force' and 'Marshall's Column or Force' after the commanding officers of each Corps. During the campaigns of 1917 and 1918 there were several ad hoc formations of infantry, artillery and cavalry, often with air reconnaissance attached or sometimes naval forces, and named after Brigadier Generals or Lieutenant Colonels, that made moves against the Turks. Kerry's and MacClachlan's are examples.

Commanding Officers

15 November 1916	Lieutenant General Sir Alexander Stanhope Cobbe

Lieutenant General Sir Alexander Stanhope Cobbe – See Tigris Corps

Composition

Division	From	To
13th	15/11/1916	01/12/1916
3rd (Lahore) Indian	15/11/1916	16/03/1918
7th (Meerut) Indian	15/11/1916	11/12/1917
17th Indian	25/08/1917	30/10/1918
Cavalry in Mesopotamia	01/11/1917	30/10/1918
18th Indian	24/12/1917	30/10/1918

Battle Honours

Advance to the Hai and Capture of the Khudaira Bend 14 December 1916–19 January 1917 (3rd (Lahore) Indian Division)

Battle of Kut Al Amara

> Capture of the Dahra Bend 9-16 February 1917 (3rd (Lahore) Indian Division)

> Capture of Sannaiyat 17-24 February 1917 (7th (Meerut) Indian Division)

Operations on the Tigris Right Bank 9-10 March 1917 (7th (Meerut) Indian Division)

Occupation of Baghdad 11 March 1917 (7th (Meerut) Indian Division)

Action of Mushahida 14 March 1917 (7th (Meerut) Indian Division)

Occupation of Falluja 19 March 1917 (3rd (Lahore) Indian Division)

First Action of Jabal Hamrin 25 March 1917 (3rd (Lahore) Indian Division)

Action of Istabulat 21-22 April 1917 (3rd (Lahore) Indian & 7th (Meerut) Indian Divisions)

Occupation of Sammarah 24 April 1917 (7th (Meerut) Indian Division)

Attack on Ramadi 11 July 1917 (3rd (Lahore) Indian Division)

Action of Daur 2 November 1917 (Cavalry in Mesopotamia, 7th (Meerut) Indian Division)

Action at Tikrit 5 November 1915 (Cavalry in Mesopotamia)

Third Action of Jabal Hamrin 3-6 December 1916 (Cavalry in Mesopotamia)

Action of Fat-ha Gorge and on the Little Zab 23-26 October 1918 (Cavalry in Mesopotamia, 17th Indian & 18th Indian Divisions)

Battle of Sharqat 28-30 October 1918 (Cavalry in Mesopotamia, 17th Indian & 18th Indian Divisions)

Affair of Qaiyara 30 October 1918 (Cavalry in Mesopotamia)

Headquarters

15 November 1916	Wadi River at Falahiyeh
11 December 1916	Arab Village or Sandy River at Falahiyeh
10 January 1917	Sinn Abtar
21 January 1917	Falahiyeh
4 March 1917	Sama Bend
5 March 1917	Aziziyah
6 March 1917	Zeur
7 March 1917	Bustan
8 March 1917	Bawi
9 March 1917	Dialah
10 March 1917	708 Central
11 March 1917	Baghdad
14 March 1917	Near Mushaidie
15 March 1917	Tel Gosh
16 March 1917	Hassaiwa
17 March 1917	Baghdad
17 April 1917	Hassaiwa
18 April 1917	Fort Kermeah
20 April 1917	Sinijah
22 April 1917	Dujail River
23 April 1917	Samarrah Station
15 May 1917	Baghdad
22 September 1917	Samarrah
2 November 1917	In the Desert
9 November 1917	Samarrah
24 March 1918	Daur
29 March 1917	Samarrah
18 May 1918	Baghdad
8 October 1918	Samarrah
13 October 1918	Tikrit
23 October 1918	Baiji

Mesopotamia III Indian Corps

See I Corps for move from France, and formation in Mesopotamia.

Commanding Officers

15 November 1916	Lieutenant General Sir William Raine Marshall
18 November 1917 to 30 October 1918	Lieutenant General Sir Raleigh Gilbert Egerton

Lieutenant General Sir William Raine Marshall – See Tigris Corps (IEF D)

Lieutenant General Sir Raleigh Gilbert Egerton, KCB, KCIE, (25 September 1860-2 May 1931) was commissioned into the Leicestershires in 1897, promoted to Lieutenant in 1881, Captain by 1892, Major by 1896 and Lieutenant Colonel by 1908. He served in the Hazara Expedition in 1888, the Isazai Expedition in 1892, the Waziristan Campaign 1894-95, the Chitral Campaign in 1895, the Dongola Campaign in 1896 and the Waziristan Campaign from 1901-02. From 1909-11 he was Commandant of Queen Victoria's Own Corps of Guides. In the war he served as commander of 7th (Ferozepore) Indian Brigade from the start of the war to 11 May 1916 by which time he had led them in France and overseen the transfer to the Middle East. He was promoted to Major General to command the 14th Indian Division in the Tigris Corps and then III Indian Corps. When Maude died, Marshall took command of Indian Expeditionary Force D and Egerton was promoted to Lieutenant General to command the III Indian Corps, a post he held until the end of the war. He was appointed Knight Commander of the Order of the Indian Empire (KCIE) in August 1917 and Knight Commander of the Order of the Bath (KCB) in December 1916.

Composition

Division	From	To
14th Indian	15/11/1916	30/10/1918
13th	01/12/1916	30/10/1918

Battle Honours

Battle of Kut al Amara 13 December 1916–25 February 1917 (British 13th Division)
Advance to the Hai and Capture of the Khudaira Bend 14 December 1916–19 January 1917 (14th Indian Division)
Capture of the Hai Salient 25 January–5 February 1917 (British 13th & 14th Indian Divisions)
Capture of the Dahra Bend 9-16 February 1917 (British 13th & 14th Indian Divisions)
Capture of Sannaiyat 17-24 February 1917 (14th Indian Division)
Passage of the Tigris 23-24 February 1917 (14th Indian Division)
Passage of the Diyala 7-10 March 1917 (British 13th Division)
Occupation of Baghdad 11 March 1917 (British 13th Division)
Delli 'Abbas 27-28 March 1918 (British 13th Division)
Duqma 29 March 1917 (British 13th Division)
Nahr Kalis 9-15 April 1917 (British 13th Division)
Passage of the Adhaim 18 April 1917 (British 13th & 14th Indian Divisions)
Action of the Shatt al 'Adhaim 30 April 1917 (British 13th & 14th Indian Divisions)
Second Action of Jabal Hamrin 16-20 October 1917 (British 13th & 14th Indian Divisions)
Third Action of Jabal Hamrin 3-6 December 1917 (British 13th & 14th Indian Divisions)
Tuz Khurmatli 29 April 1918 (British 13th Division)

Headquarters

15 November 1916	Sheikh Saad & Sinn Abtar
1 December 1916	Arab Village near Fallahiyah
1 January 1917	Atab
24 February 1917	Husifiyah
25 February 1917	Shumran
26 February 1917	Imam Mahdi
26 February 1917	B'Gaibuh
3 March 1917	Aziziyah
5 March 1917	Zeur
6 March 1917	Ctesiphon
7 March 1917	Bawi
11 March 1917	Hinaidi

13 March 1917	Baghdad
16 October 1917	Shahraba
24 October 1917	Baqubah
3 December 1917	Qalat al Mufti
9 December 1917	Baqubah
25 April 1918	Dali Abbas
26 April 1918	Ain Lailah
27 April 1918	Near Umr Mandan
30 April 1918	Umr Mandan
3 May 1918	Tuz
9 May 1918	Tauq
15 May 1918	Tuz
16 May 1918	Baqubah
25 May 1918	Baghdad
5 October 1918	Duwalib
13 October 1918	Hambis

Appendix 1 - Commanding Officers

Lieutenant General Sir Edwin Alfred Hervey Alderson	Canadian Corps (13 September 1915 to 29 May 1916)
Lieutenant General Edmund Henry Hynman Allenby	Cavalry Corps (10 October 1914 to 19 April 1915), Cavalry Corps (4 May 1915 to 7 May 1915), V Corps (8 May 1915 to 23 October 1915)
Lieutenant General Sir Charles Alexander Anderson	Indian Corps (7 September 1915 to 9 December 1915), XVII Corps (9 December 1915 to 12 February 1916), XI Corps (13 August 1916 to 30 September 1916), I Corps (30 September 1916 - 11 February 1917)
Brigadier General Charles Johnstone Armstrong	VII Corps (4 November 1918 to 11 November 1918)
Lieutenant General Sir Fenton John Aylmer	Tigris Corps (9 December 1915 to 12 March 1916)
Lieutenant General James Melville Babington	XIV Corps (15 October 1918 to 4 November 1918)
Lieutenant General George de Symons Barrow	XIV Corps (20 March 1918 to 29 March 1918)
Lieutenant General The Hon Sir Cecil Edward Bingham	Cavalry Corps (23 October 1915 to 12 March 1916 1916)
Lieutenant General Sir William Riddell Birdwood	ANZAC Corps (21 December 1914 to 27 January 1916), II ANZAC Corps (15 February 1916 to 28 March 1916), I ANZAC Corps (23 March 1916 to 15 November 1917), Australian Corps (15 November 1917 to 31 May 1918)
Lieutenant General Sir Walter Pipon Braithwaite	XXII Corps (27 August 1918 to 12 September 1918), IX Corps (13 September 1918 to 11 November 1918)
Lieutenant General Charles Briggs	XVI Corps (17 May 1916 to 30 September 1918)
Lieutenant General Sir Edward Stanislaus Bulfin	XXI Corps (18 August 1917 to 13 June 1918), XXI Corps (19 August 1918 to 30 October 1918)

Lieutenant General Sir Richard Harte Keatinge Butler	III Corps (26 February 1918 to 11 August 1918), III Corps (11 September 1918 to 11 November 1918)
Lieutenant General the Honourable Sir Julian Hedworth George Byng	Cavalry Corps (19 April 1915 to 4 May 1915), Cavalry Corps (7 May 1915 to 16 August 1915), IX Corps (24 August 1915 to 8 February 1916), XVII Corps (27 February 1916 to 25 May 1916), Canadian Corps (29 May 1916 to 9 June 1917)
Lieutenant General Sir John Philip Du Cane	XV Corps (29 September 1916 to 12 April 1918)
Major General John Edward Capper	I Corps (11 February 1917 to 19 February 1917)
Lieutenant General Henry 'Harry' George Chauvel	Desert Mounted Corps (12 August 1917 to 30 October 1918)
Lieutenant General Sir Philip Walhouse Chetwode	XX Corps (2 August 1917 to 20 August 1917), XX Corps (31 August 1917 to 30 October 1918)
Lieutenant General Sir Alexander Stanhope Cobbe	Tigris Corps (23 August 1916 to 15 November 1916), Mesopotamia I Indian Corps (15 November 1916 to 30 October 1918)
Lieutenant General Sir Walter Norris Congreve, VC	XIII Corps (15 November 1915 to 10 August 1916), XIII Corps (16 August 1916 to 12 June 1917), VII Corps (3 January 1918 to 13 April 1918), X Corps (15 April 1918 to 24 May 1918)
Lieutenant General Sir Arthur William Currie	Canadian Corps (9 June 1917 to 11 November 1918)
Lieutenant General Sir Francis John 'Joey' Davies	VIII Corps (8 August 1915 to 27 January 1916), IX Corps (8 February 1916 to 22 April 1916)
Major General Sir William Douglas	VIII Corps (24 July 1915 to 8 August 1915)
Lieutenant General Sir Raleigh Gilbert Egerton	Mesopotamia III Indian Corps (18 November 1917 to 30 October 1918)
Major General Sir Vere Bonamy Fane	XXI Corps (13 June 1918 to 14 August 1918)

Lieutenant General Edward Arthur Fanshawe	V Corps (5 July 1916 to 11 August 1916), XIV Corps (11 August 1916 to 17 August 1916), V Corps (17 August 1916 to 28 April 1918)
Lieutenant General Sir Hew Dalrymple Fanshawe	Cavalry Corps (16 August 1915 to 23 October 1915), V Corps (23 October 1915 to 5 July 1916)
Lieutenant General Sir Charles Fergusson	II Corps (19 August 1914 to 21 August 1914), II Corps (1 January 1915 to 28 May 1916), XVII Corps (25 May 1916 to 11 November 1918)
Lieutenant General Sir Alexander John Godley	I ANZAC Corps (15 February 1916 to 23 March 1916), II ANZAC Corps (28 March 1916 to 15 November 1917), XXII Corps (31 December 1917 to 27 August 1918), III Corps (11 August 1918 to 11 September 1918), XXII Corps (12 September 1918 to 11 November 1918)
Lieutenant General Alexander Hamilton Gordon	IX Corps (20 June 1916 to 16 July 1918), IX Corps (30 July 1918 to 10 September 1918)
Lieutenant General Sir George Frederick Gorringe	Tigris Corps (12 March 1916 to 11 July 1916)
Lieutenant General Hubert de la Poer Gough	I Corps (13 July 1915-1 April 1916), Reserve Corps (4 April 1916 to 12 May 1916)
Lieutenant General James Moncrieff Grierson	II Corps (5 August 1914 to 19 August 1914)
Lieutenant General Sir Douglas Haig	I Corps (5 August 1914-26 December 1914)
Lieutenant General Sir Richard Cyril Byrne Haking	XI Corps (4 September 1915 to 13 August 1916), XI Corps (30 September 1916 to 11 November 1918)
Lieutenant General Aylmer Haldane	VI Corps (8 August 1916 to 11 November 1918)
Lieutenant General Sir George Montagu Harper	IV Corps (11 March 1918 to 11 November 1918)
Major General Harold Whitla Higginson	IX Corps (22 July 1918 to 30 July 1918)

Lieutenant General Arthur Edward Aveling Holland	I Corps (19 February 1917 to 19 September 1918), I Corps (4 October 1918 to 11 November 1918)
Lieutenant General Henry Sinclair Horne	XV Corps (12 January 1916 to 12 April 1916), XV Corps (22 April 1916 to 29 September 1916)
Major General Arthur Reginald Hoskins	XXI Corps (14 August 1918 to 19 August 1918)
Major General Havelock Hudson	I Corps (4 September 1916 - 30 September 1916)
Lieutenant General Sir Aylmer Gould Hunter-Weston	VIII Corps (24 May 1915 to 17 July 1915), XVIII Corps (22 June to 2 July 1918), VIII Corps (18 March 1916 to 11 November 1918)
Lieutenant General Claud Jacob	II Corps (28 May 1916 to 11 November 1918)
Major General Sir Hugh Sandham Jeudwine	I Corps (19 September 1918 to 4 October 1918)
Lieutenant General Sir Charles Toler MacMorrough Kavanagh	I Corps (1 April 1916 - 4 September 1916), Cavalry Corps (4 September 1916 to 11 November 1918)
Lieutenant General John Lindesay Keir	VI Corps (27 May 1915 to 8 August 1916)
Lieutenant General Sir Percy Henry Noel Lake	Indian Expeditionary Force D (18 January 1916 to 28 August 1916)
Lieutenant General Frederick Rudolph Lambart, the 10th Earl of Cavan	XI Corps (29 August 1915 to 4 September 1915), XIV Corps (11 January 1916 to 11 August 1916), XIII Corps (10 August 1916 to 16 August 1916), XIV Corps (10 September 1916 to 10 March 1918)
Major General Richard Phillips Lee	III Corps (16 February 1918 to 26 February 1918)
Lieutenant General Sir Henry de Beauvoir de Beauvoir De Lisle	IX Corps (16 August 1915 to 24 August 1915), XIII Corps (13 March 1918 to 12 April 1918), XV Corps (12 April 1918 to 11 November 1918)
Major General Edward Charles William MacKenzie-Kennedy	XII Corps (4 January 1917 to 11 January 1917)

Lieutenant General Sir William Raine Marshall	Mesopotamia III Indian Corps (15 November 1916 to 18 November 1917), Mesopotamian Expeditionary Force (18 November 1917 to 30 October 1918)
Lieutenant General Sir Frederick Stanley Maude	Tigris Corps (11 July 1916 to 23 August 1916), Mesopotamian Expeditionary Force (28 August 1916 to 18 November 1917)
Lieutenant General Sir Frederick Ivor Maxse	XVIII Corps (15 January 1917 to 22 June 1918)
Lieutenant General Frederick William Nicholas McCracken	XIII Corps (17 June 1917 to 13 March 1918)
Lieutenant General George Milne	XVI Corps (17 January 1916 to 17 May 1916)
Lieutenant General John Monash	Australian Corps (31 May 1918 to 11 November 1918)
Colonel Lord Henry Francis Montagu-Douglas Scott	VII Corps (23 October 1918 to 4 November 1918)
Major General the Honourable Edward James Montagu-Stuart-Wortley	XVII Corps (12 February 1916 to 27 February 1916)
Lieutenant General Sir Charles Carmichael Monro	I Corps (26 December 1914-13 July 1915)
Lieutenant General Sir Thomas Lethbridge Napier Morland	X Corps (15 July 1915 to 15 April 1918), XIV Corps (17 August 1916 to 10 September 1916), XIII Corps (12 April 1918 to 11 November 1918)
General Sir John Eccles Nixon	Indian Expeditionary Force D (9 April 1915 to 18 January 1916)
Major General Oliver Stewart Wood Nugent	V Corps (11 August 1916 to 17 August 1916)
Lieutenant General Sir William Eliot Peyton	X Corps (24 May 1918 to 3 July 1918)
Lieutenant General Sir Herbert Charles Onslow Herbert Plumer	V Corps (8 January 1915 to 8 May 1915)

Lieutenant General Sir William Pulteney Pulteney	III Corps (5 August 1914 to 16 February 1918), XXIII Corps (16 February 1918 to 7 May 1918), XXIII Corps (5 August 1918 to 11 November 1918)
Lieutenant General Sir Henry Seymour Rawlinson	IV Corps (5 October 1914 to 22 December 1915)
Lieutenant General Michael Rimington	Indian Cavalry Corps (14 December 1914 to 3 March 1916)
Major General John Stuart Mackenzie Shea	XX Corps (20 August 1917 to 31 August 1917)
Lieutenant General Cameron Dinsdale Dean Shute	V Corps (28 April 1918 to 11 November 1918)
Lieutenant General Horace Smith-Dorrien	II Corps (21 August 1914 to 1 January 1915)
Lieutenant General Sir Thomas D'Oyly Snow	VII Corps (15 July 1915 to 3 January 1918), XXIII Corps (7 May 1918 to 5 August 1918)
Lieutenant General Sir Reginald Byng Stephens	X Corps (3 July 1918 to 11 November 1918)
Lieutenant General the Honourable Sir Frederick William Stopford	IX Corps (17 June 1915 to 16 August 1915), VIII Corps (17 July 1915 to 24 July 1915)
Major General Edward Peter Strickland	IX Corps (10 September 1918 to 13 September 1918)
Lieutenant General Sir Herbert Edward Watts	XIX Corps (4 February 1917 to 11 November 1918)
Major General Sir Robert Dundas Whigham	VII Corps (3 April 1918 to 19 June 1918), IX Corps (16 July 1918 to 22 July 1918)
Lieutenant General Sir James Willcocks	Indian Corps (29 October 1914 to 7 September 1915)
Lieutenant General Sir Henry Fuller Maitland Wilson	XII Corps (5 September 1915 to 4 January 1917), XII Corps (11 January 1917 to 30 September 1918)
Lieutenant General Sir Henry Hughes Wilson	IV Corps (22 December 1915 to 1 December 1916)
Lieutenant General Sir Charles Louis Woollcombe	IV Corps (1 December 1916 to 11 March 1918)

Lightning Source UK Ltd.
Milton Keynes UK
UKHW021836261020
372278UK00005B/293